HOW TO GO TO

COLLEGE

Almost ^ FOR FREE

HOW TO GO TO
COLLEGE
Almost ^
FOR FREE

The Secrets of Winning Scholarship Money

By Benjamin R. Kaplan

WAGGLE DANCER BOOKS
Gleneden Beach, Oregon
www.waggledancer.com

WAGGLE DANCER BOOKS
P.O. Box 860, Gleneden Beach, OR 97388
World Wide Web: www.waggledancer.com

ISBN: 0-933094-30-2
Library of Congress Catalog Number: 99-75701

Printed in the United States of America
10 9 8 7 6 5 4

To Mom & Dad,
whose recipe for love & encouragement
demonstrates that they are indeed master chefs.

ACKNOWLEDGMENTS

If winning scholarships is a game, then writing a book about winning scholarships is a no-holds-barred, in-your-face, full-contact, team sport. I'd like to take this opportunity to give a round of applause to the many individuals and organizations who were invaluable members of this team:

To Kurt Mueller, for the many wonderful drawings and graphics he contributed to this book. (Did somebody say "gorilla"?) Get your pen ready, Kurt, more books are on the way! To Colin Park, for his terrific cover portrait. Next time I need to practice leaning against an imaginary wall, I'll know where to come. . . To Roger Swanton, for his design skills, promotional insights, and unending patience in helping create the wonderful book cover. Thanks a million, Roger. To Chris Ries, for his computer expertise, and for patiently answering many technical questions. To the folks at Waggle Dancer Books, for their helpful insights, promotional wizardry, and faith in this book. I'd like to especially thank Gary Michaels for his editing prowess, guidance, and many useful suggestions. You guys are the best!

I would also like to thank Nancy Sharkey and Pam Noel at *The New York Times*, and Shaheena Ahmad and Anne McGrath at *U.S. News & World Report* for publishing the articles that led to this book.

And high-fives go out to my good friends and roommates at Harvard—Daniel "The Peruvian Prince" Alarco, Sid "Kristin called" Burke, "Cowboy" Clay Cowan, and Greg "G-Force" Lau—for constantly harassing me about not having this book finished. A special thanks goes out to Greg for allowing me to bounce plenty of book ideas off him.

Not only am I thankful for the many people who have contributed to this book, but I am also eternally grateful to all who have assisted in my scholarship quest:

First, my heartfelt appreciation goes out to the many corporations, organizations, foundations, and individuals whose scholarship programs helped turn my educational dreams into reality. Your generosity has made all the difference in the world.

I would like to extend special thanks to everyone at South Eugene High School who has helped me over the years. You have provided me with numerous opportunities, encouraged me to do my best, and have always supported me on my scholarship journey. Deserving special mention are Sue Barr, Lynne George, Larry Perry, and Chuck Vaughn, without whom none of this would have been possible. Each of you has made a tremendous difference in my life.

And, of course, to my family:

Much love and gratitude goes out to Grandma and Grandpa, who read an early version of this book and provided very helpful comments. How 'bout those Las Vegas editors!

A standing ovation is in order for Grandma E and Apisith Sae-Choi, my always encouraging book cheerleaders. A special thanks to Grandma E for all of her love, support, and radiant smiles!

No book acknowledgments would be complete without thanking Dudley, my very ferocious toy poodle who scared away countless numbers of evil book saboteurs with his menacing bark and intimidating seven-pound frame.

But most of all, I'd like to thank my parents for all of their support in making this project a success. Everything I have ever done, or will ever do, I owe to them.

What's Inside

p. 13   "The Game"

p. 15   Introduction: Let the Games Begin. . .

PART I: THE RULES OF THE GAME

p. 31   **Chapter 1: The Playing Field**
Knowing the Lingo	32
Sizing Up the Game	41
Chapter 1 Summary	44

p. 45   **Chapter 2: Players & Principles**
Who Can Apply?	46
The Other Players	51
Exploding 7 Myths	54
Chapter 2 Summary	58

Intermission #1: What Parents Can Do To Help   **59**

PART II: GETTING READY TO PLAY

p. 67   **Chapter 3: "Show Me the Money!"**
Finding Your Pot of Gold	68
Searching Internet Databases	69
Using School Resources	76
More Web Surfing Secrets	79
Books & Directories	82
Community Canvassing	82
Widening Your Net	85
Requesting Materials	87
Chapter 3 Summary	89

p. 91   **Chapter 4: A Winning Game Plan**
Maximizing Your Chances	92
Setting a Schedule	100
Chapter 4 Summary	102

Intermission #2: The Unforgiving Minute   **103**

PART III: STRATEGIES THAT GIVE YOU THE EDGE

p. 115   **Chapter 5: Painting Your Own Portrait**

Knowing the Person	116
The Painter's Touch	117
Employing Your Theme	119
9 Winning Themes	124
Chapter 5 Summary	135

p. 137   **Chapter 6: "Hidden" Judging Criteria**

The Unseen Evaluators	138
Ten Golden Virtues	150
Chapter 6 Summary	158

p. 159   **Chapter 7: Scoring Points**

Content Strategies	160
Packaging Strategies	163
Putting It All Together	169
Chapter 7 Summary	172

Intermission #3:   Creating Opportunities   **173**

PART IV: WHEN THE WHISTLE BLOWS. . .

p. 181   **Chapter 8: Essay Excellence**

Principles of Winning Essays	182
Recycling Essays	187
Getting in the Flow	191
Honing Your Essay	193
Tips for Specific Topics	197
Short-Answer Questions	199
Chapter 8 Summary	201

p. 203   **Chapter 9: Glowing Support Letters**

Star Witnesses	204
Qualities of a Great Letter	212
Chapter 9 Summary	214

p. 215   **Chapter 10: Filling in the Blanks**

Paperwork Prowess	216
The Stat Sheet	219
Activity Lists	219

Awards & Honors Lists   222
The Transcript   223
Additional Materials   226
Mailing Your Application   226
Chapter 10 Summary   228

p. 229 ## Chapter 11: Acing the Interview

Interview Mastery   230
Preparing for the Interview   230
The Big Day   234
The Main Event   235
Chapter 11 Summary   238

Intermission #4: Being Smart About Your Studies   239

PART V: WHEN THE BUZZER SOUNDS

p. 245 ## Chapter 12: Parting Shots

The Home Stretch   246
Keeping Track of Your Winnings   246
Slashing Your College Costs   250
What We've Learned   252

THE APPENDICES

A-1 ## Appendix A: Directory of Scholarships

B-1 ## Appendix B: Library of Sample Materials

C-1 ## Appendix C: State Scholarship Agencies

p. 311 Index

Ask the Coach. . .

. . . About fee-based services   p. 72
. . . About finding the time   p. 101
. . . About ethnic themes   p. 134
. . . About small-town opportunities   p. 149
. . . About younger students   p. 157
. . . About bad grades   p. 171
. . . About older applicants   p. 227

Guerrilla Tactics

#1 . . . . p. 75
#2 . . . . p. 78
#3 . . . . p. 81
#4 . . . . p. 95
#5 . . . . p. 97
#6 . . . . p. 98
#7 . . . . p. 99
#8 . . . . p. 156
#9 . . . . p. 162
#10 . . . . p. 168
#11 . . . . p. 196
#12 . . . . p. 205
#13 . . . . p. 210
#14 . . . . p. 217
#15 . . . . p. 224
#16 . . . . p. 233

THE GAME

Winning scholarships is a game—

A game with high stakes and huge rewards.

To succeed you must learn the rules and understand the players.

You must internalize the principles, strategies, and guerrilla tactics that lead to victory.

Then it's a matter of preparing, practicing, and perfecting: Enhancing your record in key areas, strengthening your self-promotional skills, and refining your application materials.

And when the whistle blows you'll be ready.

And when the buzzer sounds you'll have won.

Winning scholarships is a game.

The best way to master the game is to learn from someone who has played it well.

Let the
Games
Begin...

HOW IT ALL BEGAN

In the twentysomething movie *Reality Bites*, a jobless and penniless college valedictorian named Lelaina Pierce (played by the charming Winona Ryder) discovers, among other things, just how much mini-mart food she can buy on her father's gas card. And back in early 1994, when the movie was in theaters, I found myself in a related predicament. No, it wasn't that I shopped at the corner gas station. Nor did I regularly eat Chevron cuisine.

Rather, it was that, as a junior in high school, reality had just bitten *me*—and bitten me hard. It happened one day, as I was leafing through glossy college catalogs with dreams of wild collegiate adventures dancing in my head. All of a sudden, I felt the reality of having to *pay* for my under-graduate education sink its ugly teeth. I hoped to at-tend a top university, but how would I ever pay the six-figure tab at the college of my choice? Even if I could somehow cover the cost, was I destined to be buried alive beneath a mountain of student debt?

Granted, this wasn't a memorable scene from a slick Hol-lywood movie, but still, it was *my life*. And unlike Lelaina, I didn't have my father's gas card. . . and even if I did, the cor-ner Chevron station didn't have any diplomas for sale.

Reality Bites. . . But It Doesn't Have To

A magical gas card never did come to my rescue. But I suppose, in a strange way, a benevolent credit card did save the day. You see, one day at my high school's career center, I came across an application for a nationwide scholarship con-test sponsored by the Discover Card corporation. As I held the application in my hands, my mind raced with questions. Were there a lot of merit-based scholarships like this one? Could I win them? Did a kid from a public high school in Eugene, Oregon actually have a chance? There was probably some child prodigy out there who had mastered calculus at age 5, been an Olympian by 9, and discovered a cure for can-cer before hitting puberty.

Despite my doubts, I decided to enter the contest. I dili-gently filled out the forms, rounded up several letters of recommendation, and crafted some essays. And to my amaze-ment, I actually won! And I won BIG—to the tune of $17,500. Then I made another fantastic discovery: **Plenty of other organizations can't wait to give money away!**

So I entered other scholarship contests. I won again! And again! Now don't get me wrong: it wasn't as if I had just writ-ten a couple of essays and suddenly money began magically falling from the sky. In fact, it was a lot of hard work, and I lost my share of scholarship competitions, too.

But through a process of trial and error, I formulated winning strategies, developed foolproof procedures, and con-cocted "guerrilla tactics." When the dust finally settled, I had amassed nearly $90,000 and had paid for virtually the entire cost of my Harvard education.

I combined my scholarship winnings with a year's worth of Advanced Placement college credit (which I accumulated in high school). This covered virtually the entire cost of my Harvard under-graduate degree.

Biting Back

So is entering scholarship contests worth the effort? Most definitely! I'm living proof of it. Can *you* win these contests? You bet! All it takes is a little knowledge and a bit of elbow grease. What's the best way to get started? Read this book!

A few years ago, when I faced the daunting task of trying to pay for my college education, there wasn't anyone out there to show me the ropes. But when I discovered that **thousands of organizations give away hundreds of millions of dollars in scholarship prizes,** I saw rays of financial hope beckoning me to take up the quest anyway.

Now I can't guarantee that you'll pay for *all* of your college expenses by winning scholarship contests (for to do so also takes a bit of good luck), but with my guidance plus your hard work and determination, I know that we can make a significant dent in your financial burden.

Reality may indeed bite, but winning college scholarships can help enterprising students bite back.

"BIG" MONEY:
I was thrilled to be awarded this large scholarship prize by (flanking me left to right) E. Don Brown, President of the National Association of Secondary School Principals, and Robert Muir, Senior Vice President of Sylvan Learning Systems. But can you believe it, I didn't get to keep the giant-sized check!

MASTERING THE GAME

Scholarships are within the reach of all students. You don't have to be some kind of academic whiz to win cash for college. You don't have to possess the service record of a Mother Teresa or the moves of a Michael Jordan either.

I may not have a Ph.D. in Scholarship Science hanging on my wall, but through the process of accumulating my own pot of gold, I have become somewhat of an expert at winning the college scholarship game. And, as you read a few pages ago, winning money for higher education is indeed a game. To succeed you must learn the rules and understand the players. You must internalize the principles, strategies, and guerrilla tactics that lead to victory. It then becomes a matter of preparing, practicing, and perfecting: enhancing your record in key areas, strengthening your self-promotional skills, and refining your application materials. The book you are now holding teaches you how to master this important game.

There is, however, a very odd thing about this particular game: As important as the game is, the referee never even bothers to explain the rules. Sure, scholarship administrators publish formal judging criteria, but this only scratches the surface of what it really takes to win. There's another entire set of "hidden rules" that govern the outcomes of these contests. So how do you succeed in a game when you're not even sure how to play?

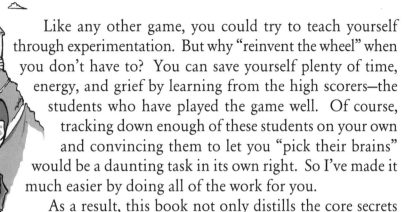

Like any other game, you could try to teach yourself through experimentation. But why "reinvent the wheel" when you don't have to? You can save yourself plenty of time, energy, and grief by learning from the high scorers—the students who have played the game well. Of course, tracking down enough of these students on your own and convincing them to let you "pick their brains" would be a daunting task in its own right. So I've made it much easier by doing all of the work for you.

As a result, this book not only distills the core secrets learned from my own scholarship quest, but also adds to the mix many valuable insights from dozens of other scholarship winners I've interviewed. (As simple as it sounds, surveying top winners is a task that has *never* been done before by an author in the field.)

"To know the road ahead, ask those coming back."

Chinese Proverb

By following the advice contained in these pages, you can avoid many of the mistakes these scholarship winners (including myself) have made, and can learn from our greatest successes. Winning scholarships may be a game, but it's a game that can be learned—and learned quickly, too.

Reaping the Rewards

This journey we're about to begin may sound like a lot of work, but I can't emphasize enough that this relatively small investment of your time can reap enormous rewards. And these rewards can be measured in *more* than just dollar terms. During my senior year, I zigzagged across the nation nearly a dozen times, attending various scholarship award ceremonies. The Discover Card Tribute Awards, for instance, sent a film crew to my hometown to shoot a mini-documentary about me, paid for my entire family to fly from Oregon to Washington D.C., treated us to limousine service and five-star accommodations, and then took us on a four-day sightseeing tour of our nation's capitol! I combined this trip with visits to several east coast colleges I was considering, and Discover Card even agreed to pick up the airfare of my extended tour.

For several scholarships, I had the opportunity to do interviews with local television stations and newspapers. For many others, I got the chance to meet interesting students from across the nation, as well as notables such as Hillary Clinton, Olympic Gold Medalist Scott Hamilton, Grammy-award winner Trisha Yearwood, Supreme Court Justice Ruth Ginsberg, and Ed Bradley of *60 Minutes* fame.

More importantly, the experience of entering these contests impacted my life in profound ways. I dramatically enhanced my writing skills, clarified my life and career goals, and began a process of self-analysis that led to dramatic self-improvement. In addition, scholarship contests gave me a tremendous head start when it came time to apply to college: I already had essays ready to go, a menu of recommendation letters to choose from, and well-constructed summaries of my extracurricular activities.

College admissions officers have told me how winning merit-based scholarship contests can greatly enhance a student's high school record. Many students have used these added credentials to get into colleges they wouldn't otherwise have been admitted to.

Entering scholarship contests also provided me with valuable feedback about what works (and what doesn't) on an application. This accumulated experience played a major role in helping me gain admittance to the college of my choice (Harvard). And learning the art of self-promotion—what the scholarship game really trains you to do—helped me secure several summer internships and job offers once I became a college student. So regardless of what monetary prizes one does or doesn't win, just entering scholarship contests is a very rewarding endeavor in and of itself.

You Can Do It Too!

Don't make the mistake of thinking "scholarships are great and everything, but they just aren't for students like me." I'm here to tell you otherwise. Scholarships are within the reach of *all* students, as long as they are willing to put in the time and effort. In fact, judging from the extremely diverse group of scholarship recipients I've met at various award ceremonies, virtually every type of student with practically every type of interest and background are represented in the scholarship winner's circle.

You don't need a stellar GPA to win scholarship money. In fact, numerous competitions don't even consider grades.

Throughout these pages, I'll be your personal scholarship advisor, helping you to build upon the things you've already done, isolate the strategies that are best for you, and then enhance your applications in key areas to achieve maximum results in minimum time. You'll find that much of what contributes to your scholarship success involves what you do *after* you decide to step on the court and start playing the scholarship game. And once again—I can't emphasize this enough—if you're determined to succeed and willing to put in the necessary preparation and perspiration, nothing can stand in your way.

WHO SHOULD READ THIS BOOK

This book is for *any* student in search of scholarship money for higher education—including students currently enrolled in high school, vocational school, two- and four-year colleges, and graduate school. The book is also ideal for returning students, interested parents, and younger students wanting to get an early start. Furthermore, the topics covered in this book are of special importance to families caught in the "middle-income financial aid crunch"—the dilemma families face when they have *too much* income to qualify for substantial need-based financial aid, but *not enough* money to comfortably pay off high-priced college tuition bills. This book will teach you how to win unrestricted merit-based scholarships—funds awarded on the basis of merit that you can use at the institution of your choice.

If you're a junior or senior in high school, applying the material in this book will provide you with a powerful tool in winning your fair share of the cornucopia of scholarships available to you in the next year or two. Indeed, the greatest share of scholarship money is available to students about to embark on their college careers.

Likewise, if you're already enrolled in college and could benefit from additional funds, this book is also for you. I'll show you how to stake your claim to the huge amount of scholarship money targeted at college freshman, sophomores, juniors, and seniors. Furthermore, the tactics detailed in this book are essential strategies to employ when applying for fellowships, grants, and scholarships for graduate-level work.

To enter the Optimist International Oratorical Contest, for instance, a student must be under 16 years of age.

And for younger students—high school freshmen and sophomores, as well as middle school students—this book can help provide what could be the most dramatic monetary results. A surprisingly large number of scholarship contests are geared toward younger students. But more important than the *immediate* contest options is the chance for younger students to prepare early and position themselves for scholarship winnings (and other exciting opportunities) in later years. Determined students who, years in advance, make a point of preparing themselves to win future scholarships become favorites to win a bounty of valuable awards. Although I didn't begin my search until late in my junior year, if I could do it all over again, I would start preparing for scholarships as early as my seventh- or eighth-grade year.

The scope of this book is also designed to appeal to students who exhibit a broad range of backgrounds, achievements, and interests. If you've had a rocky academic history, special sections show you how to distinguish yourself in other ways. If you have particular vocational or career goals, the book details creative methods for demonstrating passion and talent in a field. If you've been confronted with significant obstacles in your life, the book shows you how to use these challenges to demonstrate courage and determination, and create a powerfully compelling story in the process. If you attend a high school with fewer opportunities and resources than other schools, the book documents ways to create your own opportunities and piggyback on outside resources. If you're a student hoping to attend one of the nation's most competitive colleges (such as an Ivy League school), the book shows you how to round out your résumé and turn your best skills into standout talents.

WHY YOU NEED THIS BOOK

When I immersed myself in my scholarship quest four years ago, I knew that I needed to win numerous scholarships if I was going to cover the big-time costs of an Ivy League school. And because, like most students, I lacked a singularly amazing achievement, developing superior application strategies was critical. So I ventured to libraries and bookstores, looking for anything to give me an edge. But what I soon discovered was that the typical scholarship book was not much more than a list of available scholarships (most of which were not applicable to me). What these books did offer in the way of guidance was extremely vague, lacked specific examples, and didn't offer advice much beyond common sense.

Furthermore, most books were from the perspective of an educator or college admissions officer. Although such an approach lends insight to understanding the judge's point of view, it tells readers nothing about the winning techniques and behind-the-scenes strategies that successful scholarship applicants have employed.

Consequently, books were not a big help in my money quest. None of the many books I read even recognized that success in this type of venture could be cultivated through the mastery of a fundamental skill set. I had to discover this the hard way.

So after I had paid for my Harvard education and discovered—through a process of trial and error—the secrets of the scholarship game, I set out to pass along the knowledge I had accumulated. I felt strongly (and still do) that education is something far too important to be dictated solely by financial considerations. Unfortunately, the financial climate is becoming even more scorching: **Over the past 10 years, college tuition rates have skyrocketed by 6-7 percent per year. An annual rise of 7 percent in tuition costs translates into a doubling of a typical college bill every 10 years!**

Other statistics indicate that college tuition costs are rising 10 times faster than family income.

Although the cost problem seemed to be growing at an alarming rate, what really shocked me was the realization that none of the critical information and strategies that I had stumbled upon had been chronicled elsewhere. In light of this fact, it was no wonder that the *same* schools and communities—the ones in which past scholarship winners had grown up and passed on this critical information—dominated scholarship awards ceremonies year after year.

This book is the culmination of my attempt to level the playing field by centralizing the critical strategies, tactics, and techniques of winning scholarships into one accessible volume. I have poured my heart and soul into making this book everything that I could have used when the financial realities of paying for college were staring *me* square in face.

I have also tried to incorporate the questions and suggestions of the many students who have e-mailed and telephoned me after hearing about my scholarship success in such publications as *The New York Times* and *U.S. News & World Report*. So to all of you whom I have promised—and especially to those who have faithfully reminded me in writing—I am finally delivering the goods. Here it is: Your very own scholarship success guide.

FEATURES OF THE BOOK

Several features of the book are designed to make the material especially useful. Because I believe in being as specific as possible, the book is chock full of examples from actual scholarship contests. Throughout the text, I've reprinted many examples from my own scholarship applications—including a lot of winning material from contests you're likely to enter. In Appendix B, the Library of Sample Materials, I've aggregated plenty of winning submissions from other scholarship applicants—all of which have been annotated with my comments. In this way, you'll be able to see for yourself the qualities of a winning scholarship contest submission.

I have also drawn upon the monumental dialogues of the great Athenian philosopher Plato to create my own "Ask the Coach" scholarship dialogues. In sidebars throughout this book (identified by the icon shown at left), a variety of prototypical students pose questions to a "scholarship coach." You'll undoubtedly find that many of these dialogues relate to your own situation and experience.

In this way, Ask the Coach sections have helped me to avoid the one-size-fits-all approach found in most how-to books. Dialogues have been specially designed for students

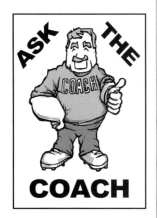

in their early teens, applicants already enrolled in college, and individuals with diverse ethnic backgrounds, among others.

Wide margins on the side of each page allow space for additional comments. These side notes are an integral part of the book, and often are used to cite further details, tips, and examples related to the information being covered in the main text. These margins also contain relevant quotes from top scholarship winners. In addition, margin comments are used as a cross-referencing tool, linking various parts of the book together.

If you happen to see a gorilla (like the one shown at left) accompanied by a shaded box of bold text, it signifies that the information is one of the special "Guerrilla Tactics" contained in the book. Guerrilla tactics are unconventional, yet extremely effective, techniques that provide a scholarship applicant with the competitive edge over other scholarship seekers. A complete listing of where all the Guerrilla Tactics are found in this book is shown on the last page of the *Table of Contents* and in the *Index.*

I've also included four "Intermissions" that fall between each major segment of the book. These intermissions cover subject matter that may be tangential to the immediate demands of your scholarship quest, but that can nevertheless dramatically improve your efficiency and effectiveness. Topics include time management, creating opportunities, getting better grades, and utilizing parental resources.

At the conclusion of each chapter, I've written a Chapter Summary that distills the main points covered in the preceding pages. Each summary is designed to reinforce, in a compact way, the book's most important concepts.

Finally, the last chapter of the book contains special bonus material. In these sections, I describe how to keep track of and manage all of your scholarship winnings, as well as how to apply a little-known technique for slashing an immediate 25 percent off the cost of attending college.

Other directories are comprised mostly of scholarships with very specialized eligibility requirements—such as a parent who works for a particular company, affiliation with an obscure organization, or enrollment at a specific college or university. Both Appendix A and the full Scholarship Sleuth directory focus on scholarships that everyone can win.

To find out more about the complete Scholarship Sleuth directory, see page A-38 in Appendix A.

See the bottom of this book's copyright page (the fourth page from the front) for your access password.

Appendix A: Directory of Scholarships

The directory of scholarships contained in Appendix A is excerpted from my companion volume, *The Scholarship Sleuth*—a comprehensive directory of scholarship contests unlike any other on the market.

In constructing Appendix A, I have specially selected several dozen scholarship contests—some of the biggest and best—so that you can get started on your scholarship quest right away. Just like the complete *Scholarship Sleuth* listings, this appendix features in-depth, full-page descriptions of contests and programs that award *unrestricted* scholarship prizes—scholarships that you can use **at the college of your choice**.

In addition, the unique *Scholarship Sleuth* format used in Appendix A provides helpful advice and insider tips specific to each scholarship competition—via special sections titled "Sleuth Says." In creating these sections, I've drawn upon interviews with contest administrators and top scholarship winners, as well as upon my own experiences with many of these programs. Such tips can be extremely valuable, as contest insiders and past winners often reveal information and share insights that extend far beyond the official published guidelines.

The Reader's Resource Room

As a valued reader of this book, you also have access to a special Reader's Resource Room—located on the Internet at **www.winscholarships.com**, the Web's best scholarship portal. The Resource Room provides interactive scholarship coaching, updates to the Appendix A scholarship directory, additional sample material, special question and answer postings, as well as a variety of ready-to-use forms and templates. When you reach the winscholarships.com home page, click on the "Reader's Resource Room" icon, and you will be prompted to input an access password. The password you should use is located at the front of this book, on the bottom of the copyright page, under the heading "Use of Companion Web Resources."

HOW TO USE THIS BOOK

I recommend first skimming the entire book once through to provide yourself with a sense of where we're headed. You may even want to first read each of the chapter summaries to get an overview of the book's major concepts.

Subsequently, I suggest reading the chapters in the order presented, as each chapter builds upon the prior ones. If you want to skip to a topic of special interest, however, use the *Table of Contents*, or check out the *Index* located at the back of the book.

If you're already familiar with how scholarship contests work and you're eager to get going right away, you may want to jump to Chapter 3 (which details how to conduct your own personalized scholarship search). Don't forget to come back to Chapters 1 and 2, however, as these sections provide you with a good sense of the overall scholarship landscape. You also might want to browse the Appendix A scholarship directory right away, and start requesting applications for scholarships you're interested in.

WHAT IT TAKES

Put in one hour every two months and win $50,000! Just fill out a form and college is free! Five easy steps and you're in the money! If you embark on your scholarship quest believing claims like these—and I hope that you don't—you're setting yourself up for failure.

But if you're willing to put in the time, effort, and hard work that the process demands, great success is yours for the taking. So go for it! You have nothing to lose, and a better future to gain. A college education is far too important to settle for the cheapest path. Rebel against those who say that financial constraints make it impossible for you to attend this or that school. Fight back against college budget offices that habitually increase tuition bills, while their financial aid allocations fail to keep up. And above all, have fun making a great future happen.

Now let's get going. . .

PART I

The
Rules
of the
Game

The Playing Field

In this chapter,
we discuss the many
types of scholarship
programs that exist,
and describe the
basics of how you
apply to win these
awards.

CHAPTER CONTENTS

- What are merit-based scholarships?
- The 3 types of merit scholarships
- The components of a typical scholarship application
- The differences between national, state, and local contests

KNOWING THE LINGO

According to a survey conducted by Gallup and Robinson, most parents of college-bound students have saved only 25 percent or less of college costs.

To make sure that we're all talking about the same thing, it's important to first distinguish between the various types of financial aid for college. Almost all aid comes in one of two varieties: grants or loans. Both grants and loans can be paid directly to the student, to the student's school, or to the student's parents. The key distinction is that loans have to be paid back, whereas grants do not.

The premise of this book is that by winning grants, students and their families can substantially lower their debt burden, or even avoid borrowing money altogether. This is especially important in a debt-ridden era where increasing numbers of parents resist taking out new loans for college expenses, opting instead for less-expensive schools. Grants allow each student to take control of his or her educational destiny, choosing the right college regardless of family financial limitations.

The Various Types of Grants

Grants generally come in two flavors: **merit-based** and **need-based**. Merit-based grants, as you'd expect, are awarded on the basis of student achievement. As we'll see later in this chapter, the judging criteria used to evaluate achievement varies substantially among grant programs—frequently taking into account a wide range of student talents and interests.

Need-based grants are awarded solely on the basis of financial need, as determined by formulas that weigh financial resources against living expenses—and parental assets, income, and expenses if the student is a dependent. The largest need-based grant program is the Pell Grant (sponsored by the federal government), which awards money to students from lower-income families. A relatively small number of grant programs use *both* merit-based and need-based criteria in making awards.

Institutional aid is awarded by colleges and universities from their own coffers. The majority of this aid comes in the form of discounts off published sticker prices and is, for the most part, distributed according to financial need. Need-based grants are sometimes offered by foundations and other organizations, but such programs are less common.

There are several problems, however, for a student who relies solely on need-based aid to finance an education. First, there just aren't enough need-based funds to go around. Most colleges have strict financial aid budgets, restricting the amount of need-based grants they can award. I have yet to find a student who felt that a financial aid office *overestimated* their family's financial need. On the contrary, most students soon discover that a financial aid office's estimate of "need" is very different from the realities of a family's cash flow and bank accounts.

Second, students from middle-income families often find themselves caught between "a rock and a hard place." Such families aren't wealthy enough to cover all of the costs on their own, but don't have low enough incomes to qualify for substantial levels of need-based aid. Having to send more than one child to college further aggravates the situation.

Even though a college may claim that a "significant percentage of its student body receives financial aid," such statements can be misleading. Loans are classified as "financial aid" when they carry an interest rate below the current market level and don't have to be paid back until after graduation. What college students and their families soon discover, however, is that these types of low-interest loans make up the bulk of most financial aid packages. And although such loans are helpful in *delaying* payment, they still have one overwhelmingly undesirable feature: they have to eventually be paid back.

The message here is straightforward: Don't rely solely on need-based aid. As Forrest Gump's momma would say, "Need-based grants are like a box of chocolates. . . you never know what you're going to get."

As a result, many students are forced to commit themselves to a long string of post-college debt payments—a financial burden that can negatively impact their choices for years to come. Students interested in attending graduate schools may have to delay or forgo such plans because of this debt. Students entering the work force may have to turn down exciting, but low-paying, career opportunities in favor of better-paying, but less-interesting, jobs.

It should also be noted that need-based grants are determined, for the most part, by circumstances outside of a

Share your financial aid stories and learn from the experiences of others in my companion Reader's Resource Room at winscholarships.com

Making Your Presence Felt

The rising costs of higher education, combined with only minimal relief from college financial aid offices, has made merit-based grants an even more critical source of funding in recent years.

student's control: the family's income, assets, and debts. Although families can take some steps to maximize their need-based aid (by utilizing smart money management techniques and by negotiating with financial aid offices), the extent of anyone's influence over the need-based allocation process is extremely limited.

Quite simply, merit-based grants are monetary prizes awarded on the basis of some measure of achievement. What constitutes achievement depends on who is awarding the money, but you'll soon discover that merit-based grants are targeted at virtually every type of student. Unlike scholarships based on need, an enterprising student can exert tremendous influence over the amount of merit-based grants he or she receives. I learned how to do this well, and in the pages that follow, I'll show you how you can do it, too.

Merit-based grants (what most people generally mean when they use the word "scholarships") are awarded by corporations, nonprofit groups, foundations, service clubs, state and federal governments, and other organizations. In addition, some colleges offer merit-based scholarships to students who enroll at their institutions, although this is rare at more competitive schools (because such schools don't have to offer this type of financial incentive to attract students).

As I mentioned in the introduction, I believe that financial considerations shouldn't dictate the choice of a particular school. For that reason, this book prepares you to win merit-based scholarships that you can use at *any* institution. There's actually an abundance of these unrestricted scholarships for high school and college students alike (and even younger students, too). The $90,000 I accumulated was comprised almost entirely of such awards.

If you've already developed an interest in a particular school (or are already enrolled in college) and want to apply for a merit-based scholarship offered by that institution, most of the strategies I outline in this book will also apply. Where tactical considerations may differ, I've noted this in the text.

A SAMPLER OF SCHOLARSHIP CONTESTS

Type 1: Specified Tasks	Type 2: Past Achievement	Type 3: Hybrid Contests
Optimist International Essay & Oratorical Contests	Discover Card Tribute Awards	America's Junior Miss
ThinkQuest Internet Challenge	Principal's Leadership Award	Intel Science Talent Search Coca-Cola Scholars Program
BMI Composer Awards	Tylenol Scholarship	Siemens Westinghouse Science & Technology
Scholastic Art and Writing Awards	Target All-Around Scholarship	Competition

The Three Types of Merit-Based Scholarships

We can divide merit-based scholarships into three fundamental types. The first type of scholarship award is based upon a student's performance on a specified task (such as writing, artwork, speeches, or Web-page design). A second type of scholarship is awarded on the basis of past achievement in particular areas (such as extracurricular activities, academics, athletics, or community service). The final type is a hybrid of the other two, and evaluates applicants according to both specified tasks and past achievement. Hybrid competitions are generally not as prevalent as the other two categories. The box shown above demonstrates the wide range of scholarships in each of the three types.

Type 1 Scholarships

*Performance On
A Specified Task*

Due to the varied nature of scholarships in Type 1—money for everything from weaving to oration, and from essays to arc welding—application requirements can be quite different. Essay competitions are the most prevalent of these contests, and most essay competitions require compositions between 300 and 1,000 words in length—with a 500-word limit about average. It's quite unusual to find an essay contest that requires longer than a 1,500-word composition (because most organizations don't have the staffing to devote to judging such lengthy expositions). All of this is good news: Less work for you, and more scholarship bucks per word!

Performance-oriented competitions generally first require the submission of video or audio tapes, with finalists selected to attend all-expense-paid live auditions. For example, in the music portion of the Arts Recognition and Talent Search, applicants first submit taped performances that are 20 to 30 minutes in length. Finalists for five levels of awards are flown to Miami, Florida for further auditions.

The National "Make It Yourself From Wool" contest asks students to sew and model a garment made of at least 60 percent wool fabric. (No polyester leisure suits allowed here!)

Type 2 Scholarships

Past Achievement

Many scholarships that are based upon past achievement focus on a student's overall record—with such criteria as leadership, community service, extracurricular activities, and academics frequently employed in the official judging. Other programs look at past achievement in a particular area only. Type 2 scholarships tend to be based upon a few basic application components: an essay, a description of extracurricular activities, possibly a grade transcript, and letters of recommendation. Some scholarships may add other evaluation tools to the mix such as interviews, lists of awards and honors, or test results. The basic format, however, tends to be the same.

Below, I've described each of these standard evaluation tools. Note that very few contests require the submission of all of these components; particular scholarships emphasize different ones. Because of the substantial overlap in requirements among Type 2 competitions, entering multiple contests is a lot less work than one might expect. Later, I'll show you how to adapt older entries to newer contests, thereby increasing your odds of winning more money.

Essays & Short-Answer Questions

For Type 2 scholarships, essays tend to be less lengthy than in Type 1 contests because more types of application materials are being used to evaluate students. In fact, essays in Type 2 contests can seem more like short-answer questions. The Tylenol Scholarship program, for instance, requires that students submit 100- to 200-word essays describing goals and aspirations, as well as two or three sentences about "experiences or persons [that] have contributed to your achievements." Basically, the program's creators expect you to summarize your entire future (and thank those who will help you get there) in less words than what's on the packaging of a Tylenol bottle itself! (That's enough of a challenge to produce a headache right on the spot...)

These mini-essays can actually be quite challenging because it's difficult to pack a lot of compelling information in such a small space.

Extracurricular Activity Lists

When scholarships ask for information about extracurricular activities, they basically want a summary of everything that you do outside of class time. This includes school clubs, sports, jobs, independent projects, volunteer activities, and everything in between. Sometimes scholarship applications will distinguish between different types of extracurricular activities. To use the Tylenol scholarship as an example, the application requests information about two separate categories of extracurriculars: (1) school-related activities and (2) community and volunteer services.

Most applications request the information in some type of list format. Some contests will limit you to the space provided on the physical application, while others will let you attach additional sheets. In addition to requesting a brief description of the activity itself, contest applications may also ask for information about the time commitment devoted to the activity, any leadership positions or offices held, and any awards or honors received from the endeavor.

Grade Transcripts

Although not all Type 2 scholarships request information about a student's academic record, a substantial number do, in fact, make this part of the judging criteria. The way in which this is taken into account, however, can vary tremendously. For scholarships such as the All-USA Academic Team sponsored by *USA Today*, grades are an important part of the judging criteria. On the other hand, many contests only use grade *cutoffs*, in which strong grades do not yield any special advantage. In the Discover Card Tribute Awards, for instance, students are required to have at least a 2.75 grade point average (on a 4.0 scale), but GPAs above the 2.75 minimum are not a factor in the judging criteria. In fact, Discover Card calls itself a program that "understands not every student's achievements can be measured in grade points alone."

It's also important to note that most high school transcripts include more information than just grades (such as test scores, awards, etc.). Knowing what's on your transcript, what you want submitted to scholarship judges, and how to shape this information to fit your tactical objectives is an important strategic consideration we'll discuss later.

Letters of Recommendation

Just like the college admissions process, letters of recommendation are an integral part of many Type 2 scholarships. Some contests ask recommenders to answer specific questions or evaluate the applicant in terms pertinent to the judging criteria. Others give the recommenders free reign.

Most scholarships that request recommendation letters ask for one or two letters—three recommendation letters for one application is typically the most you'll encounter. The majority of contests leave the choice of recommender up to you. If you can't think of someone off the top of your head who would write you a strong recommendation, don't worry. Later in the book, I'll show you how to "sow the seeds" for great recommendation letters.

Last, it's important to note that unlike application essays, most contests do not specify a word limit for recommendation letters. In Chapter 10, I'll show you how to use this flexibility to your strategic advantage.

Interviews

The written application may be the foundation of most Type 2 scholarships, but some contests do include interviews as well. Scholarship interviews can take place over the phone

Many people assume that all scholarship winners have top grades, but this is actually far from the case (see Chapter 2's "Exploding Seven Myths").

Some competitions may request one letter from a teacher at your school and another from someone who knows you in a different capacity (employer, coach, club adviser, etc.).

or in person. They can be conducted by an individual interviewer, or by a panel of judges. For prominent national scholarship contests, however, such interviews generally occur only *after* a number of finalists have been selected from the full pool of applicants. In contrast, local competitions may make interviews a part of the preliminary judging.

Although interviews are important components of several well-known scholarship contests, the majority of Type 2 contests do *not* include interviews. Furthermore, when interviews are required, they are frequently only used to group winners into different *levels* of awards (separating top scholarship winners from recipients of smaller scholarship prizes).

Typical interview questions include "Where do you see yourself in 20 years?", "Who are your role models?", and "Do you sleep in the nude?" (just kidding on that last one).

Awards and Honors

Although far less prevalent than essays, extracurricular activity lists, grade transcripts, and recommendation letters, some applications also request summaries of any awards and honors a student has received. Typically, this is limited to the high school or college years only (although such lists are not limited simply to school-related activities). The definition of what exactly constitutes an "award and honor" is typically quite vague. Generally, you'll want to include not only trophy-type awards, but also honors that are less tangible (such as when you represented your school at a conference on reducing youth violence). In Chapter 10, I'll show you how to use awards and honors lists to best suit your strategic objectives.

Test Results

When students see the words "test results," they naturally think in terms of the PSAT, SAT, or ACT—those annoying standardized tests designed by some balding exam writer in a diabolical plot to bring pain, suffering, and #2 pencils into the lives of otherwise happy high school juniors and seniors.

It's natural to be concerned about whether scholarship contest judges take your scores on these tests into account.

Although some of the most academically focused scholarships do—such programs as National Merit or the All-USA Academic Team—many scholarships do not. If you're a student with scores lower than you'd like to have, here's some good news: There are plenty of scholarships that *don't* take test scores into account. However, if you're a student who happens to have marks in the stratosphere, I'll show you how to include these impressive scores in scholarship applications (such as in the official transcript) even when the contests don't specifically request them.

Sometimes, there are test scores relevant to scholarship applications that have nothing to do with those heinous tests you take to get into college. The Century III Leaders program, for instance, administered a 50-question current events exam. Scholarships that involve foreign language achievement, may administer written or spoken tests. The inclusion of such specialized tests, however, is relatively unusual.

Type 3 Scholarships

Hybrid Contests

As I've already mentioned, Type 3 scholarship competitions combine an evaluation of past achievement with performance on a specified task. Such scholarships typically combine elements of Type 2 written applications with some type of activity in which performance is evaluated. For science-focused competitions, the performance activity may involve a formal presentation of scientific findings from research a student has conducted. In music- or drama-related scholarships, live auditions may be required.

Incidentally, the longstanding Century III Leaders program was recently phased out due to lack of corporate sponsorship.

Contests that stress leadership qualities will sometimes require more elaborate performance-based activities. For instance, in the Century III Leaders program, I first submitted an essay, recommendation letters, and extracurricular lists, in addition to undergoing an interview on the state level. When I was selected as a state winner, they flew me and the other 49 winners to a three-day National Meeting. During the big event—in which we debated and proposed solutions to societal issues—judges sat in the background, evaluating each of the participants. This type of competitive process, however, is actually quite rare due to the cost and logistics of having to assemble competitors from across the state or nation.

As you might expect, Type 3 scholarships typically have the most involved application procedures, and can be the most demanding on applicants.

"Stepping Stone" Programs

In addition to applying for these three types of merit-based scholarship competitions, high school students can apply for an additional group of "stepping stone" programs. Such programs do not provide scholarships, but offer students a variety of other opportunities—many of which lead to later scholarship winnings and stronger college applications.

Here are some examples: The United Nations Youth Pilgrimage Program sponsored by the Odd Fellows organization offers numerous students—selected through an oratorical competition—the chance to go on an all-expense paid trip to the United Nations. The Hugh O'Brian Youth (HOBY) Foundation sponsors leadership conferences in each of the 50 states for high school sophomores. Two students from each state and others from more than 20 nations are selected to attend the HOBY World Leadership Congress (a fantastic event!). For budding young scientists, the Research Science Institute (RSI) offers an intensive six-week long summer program at the Massachusetts Institute of Technology (MIT) for high school juniors with strong science and math skills.

Numerous Research Science Institute (RSI) participants have built upon research conducted at the summer program to win lucrative scholarships from the prestigious Intel Science Talent Search.

SIZING UP THE GAME

Okay, here's the bottom line: A wide assortment of scholarships exist for students with all sorts of talents, interests, and backgrounds. Although estimates vary, the general consensus is that *billions of dollars in merit scholarships of all shapes and sizes are awarded every year!*

Comparing National and Local Contests

An additional point to note is that although the scholarships with the highest profiles tend to be national competitions, a far greater number of scholarships exist on the local and state levels. In fact, many of the largest "national" scholarship contests consist of rounds in which students first compete in local and state competitions. And for many of these programs, most of the money is actually allocated to students who *don't* qualify for a national award. In the Discover Card Tribute Awards, for instance, 461 out of the 470 scholarships granted each year are awarded to state (but not national) winners. Being one of these state winners nets you between $1,250 and $2,500. Not too shabby, eh?

Like the Discover Card program, the largest national contests have many thousands of entrants (a few in the tens of thousands), but such programs may award hundreds of scholarships. Some local competitions, on the other hand, may only have a handful of entrants competing for a single scholarship award. In fact, some local scholarships go unclaimed.

Although the money, as one might expect, is often considerably larger on the national level, scholarship winnings can also be big in local competitions too. I won $5,000 and $6,500 in two scholarship contests open only to students in my district. But don't underestimate the value of local competitions with relatively small payouts ($100 to $500). Your chances of winning these contests are high, and the money can add up rather quickly.

"If you start out winning a few little scholarships, it directly leads to winning other, bigger awards. It's a totally cumulative process."

Melissa Gambol
National Scholarship Winner

Where Can the Money Be Used?

The majority of the merit-based scholarships I've seen (excluding those sponsored by particular universities) can be used at any accredited two- or four-year college in the United States. A good number of them also permit enrollment at foreign universities, but if you're planing to study abroad, you need to investigate this on a scholarship-by-scholarship basis.

For scholarships won on the local or state level, some programs may specify that the money be used at an in-state school. If you're at all considering attending an area school, you should definitely apply for such awards. The in-state requirement is also a common feature of scholarships funded or administered by state or local government agencies.

How is the Money Awarded?

Most scholarship checks are paid directly to your college's billing office (so don't expect to earn interest on the money, or to be buying a new sports car). Some scholarship winnings must be paid out in one lump-sum; others in equal annual distributions over four years. The best payment plans give the student discretion over disbursement of the funds, and may have up to a six-year window to use the money (in case you take some time off from school). On occasion, contests award cash directly to the student, but this is the exception, not the rule.

Is Scholarship Money Taxable?

The government does *not* tax any scholarship money spent on tuition, books, fees, and other bona-fide school-related expenses. As long as you don't spend the money on room and board, clothing, or transportation, the government won't take a bite out of your winnings. This is another big benefit of winning scholarships: For your parents to contribute $1,000 to your education, they must earn much more than $1,000 due to all the state and federal income taxes they must first pay. In this way, the face value of a scholarship represents an after-tax money equivalent, and is thus worth significantly more to you than the winning check amount indicates.

Are There Fees for These Contests?

Nearly all of the contests listed in Appendix A do not require entry fees. The few I've listed that do require such fees are credible programs with well-established track records (such as the Arts Recognition & Talent Search).

Unlike the hefty application fees most colleges charge, scholarship contests, for the most part, don't cost anything to enter. Occasionally, you might see a scholarship with a small processing fee (the National Honor Society scholarship charges $4), but this is relatively unusual. In fact, the only scholarship contests I've seen that cost anything more than a couple of bucks to enter are performance-oriented competitions that involve live auditions before specialized judges.

In general, if you locate an unfamiliar scholarship contest that charges substantial entry fees, proceed with caution: scholarship "scams" do exist. Signs that a contest could be a scam include guarantees that you will win, a "sketchy" application process, and numerous typos on official forms. Furthermore, just because a scholarship is sponsored by a "foundation" or "association" with an official-sounding name, doesn't necessarily mean that it's legitimate. If you suspect a contest could be a scam, contact the Better Business Bureau, your state's Bureau of Consumer Protection, the National Fraud Information Center (1-800-876-7060), or else steer clear altogether.

CHAPTER 1 SUMMARY

■ **Sponsors:** Merit-based scholarships are awarded by corporations, nonprofit groups, foundations, service clubs, state and federal governments, and other local and national organizations.

■ **Impact:** While the amount of *need-based* aid received is largely determined by factors outside of individual control, applicants can influence the amount of their *merit-based* awards.

■ **Three Flavors:** There are three fundamental types of merit-based scholarships. The first group awards prizes based upon a student's *performance* on a specified task (such as an essay or science project). The second type is judged on the basis of *past achievement* (in areas such as community service or academics). Hybrid scholarships are based upon *both* performance on a specific task and past achievement.

■ **The Application:** Scholarship applications may include such components as essays and short-answer questions, extracurricular activity lists, a grade transcript, letters of recommendation, interviews, awards and honors lists, and standardized test results. Most scholarships do *not* charge application fees.

■ **National vs. Local:** Scholarships are awarded on the national, state, and local levels. The largest national contests have thousands of entrants, but such programs may also award hundreds of scholarships. Some local scholarships may have only a handful of entrants.

■ **Taxes:** Scholarship money is not taxed as long as it is used to pay for tuition, books, fees, and other school-related expenses. This makes $1000 in scholarship winnings much more valuable than a $1000 (before-tax) paycheck.

Players & Principles

In this chapter, we discuss how scholarship eligibility works, as well as describe the people and organizations who run each contest. We'll also expose the seven most common misconceptions about winning scholarships.

CHAPTER CONTENTS

- Which scholarships can I apply for?
- Who puts up the money?
- Who runs the contests?
- How does judging work?
- Exploding the 7 myths about scholarship contests

WHO CAN APPLY?

Now that we've discussed the various types of scholarship contests, as well as the components of a typical application, the question remains: Who can apply for these awards? The answer to this question, of course, depends upon the aims of the sponsoring organization. In the following section, I describe the most common types of scholarship eligibility criteria, and demonstrate that an abundance of contests are available for students of all ages, backgrounds, interests, and talents.

Age or Grade

The most common form of eligibility criteria you'll encounter is an age or grade requirement (grade refers to your year in school, not the marks you receive in classes). In my experience, the greatest number of scholarships are targeted at students in the 12th grade—high school seniors who will soon be confronted with their first college tuition bill. But don't think that you have to wait until your final year in high school to apply for significant numbers of awards. There are also plenty of scholarships out there for high school juniors, as well as sophomores and freshmen, too.

In fact, you don't even have to be a high school student to get a piece of the scholarship action. A broad range of scholarship contests—both general competitions and specific ones for students majoring in particular fields—are targeted at college undergraduates. These programs are as wide and varied as their high school counterparts. And even if you're a dissertation-writing, coffee house-loving grad student, there still remain plenty of big money opportunities: Scholarships exist for graduate studies in general, as well as for students pursuing advanced degrees in academic or professional fields.

Furthermore, you don't even have to reach puberty to apply for scholarships. A surprising number of scholarship contests are geared toward middle school and even elementary school students (such as the Craftsman/NSTA Young Inventor Awards, the National Geography Bee, or the Bayer/ NSF Award for Community Innovation). These programs, for the most part, don't focus on an applicant's overall record.

Some scholarship contests are open to entrants of all ages, with applicants only judged against others in their age bracket. Examples of such programs include the Prudential Spirit of Community Awards (11-19 year-olds), the Toshiba/NSTA ExploraVision Awards (grades K-12), and the All-USA Academic Teams (high school and college students).

Instead, such competitions are generally Type 1 contests (specified tasks), and frequently include team projects, adult mentors, and a learning component.

Geographic Region

Other than age specifications, perhaps the most common form of eligibility criteria are geographic requirements. On the local level, particular awards may be designated to students from specific high schools, districts, or communities. This is especially true of scholarships sponsored by local businesses and organizations that hope to benefit from the publicity and community goodwill. Scholarships targeted at students from a particular state or several states are also quite common.

Organizational Membership

Some scholarship contests are open only to members of particular organizations. The National Honor Society (NHS) scholarship program, for instance, offers hundreds of $1,000 scholarships for NHS members in the twelfth grade. Other types of organizations that provide member-only scholarship awards include the Boy Scouts, 4-H, Key Club, as well as career exploration programs such as the Future Business Leaders of America (FBLA) or the Future Farmers of America (FFA). Finding out early about such scholarship programs gives you time to join and participate in any organization in which membership is required to apply for an award.

Grades & Test Scores

Although most scholarships do not have formal grade-point average or test score cutoffs, some that emphasize academics will specify minimum levels of achievement. When such cutoffs exist, they do not tend to be particularly high—generally in the 2.5 to 3.0 range for grades and the 1000 to 1100 range for SAT scores. Occasionally, scholarships will require higher achievement scores (the Robert C. Byrd Honors scholarship program requires a GPA of 3.85 and SAT scores of 1150), but such requirements are fairly unusual and limited to contests with a heavy emphasis on academics.

Indirect Affiliation

One scholarship requires that applicants have ancestors who signed the Declaration of Independence. (Does your family name happen to be Jefferson?)

Other scholarships are limited to students who are indirectly affiliated with particular organizations or historical events—typically through their parents or ancestors. Some corporations, for instance, use scholarships as an additional benefit to employees. ABC/Capitol Cities, for instance, conducts a scholarship program open only to dependent children of company staff. These types of employee-focused scholarship programs tend to be sponsored by Fortune 500 companies and other large, well-established business entities.

A number of scholarships are aimed at students whose families have military affiliation. Such programs may require that the parents or ancestors of applicants be war veterans, and may even specify other requirements (such as a particular war, army division, etc.). The United Daughters of the Confederacy Scholarship, for example, requires that applicants be lineal descendants of Confederate soldiers!

Career Interests

Some scholarships are geared for students with particular career or vocational interests. Typically, such scholarships are sponsored by industry groups and associations. Also, foundations with particular societal goals in mind frequently create these types of programs. The Washington Crossing Foundation, for instance, targets students with "an interest in government service." Like many scholarships, this government service specification is very broad: Past winners have included students interested in becoming public prosecutors, senators, National Park Service botanists, army doctors, high school teachers, and everything in between.

As a general rule, even if you're only marginally interested in a particular field or career, you should not hesitate to apply for the scholarship. Although most scholarships of this

I even found one scholarship designed for students interested in the funeral services industry. (The judges are just dying to hear from you!)

type specify that applicants have a "genuine interest" in the given field, judges recognize that for applicants who are in their teens or early twenties, virtually nothing is etched in stone—interests can, and often do, change. Scholarships with the most stringent requirements will, at most, specify that you take some courses or major in a particular area of study.

ESPECIALLY FOR INTERNATIONAL STUDENTS. . .

Although some scholarship competitions in the United States are only for U.S. citizens, other contests do allow international students to apply.

First, we should note that even limited U.S. residency can dramatically increase the number of scholarship competitions an international student is eligible to enter. If an international student has attended high school in the United States—even if only as part of an exchange program—more scholarship options are available. This is because some contests merely require that applicants be attending a public, private, or parochial high school in the 50 states or District of Columbia. Other contests, such as the Coca-Cola Scholars Program, specify only that entrants have U.S. Permanent Resident, Temporary Resident, Refugee, or Asylee status. In this way, foreign students who attend high school in the U.S. may still be able to qualify for a substantial proportion of U.S. merit-based scholarships.

Second, be aware that some form of U.S. affiliation also increases scholarship possibilities. Many U.S. programs allow entries from students at schools in the U.S. territories, at Department of Defense schools abroad, or at American-affiliated international schools.

In addition, students from nations with close political, business, or geographic ties with the U.S. may have relatively more American scholarship opportunities than those from other countries. Canadian students, for instance, are eligible to enter the longstanding Scholastic Art & Writing Awards program. The essay and oratorical contests sponsored by Optimist International are open to Canadian and Jamaican students, as well as their American counterparts.

International students who don't fall into any of the above categories can still find scholarships for use at U.S. colleges—it just takes a bit more research. (We'll discuss specific research techniques in Chapter 3.) In general, Type 1 (specified tasks) competitions are the kind most available to those from other countries. Type 2 scholarships are less common for international students, probably due to the difficulty in comparing students' past achievements across borders and in very different school systems.

International students will also want to investigate sources of funding in their own countries. According to the Institute of International Education's "Open Doors" report, for close to 10 percent of foreign students studying in the U.S., their main source of funding was money from their home government or university, a foreign private sponsor, or an international organization.

Race & Ethnicity

Plenty of scholarship money is also available to students who are members of ethnic minority groups (African-Americans, Asians, Hispanics, Native Americans, etc.). Some scholarships are open to members of any ethnic minority, while others are targeted at a particular group. One eligibility specification employed in some scholarship competitions that can make things a bit more confusing is the term "traditionally under-represented ethnic minority"—a specification which generally does not include Asians or Asian-Americans. Other scholarship programs seek to promote ethnic diversity and cultural awareness, but don't require that all award recipients actually be from ethnic minority groups.

Gender

Some scholarship contests, especially those sponsored by various women's groups, are only open to female applicants. The converse—contests open only to male students—is quite rare. For some contests open to both sexes, gender criteria may specify that one male national winner and one female national winner will be selected. In general, never assume from the scholarship title that a particular contest is open only to one gender. Always check the rules, because titles can be misleading. I won an award from the National Association of Press Women in a journalism contest that was open to both males and females.

A Cornucopia of Contests

Regardless of how well your personal circumstances and individual characteristics mesh with the above guidelines, you will undoubtedly find dozens of scholarships just right for you. In fact, there are enough generic scholarship competitions out there—contests in which the only eligibility criterion is that you are of a particular age or grade-level—to keep you busy for a very, very long time.

THE OTHER PLAYERS

We now know *who* can play the scholarship game, but that's only half the story. We still need to know about the people and organizations who run the game itself. Who puts up the money for each scholarship? Are these the same people who administer the contests? Who selects the winners? Answering these questions broadens our understanding of the scholarship landscape, and provides us with clues about where we should begin our individual scholarship searches (something we'll do in Chapter 3).

Who Puts Up The Money?

Scholarships are funded by a variety of sources, and for a variety of reasons. Large corporations are a major source of scholarship dollars, and some of the largest programs are sponsored by Coca-Cola, Discover Card, Intel, McNeil Products (Tylenol), and others. Such companies sponsor these programs not only to help students, but also because of the public relations benefits.

Foundations established by wealthy individuals and family foundations—such as the William Randolph Hearst Foundation (U.S. Senate Youth Program)—are another prime source of funding. Such organizations are generally less concerned with generating publicity, and more concerned with particular goals they have for influencing society.

Most fraternal lodges, service organizations, and veterans associations—such as the American Legion, Elks Club, Jaycees, Optimist International, Rotary Club, and Veterans of Foreign Wars—sponsor some type of scholarship program. The national headquarters of each of these groups sponsor nationwide programs, while local chapters frequently sponsor their own initiatives. In addition, student activity organizations—such as Boy Scouts/Girl Scouts of America, Key Club, 4-H, and the National Honor Society—tend to have scholarship programs as well. On the local level, banks, credit unions, newspapers, television stations, and religious groups are frequent scholarship sponsors. In sheer dollar terms, federal and state governments are the largest provider of college scholarships, although the types of awards may be limited.

Who Runs the Contests?

Think of the people who administer each contest as the gatekeepers: They're the ones you have to pass through to enter the scholarship Promised Land. So who are these gatekeepers? Well, that depends on the contest.

For scholarship contests sponsored by service organizations, fraternal lodges, veterans' associations, or family foundations, the answer is generally straightforward: The organization that puts up the money typically administers the contest as well.

The answer can be quite different for scholarship programs sponsored by corporate entities. Although a large corporate scholarship program, such as the Coca-Cola Scholars Program, may have the resources to administer the contest on its own, other companies frequently outsource the logistics of running a contest to a group that specializes in conducting such programs. Such organizations include the Citizens' Scholarship Foundation of America (CSFA), the American Association of School Administrators (AASA), and the National Association of Secondary School Principals (NASSP).

In fact, some scholarship programs—such as the Intel Science Talent Search administered by Science Service—have been created entirely by these third-party organizations (who use the corporate sponsorship angle to raise the necessary funding for the program). So when you or your school receive your winner's check, it will likely be from one of these organizations rather than from the sponsoring company itself.

For scholarship programs sponsored by federal or state governments, a state agency will administer the program. In some states, such as my home state of Oregon, all government programs reside in one particular agency. In other states, several state agencies will share administrative duties. In most instances, these agencies will only administer scholarship programs sponsored by local, state, or federal governments. In a few states, however, with Oregon being the first to do this, such agencies may also be contracted by private donors who want to avoid the bureaucratic and logistical burdens of managing a scholarship contest.

The National Association of Secondary School Principals (NASSP) administers the Prudential Spirit of Community Awards, the National Honor Society Scholarship, and the Principal's Leadership Award.

For a complete list of the government agencies in your state that administer scholarships, please see Appendix C.

Who Are the Judges?

Every scholarship contest is judged differently. Anywhere from a single judge to hundreds of judges may be responsible for evaluating entries. For contests administered by the third-party organizations discussed in the previous section, judges are generally drawn from the ranks of current or former teachers, school administrators, and organization staff members. I've found that because such organizations have had the experience of running numerous scholarship contests, the judging administered by them tends to be the most objective, and best adheres to the published judging criteria.

High-profile national contests administered by these types of organizations may also employ "blue-ribbon panels" for final judging; these panels generally include celebrities, government officials, and other notable individuals. For example, judges for the 1997 Prudential Spirit of Community Awards program included Senator Robert Kerrey of Nebraska, actor Richard Dreyfuss, and Robert Goodwin, President and CEO of the Points of Light Foundation.

On the local level, such blue-ribbon panels typically include television and radio personalities, successful entrepreneurs, and professional athletes. In contests that employ this method of judging, a limited number of finalists are usually pre-selected via more mundane judging channels, and then presented to the blue-ribbon panel for final evaluation.

For contests administered by the corporations themselves, public relations personnel may be the ones to select the winners. When judging is conducted by a public relations department, other factors such as geographical balance can sneak into the (unpublished) judging criteria. (I've had the opportunity to observe the judging procedures of one such contest.)

Programs conducted by service organizations, fraternal lodges, and veterans' associations are likely to be judged by members of the particular organization. In this way, the key tenets and values of the sponsoring organization frequently play a role in the judging.

Perhaps the most subjective judging occurs when performed by small family or historic institutions—each with a unique set of biases and viewpoints. One notable contest I

In these cases it's a good idea to "do your homework" and learn about some of the key objectives of the sponsoring organization.

entered, for instance, appeared to have a very definite political slant; most of its current winners and past winners reflected this ideological disposition.

The important thing to take away from this section is that judging is, by nature, quite subjective. Anticipating how the judging is conducted in a particular contest can give you an important strategic advantage when preparing your entry. Although scholarship contests are mostly judged on the published judging criteria, certain "hidden" criteria can enter the mix. (See Chapter 6 for more on this topic.)

EXPLODING 7 MYTHS

Hold your ears and take cover. Because in this section, we are going to explode seven widespread myths that have been perpetuated about college scholarship contests. For years now, such myths have plagued the scholarship landscape, deterring many worthy students from playing the scholarship game. But now, by revealing the real story known to scholarship insiders, we will expose these myths for what they are. In fact, just the act of exploding these myths can make your chances of winning. . . well, dynamite.

Myth #1:

"Only students with high academic achievement win merit-based scholarships."

THE REAL STORY: Scholarships are awarded to students with all sorts of talents and interests. In fact, many of the best scholarship programs are designed for students who devote their time to such diverse fields as music and the arts, foreign languages, community service, science, leadership, writing, and oratory, to name a few. Typically, these programs are entirely "grade blind"—meaning that grades are not used as a judging criteria.

Furthermore, many scholarships that do take into account grade point averages (GPAs) only use such quantitative measures as preliminary cutoff points. For instance, some scholarship contests specify that applicants have a minimum 2.5 GPA. Once you've cleared this minimum bar, grades don't impact your chances of winning.

Finally, even when GPA is used as an evaluation factor, it's only *one* aspect of a student's application. One of the largest scholarship contests, the Coca-Cola Scholars Program, is known for selecting students that do not necessarily have top grades. Other programs use a broader definition of academics that includes areas of interest and study outside of the traditional school curriculum. The bottom line is that most scholarship programs aren't myopic: They take into account that applicants have much more to offer than simply the grades that appear on their transcripts.

Myth #2:   *"Star athletes are the big scholarship winners."*

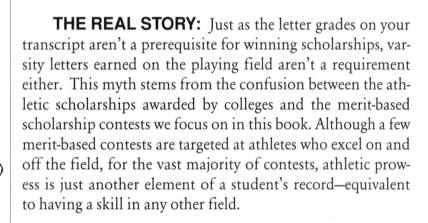

THE REAL STORY: Just as the letter grades on your transcript aren't a prerequisite for winning scholarships, varsity letters earned on the playing field aren't a requirement either. This myth stems from the confusion between the athletic scholarships awarded by colleges and the merit-based scholarship contests we focus on in this book. Although a few merit-based contests are targeted at athletes who excel on and off the field, for the vast majority of contests, athletic prowess is just another element of a student's record—equivalent to having a skill in any other field.

Myth #3:   *"The student who has the most extracurricular activities generally wins."*

THE REAL STORY: As is the case in many other aspects of life, winning scholarships is about quality, not quantity. Some people think that to win these awards you must have devoted your entire high school career to participating in extracurricular activities. On the contrary, most scholarship winners distinguish themselves by the devotion they have demonstrated to a particular activity or activities, rather than by the sheer quantity of their involvement.

Winning scholarships isn't about having the longest list of extracurriculars. Instead, it's about communicating who you are and what you care about through the activities you participate in and enjoy. And even if you can't rattle off one particular activity that you've been especially passionate about, don't worry: In later chapters, I'll show you how to find extracurricular activities that are well-suited for you.

Myth #4: *"Entering scholarship competitions is just like applying to college."*

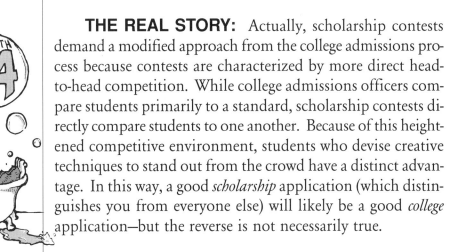

THE REAL STORY: Actually, scholarship contests demand a modified approach from the college admissions process because contests are characterized by more direct head-to-head competition. While college admissions officers compare students primarily to a standard, scholarship contests directly compare students to one another. Because of this heightened competitive environment, students who devise creative techniques to stand out from the crowd have a distinct advantage. In this way, a good *scholarship* application (which distinguishes you from everyone else) will likely be a good *college* application—but the reverse is not necessarily true.

Myth #5: *"Scholarship competitions are conducted on a level playing field."*

THE REAL STORY: Each scholarship contest has its own biases. This is not to say that scholarship judging is unfair. Rather, it's just that each contest is looking for students with particular qualities. The subjective process of valuing certain qualities over other ones tilts the playing field far from level. In this way, the ideal application for one particular scholarship contest may place you out of the money for another. Because of these biases, it's essential to define each contest's ideal applicant, and to develop a strategy that emphasizes personal attributes consistent with this definition. To paraphrase George Orwell: *Everyone is equal, but some are more equal than others.*

Myth #6: | *"The track record you've already accumulated determines whether you'll win scholarships."*

THE REAL STORY: What you do *after* you decide to apply for scholarships is just as important as the record you have already accumulated. This holds true regardless of how much time you have until a particular scholarship application is due. Content strategies, for instance, increase your chances of winning by adding depth and breadth to your existing record. Likewise, packaging strategies help make your application stand out from the crowd by creating a cohesive message that highlights talents, communicates passions, and emphasizes potential. So don't fall into the trap of thinking that your die has already been cast. What you do *now* will make all the difference in the world.

Myth #7: | *"Students should focus their time and energy on only one or two scholarship applications."*

THE REAL STORY: Some students make the mistake of thinking that they maximize their chances of winning by pouring all of their energy into one or two scholarships. Such a strategy, however, is exactly what you *don't* want to do. Applying for scholarships is a numbers game. A variety of factors outside of your control can affect the outcome of any given contest. Only by applying for large numbers of scholarships can you minimize such factors. As the saying goes, "don't put all your eggs in one basket."

CHAPTER 2 SUMMARY

■ **Eligibility:** Organizations may target scholarships at specific students according to such factors as age, geographic region, organizational membership, grades & test scores, indirect affiliation, career interests, race & ethnicity, or gender. A plethora of scholarships is available for the typical student.

■ **Sponsors:** Merit-based scholarship contests are funded by corporations, foundations, service clubs, fraternal lodges, student activity organizations, religious institutions, banks and credit unions, media outlets, as well as federal and state governments.

■ **Administration:** Service organizations, fraternal lodges, and family foundations that sponsor scholarships generally administer their contests themselves. Other groups may outsource scholarship contest logistics to third-party organizations.

■ **Selecting Winners:** Every scholarship contest is judged differently. For contests administered by outside organizations, judging is usually performed by teachers, school administrators, and organization staff members. Contests administered by corporations may employ public relations departments as judges. Scholarship judging is, by nature, quite subjective. Anticipating how judging is conducted in a particular contest can yield a strategic advantage.

■ **Exploding Myths:** A diverse group of students win merit-based scholarships. Being an academic whiz or star athlete is not necessary. Winning scholarships is about the *quality* of a student's extracurricular involvement, not about the sheer quantity of activities.

Scholarship contests are judged differently than college applications: Because students are directly compared to one another, applicants must find creative ways to make their efforts stand out from the crowd. Each scholarship contest has its own biases—understanding the tilt of the playing field yields a big advantage.

What a student does *after* deciding to enter scholarship contests is just as important as the record he or she has already accumulated.

What Parents Can Do To Help

Intermission

Congratulations! Now that you know the rules of the scholarship game, you're ready to discover the secrets of researching scholarships, as well as organizing and managing the application process. Before we move on to these topics in Part II, let's take a brief intermission—one of four "time-outs" that occur during the course of this book.

In this intermission, I describe the substantial effect that interested parents can have on the scholarship game. When reading this section, keep in mind that all of the possible parental-help tasks I describe are entirely feasible for students themselves to perform on their own. However, if mom or dad is interested in assisting with a scholarship quest, all the better. In the pages that follow, I'll illustrate how to best utilize this parental support.

Mining for Scholarship Gold

The process of *searching* for scholarships (detailed in the upcoming chapter) is one of the best ways your parents can make a substantial contribution to your scholarship success. From helping conduct an Internet scholarship search, to visiting other schools in your district when tracking down information (more on these tactics later), interested parents can really help leverage and multiply your time.

In addition, many high schools, such as my former, use parent volunteers to staff the school's scholarship library or center (typically part of the school's college and career center). So if your mom or dad is someone who frequently volunteers at the school, suggest that they volunteer at this library or center. They will quickly accumulate a wealth of expert knowledge about the key scholarship resources at your school, and will be able to help you to find those pesky scholarship applications that may be buried beneath a pile of dense paperwork on some counselor's desk.

And even if your parents don't have time to volunteer, they may, nonetheless, have better access to limited school resources. For instance, at some schools, certain scholarship resources are only accessible to students through their counselors. These same counselors, however, may be willing to give interested parents direct access to these scholarship files.

If your parents are slightly reluctant to get involved, I suggest that you show them just how much scholarship moola is out there. Tell them about some of the big money awards, and about how all of these winnings typically aren't taxed by the government (they'll appreciate that one).

Juggling the Paperwork

Managing the stacks of paperwork and keeping track of all the various deadlines can test your organizational skills—especially when you have to complete two papers, three tests, and the district tennis championships all in the same week. During these busy times, my parents would often help me in my scholarship quest by sending letters or making phone calls to request scholarship applications. And if I was extremely busy when these applications arrived, they would even help by filing them away and marking the deadlines on my scholarship calendar. (More on organizing the process in Chapter 4.)

Because some scholarship organizations may only be reachable by phone during hours when you're in class, it's especially helpful if one of your parents is willing to make a few follow-up phone calls on your behalf.

Tracking Down Background Information

Doing well on some scholarship essays may depend on compiling helpful background information in preparation for the actual writing. This presents yet another way that parents can make a significant contribution. For instance, the Washington Crossing Foundation asked scholarship applicants to include in an essay on government service any inspiration "derived from the leadership of George Washington in his famous crossing of the Delaware." Well, at the time, I knew very little about this historic event. So on the way back from running some errands, my parents stopped by the local public library and photocopied some encyclopedia articles and checked out some books on this key event.

I still had to read and process this material myself, but having it conveniently at hand made all the difference in the world.

In another contest, I wrote an essay suggesting potential reforms to the American educational system. It was important to be up to date on the latest developments in the educational reform movement, and my parents conducted a few electronic searches for the latest newspaper, magazine, and journal articles on the topic. Then they found the articles in a University library and photocopied them for my reference.

Of course, a lot of this background research I would conduct on my own, too. But during very busy times, having help from my parents was a lifesaver—allowing me to focus my energy on developing application strategies and crafting the actual application and entry materials.

Providing a Valuable Sounding Board

As for the ethics of parental help, the key point to keep in mind is that your parents should be playing a <u>supporting</u> role. They can help you brainstorm ideas, research topics, as well as proofread essays and applications—but the end product needs to be your <u>own</u> work.

In addition to helping with all of the tasks I've mentioned, parents can also be an important source of general feedback. Although far from objective (they are your parents after all!), mom and dad probably do know more about you than anyone else. So if you've left out an important experience that would work great in a particular essay, chances are they can help you jog your memory.

If your parents do a substantial amount of writing as part of their job, they may also be able to serve as great copyeditors for your scholarship applications. Aside from my own final reading, my dad conducted the final proofreading for most of my submissions.

The text in the shaded box shown below is a letter from my parents to your parents. So when you get a free moment, corner your mom or dad in the living room or kitchen, and make them read this letter!

Finally, if you're working on your application materials with your parents, try to hear out their opinions—even if you think they're dead wrong about an issue. (It does happen from time to time!) Because scholarship judging is a subjective process, if your application rubs someone the wrong way, it's entirely possible that a scholarship judge could respond similarly. Besides, there is usually a painless way to address a parent's concerns, while still keeping what you love about your original work. It just takes a bit of time and a little focused thinking. (And yes, mom, you were right!)

A LETTER FROM MY PARENTS TO YOUR PARENTS

Dear Parents of Future Scholarship Winners:

Four years ago, when our son entered his first scholarship contest, we probably felt similar to the way you do right now: We encouraged our son to apply and did whatever we could to help, but we really didn't expect a whole lot to come from it. When the scholarship checks did start rolling in, it was a wonderful surprise. The biggest shock, however, had nothing to do with all the money. It was something more important: the dramatic, even life-changing transformation we actually witnessed in our son.

You see, because of the personal nature of scholarship applications, just filling out these forms forced him to think about his strengths, to confront his weaknesses, and, most importantly, to dream about his future. In short, entering scholarship contests forced him to discover who he really was, and to begin developing a plan to fully realize his talents and passions. Not that this plan can't or won't change. Indeed, as any grown-up knows, it will change many times during the course of a lifetime. But it was this underlying sense of purpose and progress that led to Benjamin's many other successes, and that, most importantly, led him to discover the things that would make him most happy. The result was a gradual transformation in Benjamin, as he took increasing control over his own destiny. This has been very inspiring for us, and has even impacted our own life decisions.

(next)

(continued)

There are, of course, many other benefits to applying for scholarships—such things as enhanced writing skills, heightened self-promotional abilities, and substantially improved college applications (which dramatically increases the likelihood that your son or daughter will be admitted to the college of his or her choice). But these things paled in comparison to our son's personal growth. We also grew as a family through the transformational process of working together toward a common goal. The camaraderie of the quest has resulted in the forging of close ties—bonds that, we believe, supercede the expected parent-child relationship. Even when the scholarship money is used up, and the memories of award ceremonies become cloudy, these bonds live on.

If we can offer any advice to other parents it would be to strive to become a respected "sounding board," rather than a coach who tells a player what to do. Learning how to play a supporting role—instead of directing the action—is frequently the hardest lesson for a parent. Nonetheless, it is sometimes the most valuable thing you can do.

Likewise, keep encouraging your child to apply for college scholarships even if the first few bids are unsuccessful. As a family, we've come to realize that learning how to *win* first means learning how to *lose*; and in learning how to lose, you actually learn how to win. Furthermore, scholarship contest results should *never* be treated as an assessment of how good or talented your child may be. These contests are highly subjective and often unpredictable, and results should never be taken personally, or as a measure of self-worth.

In a nutshell, your role as a parent of a scholarship game player is a multifaceted one. It includes encouraging your child to apply for numerous scholarships, helping him to use time efficiently and meet deadlines, and supporting her in the midst of temporary setbacks. It may also include helping him or her fine-tune applications, conduct research, or express future goals and dreams. Moreover, being a part of your child's scholarship team will help *you*, as it helped us, to become a better parent. So even though the immediate need for college financing may motivate your child's search for scholarships, remember that regardless of outcomes, the effort is most definitely time well spent.

Best wishes,

Gary & Patana Kaplan

PART II

Getting
Ready
To Play

"Show Me The Money!"

In this chapter, we'll teach you powerful techniques for locating and researching the scholarships that are right for you.

CHAPTER CONTENTS

- Finding scholarships on the Internet
- Employing school scholarship resources
- Searching community sources
- Avoiding fee-based services
- Etiquette for requesting applications

FINDING YOUR POT OF GOLD

Legend has it that at the end of every rainbow lies a pot of gold. So you could lace up your shoes, get in your car, and whip out your best rainbow-tracking radar system... or you could use the powerful techniques outlined in this chapter to locate your very own pot of scholarship gold. (I'm sure that you're in a lot of suspense about which option I will suggest.)

In this chapter, I describe some basic—and some not so basic—techniques for finding and researching scholarship programs that are right for you. If you dutifully apply the strategies and tactics in this chapter, you'll undoubtedly find that you qualify for hundreds of scholarships—with dozens of them targeted at someone just like you.

The Golden Rule

As you embark on your scholarship quest, keep in mind a very simple, yet extremely important, rule—what I call the Golden Rule of searching for scholarships. As simple as it may be, it's a rule that most people soon forget, or at least forget to implement. It goes like this:

Additional effort invested into researching scholarships is never wasted.

To understand this principle, consider two examples: In the first case, you spend extra hours tracking down a very hard-to-find scholarship. Well, if you found it difficult to find, chances are that other people did too. So you would expect this scholarship to have fewer entries than a comparable one with better publicity. Fewer entries translates into better odds of winning. Therefore, the harder it is to find out about a scholarship program, the easier it probably is to win it. So putting the added investment into research really does tilt the odds in your favor.

Now let's examine a second example: You are entering a national scholarship contest, and you take the time to research more information than what is contained on the entry form and brochure. It takes some doing, but you locate some sample essays written by past winners. What is the result? This added information provides you with a better understanding of what the scholarship judges think is good, and your odds of winning skyrocket over other applicants. Once again, the extra investment into research pays big dividends.

Because of the Golden Rule, it is always a good strategy to invest your time into fully exploiting the techniques covered in this chapter. If you faithfully implement the steps I outline below, you'll be that much closer to finding your own pot of scholarship gold.

Using Appendix A

For more information on the complete Scholarship Sleuth directory, see page A-38 in Appendix A.

For the latest updates to the Appendix A scholarship listings, check out my Reader's Resource Room at winscholarships.com on the World Wide Web.

Start your scholarship search with the directory contained in Appendix A. This innovative directory, excerpted from *The Scholarship Sleuth*, focuses on several dozen big-money scholarship opportunities that are open to virtually every type of student, regardless of geographic residency, career interests, or college choice. This directory provides detailed descriptions of application requirements, judging criteria, and eligibility rules, as well as insider tips on each contest. In this way, Appendix A will provide you with a big jump-start on your scholarship search.

After perusing the listings, use the contact information provided to request contest applications. In general, if there's even the slightest chance that you will enter a scholarship contest, request the application. Even if you don't end up entering the contest, it's still a good idea to familiarize yourself with the various formats, components, and requirements of scholarship applications.

SEARCHING INTERNET DATABASES

Now that you've looked over the *Scholarship Sleuth* directory, you're ready to begin your own personalized search. Perhaps the best place to start this endeavor is on the Internet through the use of a variety of scholarship-search databases. These services ask for personal information such as age, gender, ethnicity, grade-point average, extracurricular activities, organizational affiliation, and career

If you don't have a computer at home, you should have access to one at your school or local public library.

interests. Then they use this information to scan their databases and provide you with a list of scholarships that fit your profile. And because the best databases are actually free-of-charge to students (they generate their revenues mainly from advertising), it won't cost you a penny to conduct these searches.

Brief reviews of the Internet's best scholarship search databases are shown below. A convenient place to link to all of these search databases is at **winscholarships.com** on the World Wide Web. In the event that the Internet addresses of these search databases change, this portal site maintains the up-to-date links. In addition, as new quality search services become available, links to them are included here. So for the latest information, be sure to bookmark winscholarships.com in your favorite Web surfing program.

FastWEB

www.fastweb.com

FastWEB claims to be the largest scholarship search database on the Internet—with more than 400,000 awards included in its database at last count. The database requires that students sign-up for a free "mailbox," which is updated periodically (and can be checked frequently) for any new scholarships that match your personal characteristics.

To manage all of the one-page scholarship contest summaries you will print out from these databases, it's helpful to use a three-ring binder organized by entry deadline, type of contest, and whether or not you've requested an application.

To conduct a search, you are required to fill out a fairly lengthy questionnaire, so plan on setting aside 20 to 30 minutes just inputting data. A strong point of the FastWEB database is the relatively detailed and accurate descriptions it provides about each scholarship.

As extensive a list of scholarships as FastWEB claims to maintain, searches yield a relatively small quantity of awards—albeit ones that precisely match the personal information you entered. The fairly generic search I conducted yielded little more than a dozen scholarship programs, most of which were the big national ones. This is partly due to the limited amount of personal information you can enter for any one search.

For instance, the database only allows you to select two potential career objectives, four hobbies, and four student ac-

In many of these search databases, holding down the "Ctrl" or "Shift" keys will allow you to select multiple items from the same category field.

tivities or skills. Because of this, you will want to submit multiple searches with varied entries. How does one do this? You can do it by either clicking on the "change personal information" option, or else by creating multiple user mailboxes.

CollegeNET MACH25
www.collegenet.com/mach25/

To use this service, you must first choose a user name and password. Next, you will input personal information into five categories: residence, personal, academics, organization, and general. One important search criterion in this database that has a large impact on results is your choice to "exclude school-specific scholarships" (located in the "general" menu). If you do not exclude these scholarships, you will be inundated with thousands of scholarship programs at universities that you're probably not considering attending. If you exclude school-specific scholarships, your list will likely contain a more manageable amount (typically a few hundred scholarships). Perhaps the best approach is to exclude school-specific scholarships in your preliminary search, and then include them in a new search when you have more time.

Some databases ask you if you want to exclude scholarships whose deadlines have already passed. In general, never exclude these scholarships. Application deadlines often change, listings can be several years old, and there's no guarantee that the deadlines stated in the database are correct.

The strength of this database is that its listings include some pretty obscure scholarship programs. This is good, as long as you are prepared to search through quite a few listings that are so specialized they probably won't apply to you. Another nice feature of the Mach25 database is its ability to save scholarships in a personal folder; this becomes available whenever you log on to the site. *Tip: To view the details about each scholarship, select the "More Detailed" check box, then click "Same."*

College Board Scholarship Search
cbweb10p.collegeboard.org/fundfinder/html/fundfind01.html

This database includes a smaller number of scholarship listings than some of the other top online scholarship search sites. The searches I have conducted in this database have mainly unearthed fairly well-known scholarship programs. These scholarships will also be uncovered by a variety of other sources. Nevertheless, the database is a good way to get some large scholarship programs summarized in one place.

COACH

In this case dialogue, the Scholarship Coach answers questions about scholarship search companies— services that charge anywhere from $10 to $200 for providing students with a list of scholarships that supposedly fit their personal attributes.

If you're still thinking about hiring a fee-based search company, you may be able to assess its legitimacy by consulting the Federal Trade Commission's Web site (www.ftc.gov).

. . . About fee-based services

Today's questions were submitted by Ivana Winn, a senior from Wantbank, Indiana.

Ivana: I recently received a brochure about a company that finds scholarships for students in exchange for a $79 fee. Should I buy the service?

Scholarship Coach: Ivana, my advice is to steer clear of such fee-based search services. After examining the listings that many students have received, it becomes clear that these companies don't have access to any better information than the free search databases. In fact, many of these fee-based services may simply input your data into the free search databases described in this chapter.

Ivana: But can purchasing such lists save me a lot of time and energy?

Scholarship Coach: No, not really. In my experience, the lists these companies provide are not particularly customized. One student paid $45 to a search firm, and received the addresses of six scholarship programs that she wasn't even eligible to apply for. Even the best of these services are no substitute for the techniques outlined in this chapter. Besides, conducting your own search isn't particularly time-consuming anyway.

Ivana: But the search promised I would win at least $1000!

Scholarship Coach: Beware of such guarantees. The Federal Trade Commission has warned that some of these search services may, in fact, be scams.

If you're having trouble printing from a given database, cut and paste the information into your favorite word processing program. Then save the file or print from that program.

Each listing is accompanied by a page that describes the rudiments of each contest. Contact addresses (but generally not phone numbers) are also provided. This online scholarship search database is a simpler version of the "Fund Finder" portion of the ExPAN software program which can be found in some high school guidance offices. Because a relatively small number of scholarships comprise this database, you will need to select multiple items from each category field to turn up a substantial number of suitable listings.

Scholarship Resource Network

www.srnexpress.com

I was pleasantly surprised when conducting searches on SRN Express. It yielded several large, well-funded scholarship programs that I had not encountered elsewhere. My search also netted more than 60 scholarships, most of which had fairly detailed descriptions.

Some sites also generate revenue by selling your profile to companies that target students through direct mail and e-mail. In most databases, however, there is an option in which you can remove yourself from such lists.

One annoying aspect of the service, however, is the requirement of typing in three-digit codes to identify many individual characteristics, instead of being able to simply click on an item to select it. The preciseness of its database categories is also questionable. For instance, scholarships targeted at students from Arkansas popped up in my search, although I had identified no college or residency within a thousand miles of Little Rock. Because you're only allowed to select three items in each category (such as three extracurricular interests), you might find it helpful to conduct multiple searches.

CASHE Online Scholarship Search Service

www.cashe.com

This online scholarship search service, sponsored by SallieMae, provides students with access to the CASHE (College Aid Sources for Higher Education) database. A fairly generic search netted two dozen or so scholarships, mostly national ones, that fit the criteria I entered. Although the listings

Most Internet databases need to be completed in one sitting. If you allow too much time to elapse in between entries (such as leaving your computer for a few minutes) you may have to re-enter everything all over again.

aren't particularly detailed, most of them include phone numbers—saving you the effort of having to send out a letter to request an application.

To use this database, you will need an e-mail account because search results are e-mailed to you within 24 hours. (On my searches it only took a couple of hours.) If you do not have an e-mail address, there are a number of sites on the Internet that provide free e-mail accounts. To locate one of these services, pick your favorite Internet search engine and type in the words "free e-mail." One of the most popular free e-mail sites is Hotmail (**www.hotmail.com**).

Overall, CASHE is a solid search service with a user-friendly interface, and a convenient mechanism for reviewing, printing, and changing information you input. Although CASHE employs perhaps the greatest number of search criteria of any major service, many of the scholarships you uncover, however, will likely be duplicates of the ones you can find through some of the other databases I've mentioned.

MOLIS: Minority On-Line Information Service
www.sciencewise.com/scholarships/

Once you're enrolled in college, the state in which you attend school may also be deemed your state of residence (in addition to your home state) by scholarship organizations. This may allow you to qualify for local scholarships in multiple states.

MOLIS provides a no-frills scholarship database geared for minority students. You simply enter your state of residence, sex, race, ethnic heritage, college major, and grade-point average, and the service provides you with a list of scholarships appropriate to someone with your interests and ancestry. There's no need to log on, register, or provide a user name. And it's also easy to use: From start to finish, a search takes under a minute. Overall, MOLIS is a great resource for identifying some excellent minority scholarship programs.

Tricks of the Trade

When these search databases ask you to define your personal characteristics, always be as broad as possible—so that you won't miss any scholarship opportunities because you selected too narrow a profile. Even if you are only marginally interested in a particular career, undergraduate major, extracurricular activity, or type of college, include it as part of your search. Remember, you will always be able to sort through the scholarships that turn up at a later date.

If a search requires you to choose between personal characteristics that are not mutually exclusive (such as if you have both Hispanic and Asian ancestry, but can only choose one ethnic category), perform the search *both ways*. Because some Internet search services require that you register with them (providing your name, address, and other information), when conducting multiple searches with different criteria, you'll have to come up with variations of your screen name to re-register. This is an especially important tactic to employ because scholarship-search databases do not always have the most up-to-date information, and sometimes misclassify scholarship programs.

GUERRILLA TACTIC #1

Conduct multiple searches in each database by varying your personal characteristics. Doing this helps you locate scholarships that may be misclassified.

It is also definitely worth your while to conduct database searches for contests you will be eligible for in future years (such as a high school junior searching for scholarships aimed at seniors). Doing this provides you with a better feel for the overall scholarship landscape, and helps you keep track of scholarship programs that currently show up in scholarship-search databases, but may drop off your search radar in future years. Furthermore, these extra searches prevent you from missing out on any scholarship contests because they happen to be classified in the wrong age bracket—a situation that has happened to me on more than one occasion.

The key concept embedded in all of these strategies is that you want to avoid leaving any potential scholarship money on the table because you didn't perform that one extra search.

Limitations of Database Searches

Although scholarship databases on the Internet are great places to *begin* your search, they are just that—*starting* points. Some students make the mistake of assuming that after a few Internet searches, they've found all the scholarships they are going to find. How wrong they are! Taking this approach is like hearing a couple of tunes on the radio, and concluding that you've discovered everything there is to know about music. In actuality, programs listed in Internet databases are only the tip of the scholarship iceberg.

Although Internet-based searches are a quick way to accumulate a list of scholarships, they do, in fact, have substantial limitations. First, these types of databases are somewhat lacking when it comes to listings of local and state scholarships. Second, Internet databases are not particularly timely: Newly created scholarships, even really large programs, will not be found in most databases. In fact, quite a few of the scholarship contests that I won have been conspicuously absent from all the online databases I've used.

USING SCHOOL RESOURCES

The above limitations make the local resources at your school—resources such as your school's guidance office, career center, or reference library—especially important research tools. My school had a filing cabinet devoted to scholarship contests, a bulletin board that listed forthcoming deadlines, and an electronic database of scholarships (similar to the Internet databases explained above).

The reason schools are a bountiful source of scholarship information is that many scholarship sponsors send applications, brochures, and other materials directly to schools nationwide in order to get the word out about their programs. This is especially true of corporate-sponsored scholarships, where merit-based contests become extensions of each firm's public relations efforts. Application materials may be sent to principals, counselors, or individual teachers. At most schools, this information is centralized—typically at a college and career center of some kind. Find out how your school works, and become an expert on the resources available.

To do this, I suggest setting up a meeting with a counselor at your school for the specific purpose of discussing scholarship opportunities. Tell your counselor that you're serious about winning scholarships, and that you would be very grateful for any help and information that he or she can provide. In general, it is always a good strategy to cultivate relationships with counselors at your school.

Because I cultivated these relationships, counselors informed me of many programs and scholarship opportunities that I would have otherwise missed. One student I know even took a job in his school's guidance office for this very reason. Doing so increased his access to scholarship opportunities, and helped him acquire excellent letters of recommendation for both scholarship and college applications.

At my high school, scholarship information letters and applications from past school years were filed away in binders for student perusal. I soon discovered the value of looking through these old materials: Sometimes information about a scholarship program may make it to your school only in an earlier year—perhaps because of reductions in the promotional budget—even though the program still exists. So if your school doesn't already file away old applications and letters, suggest that they *start* the practice!

Other resources that schools often provide include bulletin boards that list upcoming scholarship deadlines, as well as lists of past students at your school who have won particular scholarship awards. The latter can be especially useful: Noting the awards that former students have won can yield a valuable list of potential scholarship programs—especially local ones. If your school doesn't make such records available, don't be shy about making constructive suggestions.

You should also ask your teachers to inform you of any contests (typically Type 1 scholarships) they may hear about. Teachers are frequently aware of contests in their area of expertise (especially fields like creative writing, journalism, or graphic design) that don't show up on the bigger radar screens of your school's guidance office.

CD-ROM Databases at School

Many high schools and colleges also purchase scholarship-search databases on CD-ROMs that are updated each year. Such databases operate just like the Internet-based ones, except that schools purchase this software for fees ranging

Even though schools pay money for such databases, these aren't the fee-based search services I warned you about earlier. The database products that schools purchase typically come from well-respected government agencies, educational sources, or reputable publishers.

from several hundred to thousands of dollars (depending upon the number of students enrolled at the school). These databases are sometimes part of general college and career software packages such as the Career Information System.

These CD-ROM databases often contain a different mix of scholarships programs than their online counterparts, so it's definitely worthwhile to search them. In fact, because Internet sources were not nearly as developed when I was engaged in my own scholarship quest, these school-purchased databases were my main electronic option. Furthermore, a big advantage of these databases over their Internet-based counterparts is that they typically are customized to your particular school and geographic area, and thus include many more local scholarships. The same techniques I detailed for Internet search services work well with these databases too.

And Not Just <u>Your</u> School!

What if your school doesn't have all of these resources? Not to worry! You see, the enterprising scholarship seeker (that's you) won't let a few little inconveniences stand in his or her way. Instead, simply do what you would do if the corner grocery was all sold out of your favorite cereal. Go to another store! This means visiting other schools in your district (or beyond) to tap their scholarship resources too.

In fact, I highly recommend taking these field trips even if your school has *all* of the aforementioned scholarship resources. As we've seen, when it comes to scholarships, information distribution is far from uniform: The school across town may have a list of scholarship programs that just never made it to your neck of the woods.

In fact, during my scholarship search, I visited other schools in my area on a regular basis. (If you have friends at

GUERRILLA TACTIC #2

Raid the scholarship libraries and guidance offices of other schools in your area to tap their scholarship resources.

other schools, they can fill you in on the resources that are available). Of course, I didn't exactly get all decked out in my school colors and trademark logo when visiting rival high schools. . . However, even if I had mentioned that I was from a different school, I think most counselors and parent volunteers would have still been willing to help me.

MORE WEB SURFING SECRETS

Earlier in this chapter, we discussed how to utilize free Internet search databases, but that's only one aspect of what the Web has to offer. So now it's time for us to expand our Web-based search techniques. To do this, we're going to employ several widely-used Internet search engines. These engines include such portals as:

Yahoo! (**www.yahoo.com**),
Lycos (**www.lycos.com**),
AltaVista (**www.altavista.com**),
and Excite (**www.excite.com**).

As you know, finding Web sites would be virtually impossible without portals that provide you with tools to quickly and easily search for information. That's where these particular search engines come into play. They help you find your way amidst the Internet's information jungle. To use these engines effectively, however, you need to know a few key tricks. In this section, I will describe these techniques and show you the most time-effective ways to use these engines to expand your scholarship search.

First, we need to understand a little about how these search engines work. Although search engines don't store data from the Web sites themselves, they do create indexed references to Web-site pages. Most of the time, this includes the page title, the web address, as well as a summary description and list of keywords. Some Web search engines gather the summary description from the first few hundred characters of the page, while other engines look for common words or phrases on the entire page.

Using these search engines is fairly straightforward: Simply type words in the "search for" box and hit the ENTER key. I've found, however, that knowing how to properly employ the syntax in a particular search engine—this includes the use of quote marks, plus and minus signs, and capital letters—can make your scholarship searches considerably more effective. So check out the help section of your favorite search engine for more specific tips on optimizing your technique.

In the surfing I've done for scholarship information, I've found that the AltaVista (www.altavista.com) search engine works quite well.

Primary and Secondary Web Sites

As we search the Web for suitable scholarship contests, there are two types of sites we are hunting for: **primary** and **secondary** Web sites.

Primary sites are the official sites put up by the organizations sponsoring or administering scholarship contests. In the past couple of years, increasing numbers of programs have been making contest information (and even applications) available over the Internet. In fact, of the scholarship contests listed in the Appendix A scholarship directory, more than two-thirds have substantial information available over the Web.

If you're having difficulty finding a particular contest, be sure to try multiple search engines.

If you happen to know the name of a scholarship contest, or know of the organization that sponsors or administers it, then you have enough information to search for the primary Web site using the search engine techniques just discussed. If you don't know the official name of the scholarship, first try to search for it by including the word "scholarship" with whatever information you do know. If that doesn't work, try searching for the organization that sponsors or administers the contest. Once you get to the organization's Web site, you can search within the site for the contest itself.

See Appendix A for the Web addresses of specific scholarship contests.

Of course, a lot of the value of Internet searches comes from finding scholarships that you've never heard of before. You can do this by searching for generic categories of scholarships (such as ones aimed at particular career interests, fields of study, or hobbies), but the effectiveness of such an approach is limited.

This is where secondary Web sites come into play. Secondary sites are not official sites put up by contest sponsors or administrators, but rather, are sites that post lists of available scholarship opportunities. Such listings are usually not the main focus of the site, but instead are designed to be an added service for students. Frequently, these types of sites are put up by school guidance offices or associations involved with educating young people.

So how do you find such sites? All it takes is a simple, yet effective, guerrilla tactic: Type the official name of a scholarship contest you already know into your favorite search engine. (If you don't have the name of a contest on the tip of your tongue, simply pick one out of Appendix A.) Perform this task whether or not you already know the contest's primary Web site.

The reason for doing this will rapidly become apparent: Your search engine will come back with additional secondary sites that include this named scholarship in their listings. Then you can search these additional listings for information on scholarships that you don't know anything about. Repeat the exercise by typing in the name of another scholarship you're already familiar with. This, in turn, will lead you to other listings, which will subsequently lead you to still others.

Furthermore, many of the secondary sites you locate will be listings put up by high school or college guidance offices for students enrolled at their schools (most without any password or school verification). So in addition to your field trips to the guidance offices of other schools in your district, you can also "electronically visit" schools that may be physically located thousands of miles away from you. The result is a dramatic expansion in the scholarship resources at your disposal.

Keep in mind that a given scholarship contest may be referenced by Web page creators by different names. So if you don't find what you're looking for at first, try a slight variation of the name.

GUERRILLA TACTIC #3

Use Internet search engines to "electronically" visit other high school and college guidance offices and check out their scholarship listings.

BOOKS & DIRECTORIES

To obtain your copy of the complete Scholarship Sleuth directory, go directly to the publisher's Internet site at waggledancer.com on the World Wide Web.

When it comes to published scholarship directories, *The Scholarship Sleuth* is quite simply the best on the planet. Okay, I might be a slightly biased source. But the whole reason I created *The Scholarship Sleuth* in the first place was to address the glaring weaknesses of other directories on the market.

These other books are quite thick and extremely heavy, but are not as helpful as you might think. The vast majority of the listings are for very specialized scholarship programs that most students won't be able to apply for. Furthermore, many of the databases used to create these directories (there are only a handful of large scholarship databases) are the same ones you already searched via the Internet.

Despite these drawbacks, it's still worthwhile to look for scholarships in every nook and cranny. So when using these directories, don't get frustrated if you search through many pages without turning up a scholarship lead that's right for you. If a book only has a few useful listings, then you might want to simply peruse them in the bookstore and jot down a few notes. If more listings are applicable to you, then it's probably worthwhile to buy a copy. Such scholarship directories include *Scholarships: The Essential Guide* by Kaplan Education Centers (no relation to me!) and *The Scholarship Handbook* by The College Board.

COMMUNITY CANVASSING

Now that we've tackled both school and Internet resources, let's extend our scholarship search techniques to your community. The goal of this next set of scholarship search techniques is to locate those hard-to-find local scholarship programs—often the contests that have the fewest entries and thus the best odds of winning.

Local Organizations

Various service organizations, veterans associations, religious groups, and fraternal lodges are frequent sponsors of scholarship programs on the local level. Such noteworthy organizations include:

American Legion
Boy Scouts/Girl Scouts of America
Chamber of Commerce
Daughters of the American Revolution
Daughters of the Confederacy
Elks Club
Key Club
Kiwanis International
Knights of Columbus
Lions Club
National Honor Society
Odd Fellows & Rebekah Lodges
Optimist International
Rotary Club
Sons of the American Revolution
Soroptimist International
Unions (local chapters)
Veterans of Foreign Wars
YMCA/YWCA
4-H Club

For each of the groups listed above, approach the local chapter in your city, state, or region. If you are unable to locate a local chapter, try contacting the national headquarters. If you take the latter approach, be aware that each local chapter is its own entity: The national headquarters may *not* always be aware of all the programs that local chapters sponsor. So perhaps the best strategy is to ask the national headquarters about any national programs they may sponsor, and then to request contact information for the local chapter nearest to you.

Area Businesses

Area businesses are another good place to look for local scholarship programs. Banks and credit unions often sponsor contests, so drop by these financial institutions. (Don't limit yourself to banks where you actually have an account.) Ask to speak to the manager, and inquire about whether the institution is sponsoring any scholarship contests. Radio and television stations, newspapers, and department stores are also other sources that often come up on the local level.

Try to think of the businesses in your area with the highest profile or strongest community presence (especially with young people), and approach managers at these businesses too. It's not unheard of for a local business to actually create a scholarship program in response to a student inquiry. And pay a visit to your local Chamber of Commerce; it may be aware of businesses in your area that sponsor (or might be interested in sponsoring) scholarships.

State Scholarship Agencies

To look up the relevant agencies in your state, see Appendix C.

As I mentioned in Chapter 2, federal scholarship programs—such as the Robert C. Byrd scholarship—are administered by government agencies in each state. These same state scholarship commissions are also the ones who usually administer scholarship programs sponsored by state and local governments. And in states such as Oregon, the designated agency may also be contracted by private donors (who want to avoid the burdens of contest administration) to manage their scholarship programs.

For all of these reasons, contacting scholarship commissions and agencies in your state is a good strategy for generating scholarship leads. This is especially useful if you are considering an in-state college (because state-funded scholarships usually require that funds be used at an in-state school).

Family & Friends

Does your mom or dad work for a company that sponsors a scholarship program? Well, it's not as unlikely as you might think. A substantial number of companies sponsor programs that are specifically targeted at children of employees (especially large companies with a national presence). Furthermore, if your parents are members of any job-related organizations (such as unions or credit unions), investigate those possibilities as well. Locating such programs—ones with a very specific and limited applicant pool—is as good as money in the bank. In fact, when it comes to such scholarship contests, it is not at all uncommon that you could be the *only* applicant. (This *really* increases your odds of winning!)

In addition, tell your family to keep an eye out for scholarship programs advertised on television, in magazines, and in your local supermarket. Producers of consumer goods (such as Tylenol, Arizona Jeans, and Paper Mate) often promote their scholarship programs through these channels.

Similarly, it never hurts to ask relatives and family friends for any scholarship leads they might have through jobs, affiliations, or other avenues. You'd be surprised what a few friendly questions can turn up.

WIDENING YOUR NET

Some libraries may also subscribe to "Associations Unlimited," an electronic database drawn from the print version. The database (available both online and via CD-ROM) can be searched by organization name, location, subject, and other criteria. Check with your reference librarian for more information.

Now that we've discussed the basics of finding college scholarships, we're ready to explore a secondary set of research techniques that broaden the reach of your scholarship net. This new set of techniques can provide an additional avenue for finding scholarship "diamonds"–those scholarship contests that seem to be tailor-made for someone with *your* unique characteristics.

To do this, we're going to seek out a wide range of organizations and associations that are in some way related to your background, skills, interests, and goals. First, you'll need to get your hands on a copy of the *Encyclopedia of Associations* (published by Gale Research). You should be able to find a copy of this mammoth directory in the reference section of your local public library. If your local library for some reason does not carry a copy, try the nearest college library.

The *Encyclopedia of Associations* (a three volume set) is divided into a variety of categories according to the type of organization (such as commercial, educational, or cultural). To use the directory for our purposes, first go to the "keyword" list in the beginning of Volume 1 to locate subjects which are related to your hobbies, interests, career goals, or cultural background. Each keyword listing also contains the organizational categories in which the keyword appears. Next, look up these entries in each corresponding category (which are alphabetized according to keyword). Doing this will turn up a wide range of organizations and associations related to your interests and background—groups such as the Dance Educators of America, the National Society of Black Engineers, or even the National Ice Carving Association.

For each organization, the directory lists a description of the organization, as well as information on major programs, publications, and membership. Using the contact information listed, you can contact these organizations and inquire about any scholarship programs they may offer. Furthermore, because a great many organizations now have e-mail and website contact information listed, investigating scholarship programs doesn't have to run up your long-distance phone bill.

In addition, many listings contain an "Awards" section which lists major scholarship, grant, and fellowship programs the organization may run. Don't rely exclusively on the information listed in the awards section, as the information can be dated and not necessarily relevant to the individual student. (Some organizations may offer grants to groups, or awards to professionals.) Nevertheless, such information can help clue you in to which organizations are likely to offer some type of scholarship program.

Pay special attention to those associations listed in the *Education* section, as such groups place a high value on education, and are thus more likely to offer some type of scholarship program. If you already know the actual name of an organization in your field of interest, look up the name in the index at the back of Volume 3.

If you have a distinctive ethnic background, be sure to look it up in the cultural associations section.

The Foundation Directory

Another potentially useful resource available in most libraries is *The Foundation Directory* (published by The Foundation Center and edited by Jeffrey Falkenstein). First, use the "Geographic Index" located in the back of the book to locate foundations in your home region. Second, locate the "Types of Support" index (also in the back of the book), and scan the "Grants to Individuals" and "Scholarships—to Individuals" sections to find programs that might be applicable to you.

Third, use the "Subject Index" to look up foundations that deal with subjects relevant to you. Once again, use the contact information provided to further investigate your scholarship leads.

REQUESTING MATERIALS

As you come across contact information for various scholarship contests, it's always a good idea to request applications *immediately*. That way, if there are any surprises on the application (such as deadlines that have been moved up unexpectedly), you will have more time to address them. I also recommend requesting applications for scholarships that you plan to apply for in future years. Although you will eventually need to request the specific application form for the year you apply, seeing an actual application form in advance helps you better prepare for the judging criteria (perhaps by getting a relevant job, or volunteering for a related community service program).

If you've located a phone number for an organization, use it to request an application. This can save you the hassle of drafting and mailing a letter. If you don't have a phone number, you will need to request an application via good ol' "snail mail" (a.k.a. the U.S. postal service).

To save yourself time, develop a generic form letter for requesting applications. This letter doesn't need to be too fancy (although it should probably be computer printed or typed and in a standard business format). Just make sure that you clearly state the name of the scholarship application you are requesting, since some organizations sponsor multiple scholarships. Also, in addition to your mailing address, be sure to include your phone number, fax number (if you have one) and e-mail address. In general, make it as easy as possible for the scholarship sponsor or administrator to reach you.

The letter should also contain some basic information about yourself, such as your grade, school, and home town. If you want to include a few more personal details (such as your GPA or extracurricular interests), it doesn't hurt. But don't count on a couple of extra sentences about yourself in the application request letter affecting the outcome of the scholarship contest.

It's generally a good idea to include a self-addressed stamped envelope with these letters as well. Doing so will make it easier and more economical for the contact person or organization to respond to your inquiry. You may want to attach two stamps, as some of the application forms can be fairly substantial in weight.

Mailing the Letter

When you're sending out a considerable number of letters all at once, it's easy to place a letter in a wrong envelope. To avoid this, always double-check that the name and address on the envelope matches the one on the enclosed letter.

If you're provided with the specific information, address the envelope directly to a contact person at the sponsoring organization. If this information isn't provided, write "Attention: Scholarship Coordinator" on the top line, so that whoever receives the envelope can immediately forward the letter to the person who handles scholarship requests.

Sending the letter via regular mail service should be sufficient. So don't spend any extra cash on "Certified Mail" or "Return Receipt Requested." Save those verification services (if appropriate) for when you're mailing in the actual completed application.

Downloading Applications

As more organizations use the Internet for disseminating scholarship information, increasing numbers of application forms and materials will be available online for downloading to your computer. In the past year alone, I've already seen the number of applications available over the Web grow dramatically. Making applications available electronically is much more convenient, affordable, and timely for everyone involved, and will likely become the distribution method of choice in the next few years.

CHAPTER 3 SUMMARY

■ **The Golden Rule:** Added effort invested into researching scholarships is *never* wasted. Fully exploiting the techniques outlined in this chapter is always a good strategy.

■ **Directory of Scholarships:** Start out by employing the directory of scholarships contained in Appendix A of this book. Peruse the listings, and request applications right away.

■ **Internet Databases:** Expand your search by utilizing free scholarship-search databases on the Internet. Providing personal information about your interests, achievements, heritage, and geographic location yields a list of scholarships that fits your personal profile. Link to the best sites on the Internet at the **winscholarships.com** Web portal.

■ **Avoiding Fees:** Steer clear of search services that charge fees for providing lists of scholarships. Such services generally don't have access to any better information than what is available free of charge.

■ **School Resources:** Continue your scholarship search at your school's guidance office, career center, or reference library. Question counselors and teachers about scholarship opportunities. Politely "raid" other local schools to tap their resources too.

■ **Web Search Engines:** Search for both primary and secondary Web sites using special syntax rules. Target smaller sites posted by certain high school and college guidance offices.

■ **Tapping Your Community:** Seek out community organizations that are likely to offer scholarships (service organizations, businesses with a strong community presence, etc.). Contact state scholarship agencies (listed in Appendix C) to find scholarships administered by local, state, and federal governments.

■ **Targeting Organizations:** Use the *Encyclopedia of Associations* to locate organizations related to your interests. Contact these groups and inquire about any scholarships they may offer.

■ **Getting Applications:** Request contest applications immediately via phone, e-mail, or postal service. Download directly if available on the Web.

A Winning Game Plan

*In this chapter,
we'll develop a plan
of attack that maximizes
your efficiency and
effectiveness.*

CHAPTER CONTENTS

- Getting organized
- Entering multiple contests
- Developing reusable materials
- Taking a personal inventory
- Leveraging schoolwork and class time
- Cultivating important relationships
- Setting a schedule

MAXIMIZING YOUR CHANCES

If you have followed the research techniques outlined in Chapter 3, and have sifted through the directory listings in Appendix A, you're likely knee deep in scholarship application hoopla. Now what you need is a game plan: a plan of attack that maximizes your chances of accumulating substantial winnings, while minimizing your investment of time and energy. The seven components (detailed below) of the game plan I successfully employed will guide you in efficiently and effectively managing your scholarship quest.

Component #1:

Get Organized From the Beginning

Establishing a good organizational routine from the outset will save you from having to redo a lot of work in the long run. When scholarship applications you have requested arrive in the mail, remove the corresponding contest information filed away in your "Application Requests" binder (the one I suggested you create in the end of Chapter 3), and start a separate file folder for each contest.

I found it helpful to mark the deadline of each contest on the folder in big, bold letters so I could see these key dates at a glance. If you have access to a filing cabinet, it's perfect for organizing these folders (hanging ones, preferably). Otherwise, a box will work just fine.

You will want to divide your filing space into two sections: one for scholarship competitions that are upcoming (deadlines in the current school year); another for contests that you are interested in, but not yet eligible to apply for (usually because you are too young). Keeping track of contests for future years—so that you can be sure to request the current application when the time comes—will save you much work later. This is especially important for high school freshmen, sophomores, and juniors.

As you file things away, make sure to read everything first and become familiar with all of the application guidelines, rules, and criteria for each contest. This way, you're not surprised by anything later.

In each scholarship file folder, make a point of keeping all of the information you accumulate (including notes) and

Reading all materials early enough is key to implementing Component #3 of this game plan—developing reusable materials.

work you complete. Especially important is the habit of printing out and filing away all rough drafts of essays and other materials you are working on—even if the final version is very different from these earlier attempts. Because of essay word limits and other scholarship-specific factors, passages you discard in the editing process may still be very useful to you in later applications. Believe me, when you're staring at a blank page, racking your brain for ideas, these "throwaways" can prove to be useful starting points.

The last organizational technique which proved very helpful for me was the use of a large wall calendar. This is one instance where, as the saying goes, bigger is definitely better. If you happen to have a dry-erase board, it's great for this purpose. Mark each scholarship deadline on your calendar, and list in abbreviated form the application requirements so that nothing falls through the cracks. You may also want to mark a deadline *two weeks before* a given scholarship application is due. This can serve as a reminder to begin work on an application, so that you don't leave it until the last minute. (I'll show you how to fill out applications in less time than this, but ideally you should allow a couple of weeks.)

Component #2: Plan to Apply For As Many Scholarships As Possible

I've learned from experience that scholarship judging is far from an exact science. Although the strategies in this book dramatically increase your chances of winning numerous contests, your result on any one *particular* contest is unpredictable. A secretary could put your application in the wrong pile by mistake, or a particular judge could have some unusual bias. For example, in several large national scholarship contests that I thought I had no chance of winning, I somehow won. In other contests that seemed to be a sure thing, I didn't even receive an "honorable mention." Almost all of the scholarship winners I have interviewed have had similar baffling experiences.

I entered about three dozen scholarship contests, and won awards from more than two dozen of these programs.

Because of the subjectiveness of judging, and the unpredictability of factors beyond your control, you'll want to tilt the odds in your favor by entering as many contests as

"Apply for all you can, especially all the small, local scholarships. Even if the prize is only a couple of hundred dollars, the little scholarships can really add up."

Aileen Richmond
Winner of local and national
contests totaling $20,000

you can. This way, you minimize the effects of any quirks in the judging process, and leverage your chances to win sizable amounts of money. Even if the prize is only a couple of hundred dollars, I still recommend entering the contest. This might not sound like much money in the context of an entire college tuition bill, but a couple of hundred bucks can cover the cost of books for a term (unfortunately, you have to buy your own textbooks in college), or help pay for that spring break "research" trip to Cancun.

Furthermore, applying for many scholarships makes good sense in light of the learning curve that is a part of submitting good scholarship applications. After completing your first few submissions, your ability to apply the techniques covered in this book will substantially improve. You might lose your first five scholarship contests—but then win the next five. And, of course, if your objective is to go to college for free, the more scholarship contests you enter, the better your chances of reaching your goal.

Component #3:

As I rethought and refined old essays, they improved by leaps and bounds—as did my essay writing skills. This proved helpful when it came time to fill out college applications.

Develop a Suite of Generic Reusable Materials

When applying for large numbers of scholarships, creating a suite of generic reusable materials saves a great deal of time and energy. By having this suite to draw from, you will be able to focus *less* on just completing application requirements, and spend *more* time on fine-tuning and customizing the material you've already written. More than just a reduction in your work load, reusing and rethinking old materials can mean vast improvements as you repeatedly refine and edit the same passages. By employing this strategy, you gain the opportunity to fine-tune your materials with every submission. And take it from me, your tenth draft will be far better than your first.

To create this suite of generic materials, you will need to develop standard essays on perennial scholarship application themes. This should be done both ahead of time and after the fact. To prepare ahead of time, survey the scholarship landscape, and isolate common themes and requirements (whether it is a similar essay question or a comparable extra-

curricular activity worksheet). Attempt to bridge multiple applications with every sentence you write.

For instance, some applications will pose broad questions, such as asking you to propose a solution to a societal problem. Although this type of question provides a framework, the specific essay topic is up to you. So if another contest down the road poses a more specific question—perhaps asking you to critique the American education system—you may want to make *this* the societal problem you discuss in the first contest entry.

GUERRILLA TACTIC #4

Plan on creating reusable application materials that bridge multiple contests. Recycle and rethink past essays on perennial themes.

The key to bridging multiple applications is to plan ahead. After you have identified and marked on your calendar the scholarships you want to apply for, carefully survey the requirements for each.

Creating this file of reusable materials also means recycling passages and materials that may have been initially intended for other applications. Not only does this entail recycling essays on reoccurring themes—such as college plans, career goals, and future contributions to society—but it also means trying to reuse imagery, quotes, structure, and other elements of your past work. Don't just recopy such passages verbatim, but instead try to rethink, improve, and hone everything to fit the criteria of each new contest.

See Chapter 8, for more details on recycling essays.

Component #4: **Make and Regularly Update Personal Inventory Lists**

Taking a "personal inventory" means taking time to reflect on your interests, achievements, activities, as well as awards and honors. In this component of your winning game plan, you will take a personal inventory by making lists in several key areas. This process not only helps you keep track of everything you've done, but it also helps you begin to analyze specific areas in your record which may need some shoring up (a topic we'll tackle in Chapter 7).

First, type or write "Extracurricular Activities" on the top of a page, and begin listing all of the extracurricular activities in which you have participated during high school and college. For each item, include your years of participation, any leadership positions you have held, and a brief description of the activity. Include in this listing, literally *everything* you have done—even activities which may have lasted for only a weekend. In bold face or a highlighter, identify those activities which were the most significant to you.

Next, using the same format, prepare a list of any awards you have won over the years. Some of these items may be repeats from your extracurricular activities list, but that's good. Because of the space limitations and formatting constraints on some scholarship applications, having these credentials on separate lists allows us to pick and choose the best spots to include the information. When making this list, it's also important to think of awards and honors in the broadest sense possible. Anything from that math certificate you earned, to your selection as "News Editor" on your school newspaper, to being your school's representative to a special conference on cultural diversity should be included. Remember, this list is only for your *personal* review—I'll show you later how to pick and choose the most compelling information to submit.

Indeed, this is one time when all those dinky "certificate of participation" awards may come in handy.

Third, complete separate lists for service activities you have been involved with and for jobs you have held. Community service warrants a separate list all of its own because of its importance to many types of scholarship contests. If you don't have much to put down on this list, don't stress. Community service is one area of your record that can generally be quickly and painlessly enhanced.

A listing of jobs can also be critical if your extracurricular involvement has been limited. Furthermore, substantial work experience, especially to save money for college, can help communicate to judges your sincere need for the scholarship money (even when it isn't a specific judging criteria).

Finally, start a list for all of your interests and hobbies that might not be reflected in the other lists. This includes all of the things you do—from piano playing and stamp collecting, to poetry writing and break dancing—outside of school-related activities. Just because an activity isn't formalized within a school organization doesn't make it any less of an activity. Indeed, some of the most impressive types of activities that one can participate in are these individual, outside projects.

For all of these lists, I recommend completing them on a computer so that you can easily modify and update the content with minimal additional work. A word processing program like *Microsoft Word* works fine for this purpose, but if you want more versatility in formatting the lists that you'll eventually attach to applications, try a page layout program like *Adobe Pagemaker*.

Component #5: Leverage Schoolwork and Class Time

In a variety of school writing assignments, you may be able to choose your own topic. And even if this isn't the case, I've found that teachers can often be persuaded to allow you to write on related subjects that are applicable to particular scholarship contests. You have to do the schoolwork anyway, so why not make it count toward your scholarship quest?

For instance, if you're asked to write a paper on a book of your choosing, you may find it advantageous to select *The Fountainhead* by Ayn Rand. This way, you'll have a submission ready to go for the annual essay contest on this famous novel. If you're assigned a self-reflective essay, pick a personal topic that fits in well with scholarship applications you're pursuing. Leveraging class assignments saves you time and energy as you "kill two birds with one stone." Moreover, teachers can serve as a helpful source of early feedback for these potential scholarship submissions.

The second way to leverage class time is to employ the body of schoolwork you've accumulated over the years. During high school, you've undoubtedly completed notebooks full of writing assignments, essays, and papers. In completing my own scholarship applications, I found it very useful to search this "junk pile" for hidden treasure. I would rummage through my old files

---

GUERRILLA TACTIC #5

Use class-related writing assignments as an opportunity to flesh out essays for scholarship applications. Search old schoolwork for hidden scholarship treasure.

GUERRILLA TACTIC #6

Use independent study course credit to pursue self-initiated projects that enhance your record for scholarship contests.

At the time, I couldn't fit an English class into my schedule for the term. Naming the independent study course "Advanced Expository Writing" (it carried this name on my transcript) thus addressed a potential hole in my academic record.

for widely applicable topics, golden quotes, jeweled phrases, and sparkling metaphors. The treasure you dig up in this fashion can become an important contribution to your stash of reusable materials.

Finally, this technique isn't restricted merely to classroom assignments. Most schools offer some type of independent-study class credit, in which you pursue your own project under the guidance of an adviser. At many schools, you're even allowed to use a class period during the day. So instead of added classroom time, you can spend the time on self-initiated projects that substantially improve your chances of scholarship (and college admission) success. Plus, it's a great way to learn more about a really fascinating subject.

Although your school probably won't permit an independent study course on "Completing Scholarship Applications," you can use the time to pursue projects (such as an extended writing or science project) that enhance your record for scholarship contests. In high school, I created an independent study course for myself entitled "Advanced Expository Writing" (isn't it great when you get to name the course yourself!). In this course, I began writing a how-to manual about a service program I had founded. Another student I know used an independent study course to conduct a survey on the attitudes of teenagers. You can also use independent study to pursue subject matter in an area of your academic record that might otherwise be deficient.

One added benefit of pursuing this independent study option is its appearance on your official transcript (as either graded or non-graded). And, of course, if the independent study is graded, it can be a relatively painless way to raise your GPA (advisers are generally nice about grades when they see you've taken the initiative to pursue something on your own). Furthermore, cultivating this one-on-one relationship with an adviser frequently leads to glowing recommendation letters.

Component #6: Contact Past Scholarship Winners In Your Community

Past winners of scholarships often gain important insights about particular scholarship contests that go far beyond published judging criteria. In this book, I have distilled the core strategies of many national and local scholarship winners, but it's also useful for *you* to interview past winners of local contests you plan to enter. Start by locating winners in your school, community, or state. Ask them about their unique qualifications, the approach they took in filling out the application, as well as the characteristics of other winners they might have met. If you don't know someone off the top of your head, many scholarship contests will provide a list of past winners upon request.

GUERRILLA TACTIC #7

Talk to past winners of scholarship contests you are planning to enter.

Component #7: Develop a List of Potential Recommendation Writers

Letters of recommendation, another element of the typical scholarship application, also require some advance planning. It's important to note that the best recommendation letters for one contest are not necessarily the best for another. Furthermore, there can be a large variation in the writing skills of the recommendation writers you choose: Someone who thinks very highly of you may not have the writing ability to pull off a high-caliber letter, or else may not devote enough time to the task. Because of these factors, plan on obtaining as many letters of recommendation as possible.

To obtain multiple letters, you need to plan early and develop a list of potential recommendation writers. On this list, record in what contexts the person knows you, and in what areas the recommendation letter would likely highlight. Teachers, professors, school administrators, counselors, employers, coaches, and activity advisers are typically good choices for recommendation letters. A good relationship with an English or journalism teacher can lead to especially powerful letters because of his or her strong writing skills. But don't limit

Check out Chapter 9 for insider secrets on cultivating glowing recommendation letters.

yourself to traditional sources either. If you're planning to pursue a particular career or field of study, try thinking of ways to get recommendations from people who work in this field (such as your family doctor if you hope to pursue a medical career).

Put as many people on this list as you can. For the time being, don't worry too much about whether a person will give you a strong recommendation. These are just *prospective* letter writers—putting them on the list doesn't mean that you will actually request a recommendation. Besides, even if you do get a letter of recommendation which isn't that great, there's no law saying that you have to use it.

Engaging in this process will also be extremely helpful if you haven't yet applied to college.

One of the secrets of getting great recommendation letters is to start thinking about them far in advance of when you need to submit them. Start this process right away by completing your preliminary list of potential letter writers.

SETTING A SCHEDULE

Applying this game plan puts you on the steady track to scholarship success. How much time does it take to employ these seven components? Well, that depends. Ideally, starting this process three to six months before the bulk of your scholarship applications become due would give you plenty of time to get organized, talk to the necessary people, and plan your attack. I began many of these tasks the summer before my senior year in high school; this made a great (and profitable) summer project.

But don't worry if you've only got days or weeks before a bunch of scholarship applications are due. Just do the best you can. Many of these tasks can be performed at the same time that you're entering other scholarship contests. You might not have time to track down past winners, or create an independent study course, but that's okay. Your situation may not be perfect for your first batch of contests, but you'll be ready for the next set.

COACH

In this dialogue, the Scholarship Coach answers questions about the time commitment necessary to pursue scholarship contest opportunities.

... *About finding the time*

The following questions were submitted by Reilly Bizzy, a high school junior from Paydirt, Georgia.

Reilly: Scholarships sound great, but with sports, school-work, and my after-school job, I'm really busy. Do you think I have the time?

Scholarship Coach: Applying for scholarships takes some effort, but it's a *front-loaded* process. What this means is that it takes some time at the beginning to figure out what you're doing, but once you get the hang of it, it'll be a cinch to whip out quality application after quality application.

Reilly: Well, maybe I have time to enter a *few* contests, but I don't think I'll be able to jump on very many.

Scholarship Coach: Nonsense. One of the important points we emphasize is to create reusability in your applications. Once you have a couple of applications under your belt, you'll be able to modify materials you've already written to fit the requirements of other contests. So the more contests you enter, the less time it will take per application.

Reilly: But aren't your techniques really complicated and too time consuming for the average student?

Scholarship Coach: Not at all. Don't be intimidated by the size or content of this book. It's just our attempt to be comprehensive. Once you read through and start applying many of the book's strategies, they'll become second-nature.

Given the big money prizes that scholarship contests award, you simply can't afford __not__ to do it.

Reilly: How much time will applying for scholarships take?

Scholarship Coach: It should take about as much time as a typical extracurricular activity. And with the big payoffs that are possible, you could be making more than $500 per hour! That sure beats flipping burgers. . .

CHAPTER 4 SUMMARY

■ **Organization:** Getting organized from the beginning will save time in the long run. Start a separate file folder for each contest—keeping all application materials, notes, and rough drafts in this folder. Identify application deadlines on a large wall calendar.

■ **Numbers Game:** Entering as many scholarship contests as possible maximizes learning curve effects and leverages your chances to win. Don't overlook local contests with relatively small prizes, as these can add up quickly.

■ **Reusability:** Create a file of generic reusable materials on perennial scholarship themes. Survey upcoming contests, trying to bridge multiple applications with each essay. Recycle and rethink old passages to improve them for future contest submissions.

■ **Inventory Lists:** Create and regularly update personal inventory lists of your extracurricular activities, awards and honors, community service participation, jobs, and hobbies.

■ **Leveraging Schoolwork:** Use school writing assignments as an opportunity to draft essays for scholarship contests. Search old schoolwork for potential ideas for scholarship submissions. Create independent study courses and pursue self-initiated projects that enhance your record.

■ **Past Winners:** Talk to past scholarship winners in your area about the types of students who do well in specific scholarship contests.

■ **Recommendations:** Develop a broad list of people you could approach for recommendation letters. Include adults involved in school-related capacities (teachers, administrators, advisers, or coaches), as well as others who know you in different capacities (clergy, employers, community leaders, etc.).

■ **Scheduling:** If possible, begin three to six months before the bulk of your applications are due. Students without this lead time should complete these tasks as best as possible—even while simultaneously filling out other contest applications.

■ **Time Commitment:** Applying for multiple scholarships takes about as much time as a typical extracurricular activity. Following the strategies and principles in this book—especially reusability—leverages available time.

The Unforgiving Minute

Intermission

You know what I mean. . . you have probably been there before. You had it all planned out, and believe me, it was a good plan—in theory. You were going to go home and do the paper you've been putting off for several days. Three trips to the refrigerator, four sitcoms, and one great ear wax removal job later, you're still on the introductory paragraph. And all you really have to show for your brilliant plan is a full stomach and the cleanest pair of lobes in the school. But not to worry. There is always *tomorrow night* to implement your plan. And who cares if you said that *last night*. This time you *really* mean it.

So what's the problem? Why does the work which you expect to take no more than an hour, tops, sometimes keep you up until the wee hours of the morning? Or perhaps with all the other things in your life, the work sometimes doesn't get done at all. And then those good intentions degenerate into the high school version of "Dolly the sheep" (you know, the sheep those

British scientists created from another sheep's DNA), as you are forced to "clone" an assignment from a friend in your first-period English class.

Finding a Cure for Time Abuse

Does the above scenario sound familiar from time to time? Well, to conquer this problem—and free up time for you to work on your scholarship game—we'll have to transform you into an effective time juggler. Sounds easy enough, right? Unfortunately, it's easier said than done. I know from experience (and from the current state of my room) that these organizational skills are harder to master than it might at first seem.

It's also important to recognize when a job is finished. Spending extra hours, days, or weeks in order to obtain a very small payback is also a common time abuse problem. The additional hours squandered usually come out of some other important activity that you should have been doing.

Despite the obvious importance of time management, the skill is in short supply. In its place, a wide range of "task paralysis" exists. From the student who has no concept of time, to the student who is hampered by excessive planning, each strain of the disease is debilitating. What makes time abuse even more problematic is that its presence might not be detected until bad habits have already been reinforced. Even top students, who have already "breezed" through high school, often have much to learn about managing their time. This becomes all too apparent when difficulty levels, responsibilities, and distractions get cranked way up in college.

THE "GPA" PLAN

It's no accident that this plan has the same acronym as "grade point average." Following these techniques will definitely improve your grades in school.

So what's the cure for a case of task paralysis? I call it the "GPA Plan"—a three-step process of Goal setting, Prioritizing, and Action. The GPA Plan isn't just some kind of superficial, feel-good exercise that you could find in any self-help book. Rather, it's a powerful plan of attack to get you at least an extra hour in every day.

Do you ever feel out of control in your life? Do you find yourself dreaming about things you'd like to accomplish but don't? Are you stretched in too many directions by too many people? If you answered "yes' to any of these questions, then the GPA Plan is for you.

"G" is for Goals

Good ol' Yogi Berra, the colorful Hall of Fame catcher of the New York Yankees once said, "If you don't know where you're going, you'll probably end up someplace else." And when it comes to **goal setting**, this statement has never been more true: The people who care enough to write down their goals are the ones who most frequently reach them.

By writing goals down, we are taking a risk: we are putting ourselves on the line to accomplish what that piece of paper says. But, my friends, this is good! After all, the fear of failure is the single largest obstacle standing in the way of most people reaching their goals and realizing their dreams.

By having goals written down on paper, and by looking at them every so often, we reaffirm our commitment to accomplishing these goals. Furthermore, a visible reminder of the goals we've already achieved, helps us to deter burnout and frustration. Written goals thus have a therapeutic effect: They encourage us to acknowledge the progress we have already made on our journey.

Just like a detailed map helps us make good driving decisions when in an unfamiliar place, written goals help us to clarify the route and to circumvent the road blocks standing in the way of our achievement. This makes us more efficient time managers. By having a clear picture of where we want to go (and who we want to be), we can start to see ways to free up time from areas that do not contribute to this result. And believe me, this small investment of energy in the short term will save you a lot of time in the long run.

Keys to Effective Goal Setting

We've all been guilty of setting goals that have had no chance of ever being realized. Maybe you were determined to hit the weight room four times a week. . . but one month later you still were asking for directions to the gym. Or perhaps you set a New Year's Resolution to watch less television. . . but you still found yourself mesmerized by the latest brawl on *Jerry Springer*. Through the process of taking control of my own life, I've come to realize that the reason these types of goals often fall by the wayside is because they weren't set properly to begin with. So I developed seven key guidelines of goal setting that have helped me achieve results. To illustrate each of the seven guidelines, I've used examples that are applicable to the process of winning college scholarships.

1. Effective goals are specific. A primary reason goal setting doesn't work for some people is that their goals are so broad that it's hard to translate them into immediate action. The key to goal setting is to be as specific as possible. Approach the process just like you would a grocery shopping list. If you're planning to cook dinner for your family, you wouldn't just write "dinner" on your grocery list. You would instead list out all the ingredients you need—four boneless chicken breasts, one package of angel hair pasta, a container of pesto sauce, some broccoli flowerettes, a little Parmesan cheese (gosh, I'm getting hungry just thinking about it!).

Likewise, if your goal is to win $15,000 in scholarships for college, you need to break down this broad goal into many smaller ones. The "how" is the key question to be asking here. How many scholarships will you apply for? How will you enhance your record? How many letters of recommendation will you obtain? (We'll discuss the specifics of what might be on your scholarship goal-setting list in later chapters.)

2. Effective goals are divisible. It's important to have long-term "visionary" goals in mind, but it's equally important to divide these long-term objectives into preliminary short- and medium-term goals. If all your goals are long term in nature, it will be difficult to feel like you're making progress. Similarly, if all your goals are resolved in the short term, your road map is not much more than an extended "to-do" list—you will likely miss the forest for the trees. For instance, if you've made up your mind to apply for at least 25 scholarships, how many hours will you devote in the coming week to the process? How about in the following month?

"If my mind can conceive it and my heart can believe it, then I can achieve it."

Muhammad Ali

3. Effective goals are measurable. Goals need to be written in a measurable way so that you can evaluate your progress, and so that you will know when you have achieved your goal. If you are setting a goal about locating scholarships, don't just write "Find some scholarships on the Internet." Instead, write something like "I will spend five to seven hours this week researching scholarships and will identify at least 25 that I can apply for."

4. Effective goals are achievable. It doesn't make any sense to write "Enter 25 scholarship contests in the next 24 hours." Unless you have superhuman powers (in which case you might not need the scholarships to begin with), this just isn't a realistic goal. Try to make your goals ambitious, but not overwhelming.

5. Effective goals paint a picture. Much of our energy to achieve the goals we set comes from our desire to attain them. This makes good sense: The more we desire a result, the harder we'll work to achieve it. To light this fire, I've found it extremely effective to be able to vividly picture the result. You want to be able to feel the scholarship check in your hand, see the broad smile on your parents faces, hear the roar of the crowd as you stride to the podium to accept your award, and perhaps even smell the sweet fragrance of victory.

6. Effective goals are adaptable. Life always throws unexpected curves down our path. Such happenings can alter our goals either temporarily or permanently. For example, perhaps you start devoting one week to completing a scholarship application. Then suddenly, you learn of an upcoming test in your math class. It might be wise to modify your original plan so as to accommodate this new development—especially if doing well in math is another one of your goals! You may need to revamp your short-term objectives (such as your plan for the week) in order to better meet all of your long-term goals.

7. Effective goals require planning. Every goal has a series of obstacles in its path that stand in the way of its realization. The more aware you are of these challenges, the better you can deal with them. In order to win your $15,000 in scholarships, for instance, you may need to have strong letters of recommendation. Anticipating this obstacle—and consequently taking the time to cultivate relationships with potential letter writers—will increase your chances of achieving the desired result.

Finally, I should mention that although I've used examples from scholarship goal setting, for truly effective time management, goal setting needs to be incorporated into *all* areas of your life. Think of the many "roles" you assume in any given day—that of student, friend, son or daughter, athlete, etc.—and try to come up with goals for each of these roles. This will help you achieve balance in your life, and will lead you to the second part of the GPA Plan: Prioritizing.

"P" is for Prioritizing

Keep a calendar on your wall (the bigger, the better) reserved for high-priority milestones and deadlines. You will need to be able to view these upcoming events at a glance.

Perhaps you have already set goals, and know precisely where you want to go. Unfortunately, because there are only 24 hours in each day, you can't go everywhere at once. That's why **prioritizing** comes into play. Prioritizing helps you determine your most important destinations and design daily routines that will give you the greatest chance of reaching those places. Remember, not all tasks are equal. To ensure success, you must organize your schedule around what counts the most. As the classic 80-20 Rule states, "20 percent of the things you do typically yields 80 percent of your results."

So how do you decide what to do each day? And how do you determine which activities get your attention first? Here are some typical ways you might answer these two questions.

■ **The "Squeaky Wheel" Method:** Whatever squeaks the loudest gets your attention. *Problem: Just because something is loud doesn't mean its important.*

■ **The "Follow the Leader" Method:** You do whatever your teachers, parents, or friends tell you to do. *Problem: No one else but you knows the priorities and goals best suited for you.*

■ **The "Hard Core" Method:** You do the most difficult and stressful things first. *Problem: This very quickly becomes a cause of frustration and burnout.*

■ **The "Easy Does It" Method:** You try to get the minor tasks done before everything else. *Problem: This can rapidly turn into procrastination.*

■ **The "Drifting Log" Method:** You do whatever is most interesting at the moment. *Problem: There is a tendency to become sidetracked and lose all direction.*

■ **The "Falling Domino" Method:** Issues are dealt with in the order in which they arise. *Problem: It's easy for you to fall behind in your tasks and never catch up.*

"Dost thou love life? Then do not squander time, for that's the stuff life's made of."

Benjamin Franklin

None of these methods is optimally effective because none of them take into account the goal setting we've just explored. To identify your top priorities for each day, you need to rank the goals you've outlined, translate those goals into daily activities, and then combine them with some kind of "urgency factor" to account for the fact that some tasks have more immediate deadlines than others.

A good way I've found to do this is to make a chart of all of the activities I need to get done, and then to rank them according to two key criteria: **importance** and **urgency**. The best balance I've found is to *place twice the emphasis on importance than on urgency.* After all, making sure that you're headed in the right direction to begin with is more important than the time remaining to get there.

To construct this ranking system, evaluate each of your activities using the importance metric. Then, in assessing each activity's importance, try to determine which goal and sub-goals the activity is contributing to. If a given activity doesn't have a home on your goals list, you'll know that you either need to develop a new goal, or else the activity isn't particularly important. Assign an *importance* ranking using a 5 to 10 scale (with 5 representing activities of the lowest importance, and 10 representing those of the utmost importance).

Perform the same ranking procedure for the *urgency* criteria—the need to get a particular task completed immediately. To assign urgency half the weight, use a 1 to 5 scale (with 1 representing activities with very low urgency, and 5 representing activities that are extremely urgent.)

Then for each activity, add together the importance and urgency rankings to obtain the activity's overall ranking. An importance ranking of 7 and an urgency ranking of 3 would yield an overall ranking of 10 (aren't you impressed with my high-powered math skills?). Activities with the highest overall rankings are your priorities and should receive your primary attention. *Do these first things first.* Then, if necessary, you can delegate, postpone, or abandon the lower-priority ones as needed.

Prioritizing in this manner helps prevent you from becoming overextended, and naturally shapes the most practical timeline for you to follow. It also places an actual value on your time. Time is an investment: Make sure that both the immediate and long-term returns of a project are worth the time you are actually putting in.

Finally, don't forget to allocate some time for this prioritization process itself. It's ironic when someone says that they don't have enough time for prioritizing and time planning. This is the one activity that can pay anyone back many times over for the small amount of effort invested.

> *The virtue of this ranking system is that activities with high importance but low urgency (very long-term goals) are weighted in your daily routine about the same as low importance & high urgency tasks (the little errands that need to get done). But high importance & high urgency items (what should be your priorities) always trump*

"A" is for Action

Although goal setting and prioritizing are indeed critical, you won't be able to walk the path of effective time management unless you also take **action**. This, however, is easier said than done. All of us have been bitten by the procrastination bug from time to time. The recommended treatment is simply to minimize the size and frequency of these bites. We must train ourselves to refrain from turning our backs on difficult or unpleasant tasks, hoping that they will magically disappear. They won't! Listed below are some techniques I've used to help me "Nike It Immediately" (translation: "Just Do It: Now!").

■ **"Light Your Fires"**: All of us are motivated by different things. Find out what works for you. Maybe this means giving yourself a reward after two hours of work. Or perhaps it means visualizing the benefits that will result from finishing the activity.

■ **"Split the Atom"**: Break apart the task into smaller, more manageable chunks. Begin by working on just one part of the task.

Use spare moments in your day (such as those few minutes before class begins) to complete small tasks which don't require high levels of concentration. The cumulative effect of doing this is truly amazing.

■ **"Sink Your Teeth"**: It's not terribly difficult to commit 15 minutes to any task. And frequently, this is enough to get you started. Put in your 15 minutes, then stop if you need to. More often than not, you'll be ready to take bigger bites.

■ **"Naughty! Naughty!"**: Think of this method as the reverse of the above "Light Your Fires" approach. Impose small self-punishments for not getting things done. Perhaps having to do 20 push-ups or skipping your favorite television show will do the trick.

■ **"Feel the Groove"**: The song "Eye of the Tiger," from the *Rocky* movies, happens to be one of my personal theme songs. Just hearing it gets me psyched up. Find a theme song that gets you going, and play it loud when it's time to get to work.

Streamlining Your Life

We all have room for improvement where time management is concerned, but we can't make headway unless we first recognize its existence and importance. Be aware that time management skills will open doors of opportunity in *all* areas of your life. Using my GPA Plan to help you manage your scholarship quest will assist you in refining such skills. In addition, you will keep your sanity, be much happier, and still be able to achieve great monetary results without adversely impacting other important activities.

In my own life, because I began to see measurable results, I steadily increased my use of the GPA Plan—not as some warm and fuzzy, pie-in-the-sky exercise, but rather, out of sheer necessity! With schoolwork, student government, community service, athletics, and journalism (among other things) all competing for my time, I simply couldn't afford *not* to do it.

So if you want to have more control over your life, try out these GPA techniques. And get started NOW! After all—it's about time, isn't it?

PART III

Strategies
that give you the
Edge

Painting Your Own Portrait

In this chapter, I'll show you how to create a cohesive application theme that powerfully communicates who you are.

CHAPTER CONTENTS

- Building a cohesive message
- Primary and secondary themes
- A sampler of winning themes

KNOWING THE PERSON

In the process of writing this book, I've had the opportunity to inspect a wide variety of scholarship applications submitted by many different students—scholarship applications that brought home the scholarship bucks, and plenty of others that didn't. And when I put these two groups of applications side by side, the differences between them were even more pronounced than I had anticipated.

Unsuccessful scholarship applications, more often than not, resembled a laundry list of activities, awards, and accomplishments. Although these credentials were often impressive in and of themselves, reading such material felt like inhaling a random conglomeration of facts. While skimming a few of these applications, everything started to blend together; after awhile, I couldn't even remember which accomplishments and credentials went with which applicant.

When reading a winning application, on the other hand, I felt like I was actually getting to know the person who submitted it. Each application communicated the underlying motivation behind the cornucopia of credentials. I came away from each feeling like I understood the core interests, skills, and values of the individual.

This initial impression is reinforced when I think back to conversations I've had with contest judges at various scholarship award ceremonies. (If you win, you often get to meet the people who have judged the contest.) When meeting many of these judges for the first time, the most frequent comment I heard was "I already feel like I know you, Ben." They would then ask me about how the tennis season had been going for the year, or how this or that writing project was coming along—specifics that judges would have had to remember from my application.

So why do winning applications ultimately leave such strong impressions? Quite simply, *these applications create vivid portraits of the applicants*: Each one of these applications doesn't just recite accomplishments—it depicts the *person* behind all of the grades, extracurricular activities, and awards. After all, judges award scholarships to *people*, not to résumés. If a judge feels like he or she knows you—elevating your application to more than just another file in the pile—it's much harder to deny you the scholarship money.

Defining who you are thus creates a powerful emotional connection with those who evaluate you. This makes your application more memorable, and your cause more persuasive. So perhaps the best way to approach a scholarship application is to think of yourself as a painter—with the application providing a canvas and your commission to paint a vivid self-portrait that powerfully communicates who you are.

THE PAINTER'S TOUCH

Of course, painting this self-portrait is easier said than done. The biggest obstacle in the way of achieving this objective is the physical limitation of the application itself: You're often trying to superimpose years of experiences, discoveries, and thoughts onto a couple of sheets of paper. If contest judges were to shadow your every move for a week, they could probably come up with a pretty good sense of who you are and what you're like. But because your evaluators are judges, not stalkers, you'll have to convey a great deal using just ink on a white page.

So how does one paint these self-portraits I've been talking about? First, you must treat each component of the application (such as the essay, extracurricular activity list, and recommendation letter) as part of a unified whole—not as separate entities. Each essay, list, and letter contributes to the overall impression that you make, and each component makes this contribution in different ways. If you don't coordinate the message that each part sends, the overall message is unclear and jumbled.

Second, we must develop the message itself: the main idea that permeates the entire application, powerfully communicating who you really are. I call this cohesive message the application **theme**. Think of the theme as the core idea or message you are trying to communicate about yourself— the framework that puts all of your activities, interests, and credentials in the proper context. Application themes are

In my interviews with scholarship winners, the importance of having an application theme and painting a clear picture of it was repeated over and over again.

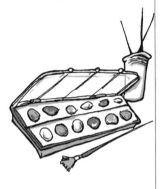

frequently created around particular activities that you're passionate about, particular interests that fascinate you, or career goals that you're striving towards.

No matter how complex you are as a human being, or how little space a contest allows you to explain yourself, your application theme should convey something truly important about who you are and what you care about. The goal here is not to explain all the facets of your life, but rather to focus on one or two key areas.

Which activities do you most enjoy? What types of disciplines and skills come naturally to you? What do you dream of doing 20 years from now? These are a few of the underlying questions that help you define a theme. Your goal should be to make this theme resonate throughout all parts of your application.

This is not to say that all of your applications must have the *same* theme. Let's say, for instance, that a student has identified three potential application themes: (1) a fascination with science, (2) extensive participation in community service, and (3) a dream of one day dancing on Broadway. For applications focused on science, her theme could be science-related. For contests emphasizing contributions to society, the theme could be built around extensive community service experience. And finally, for awards based on artistic achievement, her hard work and sacrificing while developing dancing skills would be showcased.

In Chapter 7, I'll show you how to choose a personal theme that best fits a given contest.

Primary and Secondary Themes

In my experience, the typical application should have no more than one or two major themes. Any more than this, and you start to dilute the communicative power of your message. If you want an application to have two themes, then make one of them the **primary theme**, and the other one the **secondary theme**. The primary theme should be the focal point of the application—the primary message you're trying to communicate. The secondary theme builds upon this message by illustrating another important aspect of your life, interests, and personality.

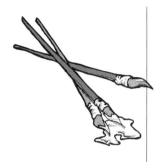

For instance, the hypothetical student discussed on the previous page might choose to make science her primary theme and community service her secondary theme for a given application. The choice of which theme should be primary depends on the agenda of a given scholarship contest—a topic we'll tackle in Chapter 7.

The primary and secondary themes can be closely linked or entirely unrelated to each other. If, however, you are able to present certain activities in such a way as to reinforce *both* themes at once, you can create an especially compelling portrait. As an example of this, consider the thematic impact of our same hypothetical student who has organized a community service program that introduces young, disadvantaged children to the wonders of science.

Enhancing Credibility

Building a cohesive theme in an application serves another important purpose. Given the competitive nature of a merit-based scholarship contest, judges recognize that all of the applicants are more or less trying to say what they think the judges want to hear. This is understandable, but judges are on the lookout for applicants who aren't just paying lip service to some lofty ideals.

Primary and secondary themes enhance an applicant's believability by communicating, and continually reinforcing, a consistent message. The applicants who seem the most credible are the ones who communicate the strongest themes.

"I tried to stick to a theme in my applications. This theme dealt with my involvement in peer education, sex education, and a lot of related issues. It became clear in my applications that this was something that I really cared about."

Alexandra DeLaite
National Scholarship Winner

EMPLOYING YOUR THEME

Perhaps the best way to understand how to employ a primary and secondary theme is to view these themes in action—as part of an actual contest application. The following excerpts are taken from my winning entry in the Discover Card Tribute Awards. My primary theme was built around my passion for writing and my deep appreciation for all forms of communication as tools for solving problems. My secondary theme focused on how I had already exhibited, and would continue to exhibit, a high level of leadership.

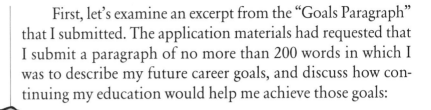

First, let's examine an excerpt from the "Goals Paragraph" that I submitted. The application materials had requested that I submit a paragraph of no more than 200 words in which I was to describe my future career goals, and discuss how continuing my education would help me achieve those goals:

> *"Because of a strong interest in writing and communication, an aptitude for analysis and problem-solving, and a fascination with the inner workings of government, I plan to pursue a career in print and broadcast journalism, as a political columnist and commentator. A well-rounded education will unlock the gates of opportunity—not only helping to clarify complex issues and providing skills for becoming a more persuasive writer and effective speaker, but also preparing me to be a responsible contributor in this world of infinite possibilities. . . . As a well-educated journalist, I will strive to broaden minds and uncover truth—thus doing my part to make a difference in the world."*

"You need a specific focus in your application to grab a judge's attention. For me, this strong selling point was my interest and involvement in politics and government."

David Weiss
National Scholarship Winner

Notice that *both* my primary and secondary themes are supported in this statement. My strong passion for writing and oral communication is reinforced both in terms of my career goal itself, and how I describe that goal. My secondary theme of empowering leadership is demonstrated by the description of how I plan to contribute to society via my journalistic endeavors.

Next, let's examine an excerpt from the first section of a criteria statement that I wrote for the Discover Card application. In this statement, among other things, I was asked to describe my "special talents."

> *"As far back as I can remember, a love for language and a passion for ideas has been an integral part of who I am. I have expressed this through the creation of poetry and short stories, active involvement in debate and public speaking, and by working in journalism and documentary filmmaking. . . . Eventually, my fascination with the power of words led to positions as Editor-in-Chief*

There's a lot to be said for being humble, but a scholarship application is not the place to do it. You have a limited amount of space and time to persuade contest judges, so you'll want to highlight your most compelling achievements.

of my middle school newspaper; News Editor of my high school newspaper, The Axe, *as a sophomore; and presently, Editor-In-Chief of this nationally-acclaimed publication. In these roles I have received recognition for both my writing and design, and have had excerpts of my political commentary on the Senator Packwood sexual harassment scandal reprinted in my local newspaper,* The Register-Guard.*"*

In the above excerpt, I have once again bolstered my primary theme by discussing different manifestations of my love of writing. I have also illustrated that this isn't just a transitory interest, by showing how the interest can be traced back to my childhood. The description of the journalism-related leadership positions I have held further strengthens my secondary theme.

In choosing letters of recommendation to include with my application materials, I picked recommendations that further enhanced my two main application themes. The first recommendation letter I submitted was written by my faculty adviser on the school newspaper. Here is an excerpt:

"Conscientious, dedicated, and persistent, Ben is the kind of individual so greatly needed in journalism. He works equally well as part of a group or independently, he is concerned about others and his community, and he is keenly interested in current affairs. . . . In addition to being one of the top writers and analysts I have seen in 15 years of advising the journalism program, he is also an adept, articulate public speaker. Ben would make an outstanding journalist, a leader in his field."

A second letter of recommendation included in the application was written by my student government adviser, and emphasized my leadership skills:

In Chapter 9, I'll show you how to cultivate recommendation letters that reinforce your application themes.

"Ben has organized school elections, played a leading role in school-wide assemblies, is a part of the budgeting process for school clubs and activities, and has worked on projects to provide for indigent people in our community. . . . Ben is confident and comfortable in a small social group or speaking to a very large audience. He learns well from each situation in which he takes part."

The Discover Card application also allowed me to attach additional supplementary materials. To further bolster my primary theme (and to show that I had the necessary skills to reach my career goals), I chose to include three articles that I had written for my high school newspaper. Among these articles, I included my political column about the Senator Packwood scandal—the same one I had referenced in my criteria statement. Another article I included brought attention to the pressing need for an important school reform; this also reinforced my secondary theme by highlighting my "leadership through journalism" approach.

One common application component that wasn't depicted in the above example was an extracurricular activity list. Activities that reinforce your primary and secondary themes should be at or near the top of your list.

Overall, this example illustrates how a theme is implemented by reinforcing it in each component of an application. This is done by placing activities and credentials that support your theme in prominent places, and by addressing the theme in essays and personal statements.

Staying Balanced

Keep in mind that building a theme *doesn't* mean omitting other areas of your record that don't fit neatly into the thematic message. I still covered all of these off-theme activities and achievements in my application, but I kept this material in the background.

Case in point: I included a third letter of recommendation, written by the co-principal of my school, which touched upon my writing and leadership themes, but also described my involvement in activities that didn't relate to my thematic message. For instance, the letter discussed my tennis ability:

LEADING THE TEAM: *Here I am going over page changes with other members of my high school newspaper,* The Axe. *This photo, taken by Discover Card for use in their winners' slide show, illustrates my two main application themes (writing/communication and leadership).*

> *"Ben is also physically talented. Currently, he is one of the best high school tennis players in the state of Oregon. In individual play in United States Tennis Association junior tournaments, he is a national caliber player ranked in the top five for his age division in the Pacific Northwest. . . . The best part is he will represent South Eugene High School tennis for the next two years."*

Indeed, as we'll show in Chapter 6, depicting your well-roundedness is an important way to address the "hidden" judging criteria.

So the message here is that you *don't* have to sacrifice depicting your "well-roundedness" to make room for your application theme. Activities that fit your theme should occupy "center stage," but there's still plenty of room on the rest of the stage for all your other credentials.

9 WINNING THEMES

Never blindly follow a theme if it doesn't feel right for you. Judges can tell if a theme isn't genuine.

In this section, I describe nine application themes that have been successfully employed by scholarship winners I've interviewed. These descriptions are meant to stimulate your thinking, and to provide you with a sampling of the wide range of themes that are possible. Keep in mind that these themes represent only nine popular ones that I've chosen to profile: Winning scholarship themes come in all shapes and sizes, and can be as individual as you are.

In each of the profiled themes, I discuss the characteristics of the typical student using the theme, as well as the tactical advantages and disadvantages of that theme. All of these examples are suitable for use as both primary and secondary themes. I also discuss strategies that scholarship winners have used to flesh out the themes, making them especially persuasive and effective. Remember, I'm only summarizing strategies that other students have used. If you can come up with your own creative ways to flesh out these themes, so much the better. So without further ado. . .

THE DO-GOODER

Characteristics: You volunteer for several community organizations. You may have even created your own service program. Community service is your passion; it dominates your extracurricular activities.

Advantages: Service to others is an important criteria in many scholarship contests. By awarding scholarship money to you, society eventually receives a benefit many times greater than its investment. Your commitment to others is refreshing and admirable.

Disadvantages: Service to others is a fine theme, but it's still a pretty broad one—and one that many of your competing applicants will likely employ. You may be overshadowed by others with different areas of expertise, who *also* do volunteer work.

The key for this type of applicant to do well is to demonstrate a core purpose behind the services you perform. Because you'll need to make your commitment to community service credible, your service theme needs to be more specific. You can do this by crafting your theme around particular types of service programs that you especially care about.

Whenever possible, use personal experiences to illustrate why you are so taken by the particular type of service. Perhaps you are especially close to your grandmother, and have found it very rewarding to volunteer to help the elderly through the *Meals on Wheels* program. Or maybe you helped raise your younger siblings, and as a result of that experience enjoy working with young children.

This isn't to say that you shouldn't participate in a broad range of community service efforts. Just try to focus a little, making one type of service endeavor your special project. If you're really interested in community service, a very personally rewarding way to build upon your theme is to create your *own* community service program.

THE CREATIVE TALENT

Characteristics: You are unusually skilled in a particular creative discipline—whether in the visual arts, dance, music, drama, or some other field. You spend countless hours practicing the discipline, derive great enjoyment from it, and hope to pursue it in some capacity in the future.

Advantages: Your special talent helps make your scholarship applications stand out. Achieving distinction in a creative discipline illustrates that you possess many of the character traits (focus, determination, and work ethic) that are ingredients of success—and worthy of financial support.

Disadvantages: Judges are also looking for well-rounded applicants. The danger here is that you could appear too focused on your special talent, to the exclusion of everything else. Furthermore, if a judge doesn't have a good appreciation for your particular discipline, the chance of you bringing home the money becomes somewhat impaired.

Creativity is highly valued in scholarship applications. By passionately discussing significant milestones on the long road to proficiency and mastery, you can make your application memorable. The critical thing here is that you don't want to look too one-dimensional—suggesting that the particular discipline you excel in is the *only* thing you do. Some applicants get around this by demonstrating how they are skilled in a wide range of creative disciplines. Others balance their special talent with solid academics, community service involvement, and other extracurricular activities.

The other important aspect of employing a creative talent theme is demonstrating your ability. If contests permit it, try to send portfolios or samples of your work. Get professional artists and teachers in your field to comment on your work's quality, and enter various competitions in your field to establish marks of distinction.

THE SURVIVOR

Characteristics: You have overcome significant obstacles in your life—things like economic hardships, family problems, medical conditions, or personal issues. Overcoming such challenges has played an important role in shaping who you have become.

Advantages: Stories of obstacles overcome can create applications of compelling human emotion and drama. Some of the most powerful contest applications I've seen have been submitted by students who have described, in dramatic fashion, how they have triumphed over tough challenges with sheer will and determination.

Disadvantages: Depending on the obstacle you've overcome, some of it could involve private matters that are difficult (or painful) to discuss in an application.

"Success is to be measured not so much by the position one has reached in life as by the obstacles he has overcome trying to succeed."

Booker T. Washington

Merely describing a tough situation you've faced is not enough. Judges are more interested in how you've dealt with this challenge. In this way, the focus of your application should not be on the obstacle itself, but rather, on how you have *responded* to this obstacle.

For example, one scholarship winner I know had been diagnosed with cancer. Yet, she was still able to transform this potential personal tragedy: Using herself as a research subject, she conducted a study on the link between hair properties and chemotherapy, and illustrated how hair might be an effective vehicle to diagnose disease.

Some types of obstacles (for example, drug abuse) may be things that initially put a negative image in minds of judges. So if the obstacle you've overcome is an obstacle created by your own doing, you'll want to clearly show how you've learned from your mistakes, and are now an entirely different person. This is also an effective strategy if there's a "black eye" on your record (such as a school disciplinary action). Such a theme can put the punishment in a more positive light.

THE BRAINIAC

Characteristics: You have a high grade point average (3.8 and above) and very strong standardized test scores. You have taken a slew of Advanced Placement, honors, and other high-level classes. Your friends call you "Doogie."

Strengths: You're going to look great with anything that requires a transcript. Your success in school demonstrates your discipline and commitment. Your results in tough classes illustrate a drive to succeed in challenging environments.

Weaknesses: Grades and high scores aren't everything. If you don't balance your academic prowess with success in other areas, you might come across as very one-dimensional. And because it's impossible to garner a GPA of 49.2 on a 4.0 scale, you need to find additional ways to distinguish yourself.

Grades alone won't bring you scholarship success, but you are in an excellent position to build on the stellar academic record you've already accumulated. There are, of course, a number of ways to do this: One way is to demonstrate that your good grades are, at a fundamental level, a result of your great curiosity and thirst for knowledge (in a wide range of fields, or one field in particular).

You could illustrate this thirst by explaining how much a particular out-of-school academic program or course of independent study has meant to you. The strength of such an approach is that it presents you as someone who will get the most out of a collegiate academic environment. Judges would likely feel that awarding you a scholarship would be money very well spent.

Another approach is to emphasize that although school work is primarily an individual task, you're interested in helping others get more out of their studies, too. Typical activities to support this theme might include tutoring other students in your school, or starting a program—such as a math tournament—to help encourage younger students.

THE ACTIVIST

Characteristics: You devote a considerable amount of time supporting and promoting various social causes that you believe in. You have helped organize rallies, petition drives, awareness campaigns, and other projects. Your first words as a baby were "Hell no, we won't go!"

Advantages: Your devotion to making society a better place is very admirable. Judges will like the fact that you are not content to just sit on your laurels, but rather, are someone who takes action and has strong convictions.

Disadvantages: Some of the causes you support may not be supported by some contest judges. You could thus alienate some judges by taking a controversial position. Furthermore, you don't want to come across as someone who takes on social causes just for the sake of being a protestor.

These days, we hear that less young people are active in social causes than in past generations. So to the extent that you work hard to better society, your efforts will definitely stand out from the scholarship application pack.

Students who employ this theme should be cautious about too heavily emphasizing controversial opinions in an application. In general, a scholarship application is *not* the place to make a bold political statement—especially one that may alienate some contest judges. You should also research any potential political leanings of the organization sponsoring or administering the contest. You wouldn't want to focus on a cause that is opposed by the organization. In general, focusing on controversial topics (like abortion) is always risky.

That having been said, you still want to be true to your convictions. Just try to balance what you want to say within the pragmatic boundaries of a scholarship application. Also, remember to highlight the leadership, organizational, and communication skills that you exhibit in your activism work.

In Chapter 7, we'll discuss how to "do your homework" and learn about the sometimes "hidden" agendas of contest sponsors and administrators.

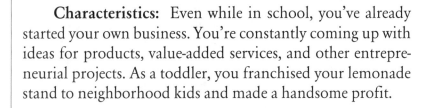

THE ENTREPRENEUR

Characteristics: Even while in school, you've already started your own business. You're constantly coming up with ideas for products, value-added services, and other entrepreneurial projects. As a toddler, you franchised your lemonade stand to neighborhood kids and made a handsome profit.

Advantages: Starting your own business demonstrates a great deal of self-initiative and vision. If your business is a success, that's quite an achievement for a full-time student. The story of how you built your business—from idea creation to implementation—makes interesting essay fodder.

Disadvantages: You could come across as overly concerned about making a quick buck. In addition, given that scholarships fund education, you don't want it to seem as though you've neglected your education to pursue your latest business plan.

Starting a business (especially a small, shoestring operation) requires that you wear many hats—acting as innovator, problem solver, marketer, customer service representative, and manager. Because of this, starting your own business provides you with fertile ground to demonstrate your abilities.

What types of businesses have winning scholarship applicants started? Everything from Internet sales operations and Web page design firms, to jewelry makers and investment advisers. Really, anything is possible. Many students have also assumed significant responsibilities in the family business.

Some applicants who have employed this theme have stressed that they are saving money generated from their business to help pay for college. This underscores how you've been taking the initiative to pay for your own education, and are worthy of additional scholarship help.

THE LEADER

Characteristics: You have been a driving force behind some type of project that has involved working well with others. You excel in the group environment, and hold leadership positions in several organizations.

Strengths: Great leaders bring out the best from others, not just from themselves. This ability to positively influence others is an important aspect of many scholarship programs. The various titles and positions you may have held contribute to your credentials and accomplishments.

Weaknesses: Leaders aren't judged by the positions they hold, but by their actions. Your application could be less-than-compelling if it comes across only as a list of offices you have held. Titles backed up by little actual results or accomplishments can seem hollow.

E ffectively demonstrating your leadership in a scholarship application takes more than just saying that you're a leader. As a result, students employing this theme often have others communicate this message for them—through letters of recommendation that specifically comment on their leadership qualities.

Leadership is a contest judging criterion in its own right. We discuss this at length in Chapter 6.

Keep in mind that leadership, by definition, involves other people and groups of people. So the emphasis here needs to be on activities you participated in as part of a team. Interpersonal skills such as your ability to get along with team members, work well in a group, gain the respect of others, and accept criticism, should be conveyed in an application.

Furthermore, because leadership ability is really measured in terms of impact, it's important to be able to show tangible results. These results will often be measured by what the overall group was able to accomplish, and how *you* helped bring about these results.

THE SCIENTIST

Characteristics: You enjoy learning about science in your spare time—whether it's building model rockets, competing in science fairs, or conducting outside research. You get excellent grades in science-related classes. You have a curious fondness for Bunsen burners.

Advantages: Quite a few scholarship programs are geared toward students who excel in science. Laboratory research can lead to impressive individual projects. Science projects outside of the school curriculum demonstrate a commitment to learning and a fascination with knowledge.

Disadvantages: Scientific jargon used too liberally can pass over the head of contest judges who don't have a strong background in science. Competition for science-related awards, credentials, and opportunities can be fierce. Developing a quality science project can take years of hard work.

Science can be a powerful application theme, but it's also important to recognize that science-minded scholarship winners frequently have done significant research and study outside of the school environment. So if science is going to be the focal point of your application, be prepared to demonstrate your interest and ability through science contests, fairs, and research projects that extend beyond the classroom.

Good science research projects often depend on finding a mentor who is willing to take you under his wing. Scholarship winners have done this by seeking out local college professors and research scientists, or by attending summer science programs on college campuses.

Working with a mentor has an added benefit: It typically yields outstanding letters of recommendation.

Because scientific research is, to a large extent, an individual endeavor, be sure to balance this out in an application by also showing participation in activities that require interpersonal and teamwork skills.

THE ATHLETE

Characteristics: You have exceptional skill in a particular sport (good enough to play college athletics), or else you have accumulated a solid record in several sports.

Strengths: Describing athletic competition can add welcome drama to an otherwise average profile. Because sports represents a microcosm of life, recounting some poignant lessons learned on the court or playing field can make you stand out from the crowd.

Weaknesses: Many students are pretty good at sports; it could be difficult to distinguish yourself. Also, some judges might not want to award you money if they believe that you are likely to receive a sports scholarship for college.

Being a good athlete is a nice attribute to have, but to translate this into a powerful theme, you need to extend what you've learned from your sport to other areas beyond the world of athletics. A good way to do this is to think about qualities and abilities you've developed on the court or playing field that have impacted other areas of your life—attitudes like determination, hard work, perseverance, grace under pressure, and teamwork.

The key to making this theme work is being able to show direct and tangible ways that the lessons of athletic participation have contributed to success in other areas of your life. Perhaps the lessons you have learned about teamwork on the basketball court have helped you manage your staff as sports editor on the school newspaper. Or maybe all of those early morning swim practices have taught you the importance of discipline—which in turn, helped you get better grades. There's a lot more you learn through sports than just how to throw a ball, or run down a backhand.

Finding Your Theme

Now that you understand what themes are, and how scholarship winners have employed them, it's time for you to think about developing your own. Keep in mind that even two applications with identical themes can look entirely different. The substance of a theme is derived from all of the supporting details; these details are unique to *you*.

In any event, your job is to develop application themes that best reflect you. If a theme doesn't come to mind immediately, that's perfectly okay. Part of this process entails taking a detailed look at your life, and searching for subtle patterns that might be nurtured and developed.

COACH

In this dialogue, the Scholarship Coach answers questions about developing an application theme built around ethnic heritage.

. . . About ethnic themes

The following questions were submitted by Ed Nicity, a high school senior from Bigbucks, California.

Ed: I'm currently filling out a scholarship application and am trying hard to develop my own theme. Since I'm an African-American student, I am wondering if my ethnic heritage can be developed into a strong theme?

Scholarship Coach: Yes, ethnicity can be a strong theme in an application. The key is that you don't want your underlying thematic message to simply be saying "I'm an African-American." Instead, you want to show how your ethnic and cultural heritage has shaped who you are, as well as communicate what you have learned from this heritage. Some applicants doing this have also broadened their theme by demonstrating their appreciation for other cultures.

Ed: Are there a lot of scholarships out there geared toward students from ethnic minority groups?

Scholarship Coach: Yes, there are quite a few. In addition, some scholarship contests—especially ones sponsored by large corporations—try to select a group of winners from diverse ethnic backgrounds. A strong ethnicity theme can thus work well in such scenarios.

CHAPTER 5 SUMMARY

■ **Winning Applications:** Unsuccessful scholarship applications resemble laundry lists of credentials. Winning applications, however, show judges the person behind the application.

■ **Painting Your Self-Portrait:** Treat each component of an application as part of a unified whole. Develop an application theme that permeates the entire application and communicates a cohesive message. Application themes are frequently based on extracurricular activities, longtime interests, or future career goals.

■ **Thematic Variety:** All of a student's applications need not have the same theme. Certain themes may be better suited for particular types of scholarship contests.

■ **Primary & Secondary Themes:** The typical application should have one or two major themes. Trying to fit in more themes than this devalues your thematic currency. If you feel an application should have two themes, make one the primary theme and the other the secondary theme. The primary theme should be the focal point of the application—the main message you're trying to communicate.

■ **Credibility:** Cohesive application themes enhance credibility by providing frameworks that give meaning and purpose to activities, achievements, and experiences. With a strong theme, this framework is reinforced throughout an application.

■ **Employing a Theme:** Themes are created by reinforcing the message in each component of an application. This is done by placing résumé items that support the theme in prominent places, and by addressing the theme in essays and personal statements.

■ **Application Balance:** Building a theme *doesn't* mean that one should omit credentials that don't fit neatly into the thematic message. Applicants should still strive to appear well-rounded. Although activities that fit one's theme should occupy the spotlight, there is always plenty of room in the rest of the application for everything else.

■ **9 Winning Themes:** Some popular themes employed by scholarship winners include: "The Do-Gooder," "The Creative Talent," "The Survivor," "The Brainiac," "The Activist," "The Entrepreneur," "The Leader," "The Scientist," and "The Athlete."

CHAPTER 6

"Hidden" Judging Criteria

In this chapter, we describe the unseen, neglected, and overlooked factors that influence contest judging.

CHAPTER CONTENTS

- Width and depth evaluators
- Analyzing perennial judging criteria
- The "Ten Golden Virtues"

THE UNSEEN EVALUATORS

The following section focuses on Type 2 and Type 3 scholarship contests—the ones that take into account a student's past achievement.

In the previous chapter, I showed you how to paint your own portrait by developing a strong application theme. In addition to communicating this overall message, we also need to be concerned about the nitty-gritty details of our application. In particular, we want to understand how scholarship judges employ contest judging criteria to evaluate and rate all of our activities, achievements, and credentials.

First, we should note that although scholarship judging criteria comes in thousands of flavors, there are definitely some perennial favorites. In fact, a good many Type 2 and Type 3 contests will employ at least one (and frequently several) of the following categories of judging criteria:

Service to Others
Academic Achievement
Extracurricular Activities
Leadership

So how do contest judges rate you in each of these categories? Well, in a general sense, they do this by comparing your activities, achievements, and overall record to those of other applicants. Of course, it would be an arduous task to compare dozens, hundreds, or even thousands of preliminary applicants on a one-on-one basis. So contest judges do this implicitly by comparing each applicant to a set of expectations for each judging category.

Where do these hidden expectations come from? Well, imagine that you have a huge iron kettle for each judging category. Then, for each contest applicant, you pour in all relevant credentials that fit this category. Subsequently, in going through this scholarship stew, you'd soon discover that applicant credentials naturally fall into certain common subcategories—the carrots, onions, and potatoes of our stew. Taken as a whole, these subcategories define the full range of activities and achieve-

The Catch

Don't worry, I'll explain what these specific terms mean in a few pages.

ments of all applicants. More simply put, these subcategories summarize the entire spectrum of activities, achievements, and credentials that judges could expect to find in a student's application.

There's just one catch: For the most part, scholarship applicants aren't aware of these subcategories. Applicants don't know about them because they haven't had the benefit of viewing all of the applications submitted by other students. Because of this, these subcategories become what I call the **unseen evaluators**—the hidden categories that judges use to compare students.

To better understand these evaluators, it's helpful to sort them into two groups. **Width evaluators** assess the range of your activities within a given judging category. The emphasis here is on having many different types of experiences and credentials. In this way, width evaluators can be thought of as a series of checklist items measuring your well-roundedness in a judging category. For example, in the *Service to Others* category, width evaluators assess whether you've done school-based, community-based, and/or self-initiated service projects.

The second group, **depth evaluators**, assess the *quality* of your record within a given judging category. They help measure what you've brought to the experience—hopefully, more than just a willingness to participate. To use the *Service to Others* example, depth evaluators weigh your time commitment, the impact of your service, as well as the leadership you have exhibited.

The specific width and depth evaluators, of course, depend upon the judging category. We can illustrate the relationship between width and depth, however, by using our *Service to Others* example. The two dimensions of evaluation for this category are shown at left.

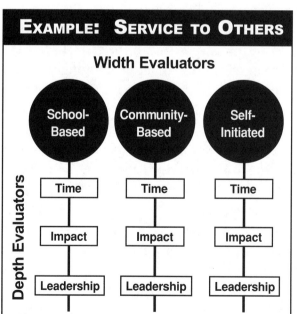

EXAMPLE: SERVICE TO OTHERS

Width Evaluators

School-Based | Community-Based | Self-Initiated

Depth Evaluators

Time | Time | Time

Impact | Impact | Impact

Leadership | Leadership | Leadership

I've also had the opportunity to watch the judging procedures of one scholarship competition up close. I know from this valuable experience that these unseen evaluators, whether explicit or not, are indeed a very real part of contest judging.

Are these evaluators always hidden? Well, not always. For example, some contests request information about any awards and honors you've received as part of an activity—even though "awards and honors" is not a specific judging category of its own. In this way, awards and honors may be used as a depth evaluator that helps assess a student's record in a broader judging category.

In this particular example, the depth evaluators (time, impact, and leadership) are identical for each width evaluator (school-based, community-based, and self-initiated). Although it works out this way for the *Service to Others* category, this is typically *not* the case for other judging criteria because certain depth evaluators may only be appropriate for particular width evaluators.

We should also note that it's perfectly acceptable for one activity to span multiple width evaluators. For instance, a community service project may be both community-based and self-initiated. Indeed, activities that bridge multiple areas are useful in that they can strengthen many aspects of your overall record at once.

So do judges actually check a list of these width and depth evaluators when they're assessing a contest application? Well, not necessarily. For many contests, these are part of the implicit judging process. Contest judges may not explicitly check off these hidden evaluators, but due to the repetitive nature of judging numerous applications, they subconsciously employ these evaluators when making comparisons between applicants.

Treating these hidden evaluators explicitly, however, can yield a big strategic advantage. Thinking in terms of these hidden evaluators helps you to assess the strengths and weaknesses in your record in comparison to the rest of the pack. This enables you to develop content and packaging strategies that highlight your strongest areas and compensate for your weaker spots (something I'll show you how to do in the next chapter). Indeed, the quickest way to improve the overall impression you make on contest judges is to better communicate how you have demonstrated competence in these unseen evaluator subcategories.

Don't feel, however, like you're expected to be able to think of an activity or credential that demonstrates competence in each of these hidden evaluators. In fact, the point is that you *won't* be able to. Even a self-proclaimed scholarship superman or wonderwoman will not be able to rattle off

140 *How to Go to College Almost For Free*

an experience for all of these width and depth evaluators. After conducting this analysis, however, *every* student will be able to find relatively painless ways to enhance their current standing.

So enough with the abstract discussion. Let's now get specific: The hidden evaluators for each of the six perennial judging categories I've isolated are discussed in the sections below. Think of these sections as your power drill, helping you bore below the visible surface criteria to learn what lies underneath.

Service to Others

Because we've already used the *Service to Others* category in a few of our examples, let's start out by discussing this perennial category in further detail. First and foremost, service to others is about using our time and energy to make a positive difference in our schools, communities, and the nation as a whole. Because *Service to Others* is such a ubiquitous scholarship judging criterion, it's especially important to be aware of its hidden evaluators. Furthermore, an understanding of these width and depth evaluators can also help guide you to broaden the extent of your community service experience.

The first width evaluator is **school-based** service, which includes service activities undertaken by a group associated with your school—projects like peer tutoring, campus cleanup drives, or a school dance to raise money for the Children's Miracle Network. It includes service projects which you may perform as part of such student groups as the National Honor Society, Key Club, or your student government.

Community-based service follows you beyond the walls of your school to areas in the community that benefit from your help. Such projects may include volunteering at the local homeless shelter, delivering meals to the elderly as part of the Meals on Wheels program, or helping with a local recycling effort. Participation in community-based service demonstrates your willingness to help solve problems outside of the structured activities of school-related service.

Self-initiated projects demonstrate your ability to recognize and address a pressing problem in your community.

EVALUATORS

WIDTH

School-Based
Community-Based
Self-Initiated Projects

DEPTH

Time Commitment
Impact
Responsibility

It's a good idea to keep a written or electronic record of all the hours you spend on each community service project. For some applications, I found it useful to include the total number of hours I had spent on community service during the year.

This includes both school-related and community-based involvement—with the key factor being an effort *you* helped create and organize.

Depth evaluators for this category help assess what you have contributed to the particular service project. A common way of assessing this contribution is through **time commitment**—generally measured in terms of the amount of hours you spent on the project (on a cumulative or weekly basis). But quantity alone doesn't communicate the results of your work. That's where **impact** comes into play: Impact assesses the positive effect of your work on the problem you're addressing. Impact can be measured both in terms of your individual efforts and that of the entire service organization. Finally, **leadership** measures the extent of your help in organizing an activity, assuming responsibility for implementing the program, and in recruiting others to participate.

Academic Achievement

EVALUATORS
WIDTH
Schoolwork
Standardized Tests
Academic Clubs
Individual Study
Research Projects
DEPTH
Grade Point Average
Class Ranking
Test Scores
Grade Trend
Class Balance
Class Difficulty
Awards & Honors

When most people think of evaluating academic achievement, they naturally focus on two self-explanatory width evaluators, **schoolwork** and **standardized tests**. Schoolwork, of course, refers to all the classes you've taken during your high school or college career. Scholarship applications that request standardized test information typically want PSAT, SAT, or ACT scores. On occasion, scores on SAT II subject tests may also be requested (although students who haven't yet taken such exams may be exempted). Scores on Advanced Placement (AP) or International Baccalaureate (IB) exams are not usually requested, but students who have done well may want to submit their scores nevertheless. If you're a freshmen or sophomore in high school, you are generally not expected to have taken any standardized tests.

What depth evaluators are typically associated with these two width measures? Perhaps the most commonly used depth evaluator is a student's **grade point average**. Because different schools have different grading standards, scholarship contests may also request a student's **class ranking** in order to assess a student's grade-point average relative to other stu-

See Chapter 9 for tips on how to get recommendation writers to discuss the aspects of your record that you need addressed.

If you want to improve your overall academic achievement (and compensate for weaker grade transcripts or standardized test performance) these three nontraditional width evaluators are especially useful.

dents in his or her school. And of course, **test scores** show academic performance relative to other test takers.

Three other depth evaluators for measuring the quality of your academic schoolwork, however, are often overlooked. First, **grade trend** is the term used to describe the overall direction a student's grades tend to be headed over his or her high school career. Do the grades seem to be getting better over time (a positive trend)? A strong grade trend can make up for sluggish grades early in a student's high school career.

Second, **class balance** poses the question of whether you have taken a broad range of classes in many different subject areas. This includes English, math, science, social studies, and foreign language.

Third, **class difficulty** measures the amount a student challenges himself by taking difficult courses. Because a scholarship judge is unlikely to be familiar with which classes are the most challenging (unless the contest happens to be open only to students in your school), the level of class difficulty is conveyed in two main ways. First, classes denoted with "AP," "Honors," or some other form of distinction will be perceived as more challenging. Second, recommendation letters that address the academic rigor of a student's course work are an effective way to communicate this subcomponent.

In addition to these overlooked depth evaluators, there are three additional width evaluators that contest winners frequently employ. These concern what goes on outside the daily grind of homework and test-taking. For instance, participation in **academic clubs and teams**—activities such as the Science Olympics, Academic Bowl, or math team—demonstrates a different side to a student's academic achievement.

Pursuing a course of **individual study** is a great indicator of self-motivation. Students who are up for this pick a topic, person, or subject area encountered in class, and study it in more depth on their own—usually under the guidance of a faculty advisor.

Finally, **individual research projects** demonstrate a type of academic achievement that is relatively unusual among most high school students. The students who conduct such projects generally find mentors in their school, community, or nearby university, and engage in some type of academic research guided by these mentors. This sounds more difficult than it is: By picking an area you are genuinely interested in, and selecting the right mentor, it can really be a lot of fun.

In these three areas above, depth of involvement is generally measured through **awards and honors** (or other forms of recognition) received.

Extracurricular Activities

SUBCOMPONENTS
WIDTH
Creative Arts
Athletics
Communications
Student Government
Vocational
Academics
Entrepreneurial
Culture & Language
Issue-Oriented
Internships
Jobs
Religious Groups
Community Service
DEPTH
Time Commitment
Leadership
Awards & Honors

I have chosen to break down *Extracurricular Activities* into thirteen width evaluators and three depth evaluators. Please note that because a wide range of after-school endeavors could be considered extracurricular activities, my list could potentially include many more entries. Instead of listing out all of the possibilities, however, I have focused on the most common types of activities—the ones that contest judges will be most on the lookout for.

The first two width evaluators are fairly self-explanatory. **Creative Arts** encompasses all sorts of artistic endeavors ranging from the visual arts (painting, sculpture, etc.) to the performing arts (dance, drama, music, filmmaking, etc.) to the literary arts (fiction writing, poetry, etc.). **Athletics** includes both school-sponsored sports and other forms of athletic involvement (such as city leagues, individual competitions, clubs, etc.).

Communications highlights such activities as the school newspaper, yearbook, or other official and unofficial publications (such as an underground newspaper). It also includes other forms of communications-oriented activities such as participation in a speech and debate club ("Four score and seven years ago. . ."), or work on the school radio station ("The love doctor is in!").

Student Government is about more than just getting elected to a class or school-wide office. It includes work you might do in conjunction with your school's student government in a nonelected capacity, as well as service on other governing bodies that may be affiliated with organizations in your

community other than your school.

Vocational activities might involve such career-oriented groups as 4-H, the Future Business Leaders of America, and the Future Farmers of America. This subcomponent also includes such diverse activities as Mock Trial ("If it doesn't fit, you must acquit!") or a car mechanics' club.

Academics deals more with fields of study than particular careers. It includes clubs devoted to such academic areas as science, literature, history, or other fields of study. This extracurricular evaluator also includes any in-depth research or independent study projects you might choose to do.

Starting your own business of some kind is classified as an **Entrepreneurial** activity. Perhaps you design Web pages for organizations in your area. Maybe you design and sell your won jewelry. Even your summer curb-address painting business counts.

Culture and Language activities and projects are noticed by contest judges and college admissions officers everywhere. This typically involves learning about foreign cultures, the study of foreign language, travel abroad, and the appreciation of various ethnic groups.

Issue-Oriented activities frequently involve the promotion of political causes—such as environmental preservation, First Amendment rights, or campaign finance reform. This also includes issues that may immediately impact your school such as youth violence, drug abuse, or educational reform.

Internships are work experiences in which learning is the primary motivation. During high school, for instance, I had an internship at a local daily newspaper. Many students arrange their own internships in careers they are interested in pursuing. Internships can be both paid and unpaid.

Jobs, unlike internships, are work experiences in which money is usually the primary motivation. This encompasses all the traditional high school and college jobs we think of—including ones that may involve the phrase, "Do you want fries with that?" Many students don't include such jobs on contest applications because they think they're not particularly impressive after-school pursuits. Such jobs, however, are

Moreover, such jobs show that you know the value of a dollar, and do, in fact, need the funds that the scholarship contest can provide.

important "real world" experiences that illustrate how you have taken on responsibilities outside of your school environment.

Any activity that you take part in because of your religious faith comes under the umbrella of **Religious Groups**. This may include regular commitments at your church, synagogue, mosque, or temple.

I should also point out that **Community Service** has been included here as an *Extracurricular Activities* width evaluator, even though we have previously treated it as a *separate* judging category. I treat it this way to emphasize that community service impacts any judging where *Extracurricular Activities* are taken into account.

As for depth evaluators, there are three primary metrics: **Time Commitment** seeks to quantify the energy and effort you have invested into a particular activity. It is frequently measured in terms of the hours you spend on the activity each week. **Leadership** examines whether you have helped organize the extracurricular activity, or even created the group on your own. Finally, **Awards and Honors** reveals any marks of distinction you have received for your involvement.

Leadership

SUBCOMPONENTS

WIDTH

Organizational
Issue-Oriented
Representative
Peer-Directed

DEPTH

Positions Held
Impact
Time Commitment
Organization Size
Awards & Honors

We've encountered leadership as an unseen depth evaluator for other judging categories. Leadership, however, has become such an important part of some scholarships, that it is frequently listed as a judging category in and of itself.

We can divide the leadership judging category into four width evaluators. **Organizational** leadership, as the name suggests, involves leading and managing an organization, or one aspect of an organization. Perhaps you manage the advertising department of your school newspaper. Or maybe you help organize activities, schedule speakers, and run meetings for your school's creative writing club.

Issue-Oriented leadership brings awareness and inspires action on a particular societal issue. Frequent issues around which this type of student leadership coalesces include environmental preservation, educational reform, freedom of speech, and youth violence.

Stepping up as a representative voice for a particular constituency is the essence of **Representative** leadership. Students frequently exhibit this type of leadership by serving on student government or by representing the student body on school steering committees. Students may be elected to such positions, or appointed by someone in a position of authority (such as a school principal).

Peer-Directed leadership focuses its energy on influencing peers in a positive way. Some students have done this by participating in groups that educate others on the dangers of substance abuse, youth violence, or sexually-transmitted diseases. In other instances, peer-directed leadership simply means being a good role model and mentor for younger students.

Leadership *depth* is typically evaluated five ways: Perhaps the most traditional way is **Positions Held**. This assesses any formal leadership positions and titles you may have held— such roles as class vice-president, captain of the track team, managing editor of the school newspaper, or treasurer of the mountain climbing club.

Being a leader, however, isn't just about having a title. For instance, some of the world's greatest political leaders— individuals such as Martin Luther King, Jr. and Mohandas Gandhi—never held an official position in government. The **Impact** evaluator acknowledges that being a leader is about *doing something*, not just being somebody supposedly important. It assesses what you've managed to accomplish in your leadership roles, irrespective of any titles or positions held.

Just as in the case of the community service and extracurricular activities judging categories, **Time Commitment** is once again a depth evaluator. The time you devote to your leadership activities provides a sense of the demands of the job. The **Organization Size** evaluator provides judges with some sense of the demands of a particular leadership role. It's likely to be more demanding to run an organization made up of one hundred students than one composed of five.

Finally, **Awards & Honors** accounts for any accolades you may have received in your leadership capacity. Although you would obviously include awards and honors won for *individual* work, you might forget to include awards bestowed on the *organization* you helped lead. You have every right to indicate that your leadership has, in fact, contributed to the organization's success. For instance, because I was editor of my high school newspaper, I would also try to communicate in an application that our newspaper had won top prizes in several national journalism competitions.

So What?

The unseen evaluator framework we've developed has several important implications for scholarship applicants. First, this framework emphasizes that many factors go into the overall impression you make in each judging category. By examining these hidden factors explicitly, you won't forget to address these areas in contest applications.

Second, the framework helps us to better understand areas where we all could use some improvement or growth. Subsequently, we can devise relatively painless ways to shore up these weaker areas in our profiles. (We'll discuss how to do this in Chapter 7.)

Don't limit what you've learned in this section to the four judging categories I've described. Instead, whatever the published judging criteria may be, break it down into width and depth evaluators like we've done here.

Third, the framework shows that we can compensate for less-than-ideal performance in one aspect of a judging category by excelling in other unseen evaluator areas. For instance, in the *Academic Achievement* category, if your grades and test scores are not as strong as you would like, you can make up for this by participating in academic clubs, pursuing independent study, and creating your own research projects. Indeed, contest judges have told me that these types of self-initiated academic projects are the types of academic endeavors that are the most impressive.

ASK THE COACH

. . . About small-town opportunities

The following questions were submitted by Smitty Limits, a high school sophomore from Momoney, Montana.

Smitty: I'm a student from a small, rural area, and there just aren't as many extracurricular activities available to me as there would be in a big city. How can I be competitive in scholarship contests with students from more populated areas?

In this dialogue, the Scholarship Coach answers questions about finding activities and opportunities when you're from a small town or rural area.

Scholarship Coach: The key is to take advantage of the resources you do have around you. For instance, I know a student from rural Alaska who used his proximity to the Exxon Valdez oil spill to study the effects of the accident on the environment. Another student I know from a small Midwest town did agricultural research on her family farm. Both converted their projects into impressive scholarship winnings.

Smitty: Well, even if I do my own individual project, what about the other extracurricular activity width evaluators that my school is missing?

Students from smaller schools or rural areas have certain advantages over their big city counterparts. For instance, competition for leadership roles in a club or activity tends to be less intense in smaller schools.

Scholarship Coach: If a particular type of club or organization doesn't exist in your area, then just start such a group yourself! Not only will the activity be on your record, but you'll also impress judges by demonstrating your individual initiative and leadership role.

Smitty: Do students from smaller towns and high schools win national scholarship contests?

Scholarship Coach: You bet! It happens all the time. You don't have to go to Fancysmancy Preparatory Academy to be competitive on the national level.

TEN GOLDEN VIRTUES

Although we've explored quite a few of the "hidden" criteria that arise in scholarship contest judging, there are some additional judging factors that lie beneath the surface. First, consider the subjective element to judging; this is rooted in the biases, experiences, and values of each individual judge. You would expect judges to be more inclined to select students who possess personal qualities that they themselves value, admire, and respect.

Because it's impossible to know the predisposition of the person or persons who will judge each of your contest applications, we'll have to resort to the next best thing. We can anticipate the types of personal qualities that judges are likely to respond well to (traits that aren't necessarily official judging criteria) by examining the types of qualities that our society as a whole respects and values. Additionally, we can look at the types of personal qualities that the most successful scholarship applicants have communicated.

When we combine these two approaches, what we come up with are the 10 Golden Virtues—the personal qualities that almost all scholarship contests look for in their scholarship winners. By illustrating in your application as many of these core virtues as you can, you gain the ability to communicate with contest judges on an emotional level. So let's first discuss these ten qualities, and then we'll explore how students can employ them in a traditional application format.

Trying to communicate these 10 Golden Virtues doesn't mean that you will be "manipulating" judges by making up false stories or emphasizing traits that you don't really have. Rather, the goal of this section is to help you take a deeper look at the things you've done and highlight the personal attributes that you're most proud of.

1. Hard Work

There's more to success than just wanting it. For every person who becomes a success story, there are hundreds of others who may have had the same goals and desires, but who weren't willing to put in the necessary hard work.

So don't hide the fact that you've been putting in those extra hours of practice and training. If you happen to dream of becoming a concert pianist, letting judges know about all of the work that you're putting in *now* to reach this goal makes your dream seem substantially more attainable. Scholarships are awarded to students who aren't afraid to invest their time and energy in things they care about.

2. Overcoming Obstacles

At the core of traditional American values is a "can-do" spirit: the notion that obstacles in one's path are challenges waiting to be faced. For some of us, overcoming obstacles may involve coming back from defeat, conquering that debilitating fear, or shoring up some of those personal weaknesses. For others, the obstacles may be something more dramatic: health conditions, unfortunate economic circumstances, or serious family problems.

Regardless of the obstacles that one faces (and we *all* face them), our culture respects those who tackle these obstacles head on. Such people are not defined by the obstacles they face, but rather by how they *respond* to these roadblocks. So if you have genuinely worked to conquer an obstacle in your life, by all means communicate this in your scholarship essays and other application materials.

3. Teamwork

Why do sports like football, basketball, and baseball receive more national attention than athletic competitions like tennis, golf, or swimming? Perhaps it's because the former are all *team* sports. From the playing field to workplace, and the schoolhouse to the statehouse, society places a premium on people working together in pursuit of a common goal.

So how can you illustrate your teamwork skills in a scholarship application? It's easy. Pick any activity in which you work with other people, and emphasize the team aspects. And if the group you're involved with has received some type of award or distinction, mention this in your application, too.

4. Perseverance

Gratification can't always be immediate. In fact, most things that are truly worthwhile take time. Usually, before you can succeed at something, you first have to pay your dues. And that's what perseverance is all about: sticking with a goal, when others quit or give up.

When I was younger, I had a fear of speaking in front of large groups. To conquer this fear, I forced myself to take the podium whenever possible. Eventually, I learned to love public speaking. In fact, it's now one of my favorite things to do.

"What counts is not necessarily the size of the dog in the fight, but the size of the fight in the dog."

Dwight Eisenhower

In order to communicate perseverance in an application, you should not hide the struggles that have helped you get where you are. Perhaps you have endured years of sitting on the bench, but after putting in countless hours of extra practice, you now start for the varsity team. Often, by illustrating how you have persevered in some difficult situation, you can make your application all the more compelling.

5. Individual Initiative

Whether we're talking about a social worker who starts a shelter for the homeless, a teenager who decides to research her family tree, or a business school graduate who creates an innovative Silicon Valley start-up company, we're illustrating the same core character trait: individual initiative.

In a nutshell, individual initiative means *taking action*. If something doesn't exist that should, create it. If opportunities and resources aren't immediately accessible, seek them out. America was settled by pioneers who possessed the individual initiative to boldly journey to far away places in search of better lives.

So how do you convey individual initiative in a scholarship application format? There are infinite ways. You can do so by describing a project that you helped initiate, either on your own or as part of a group. You can also do this by discussing an interest that you went out of your way to pursue (such as seeking out a mentor to coach you on a project). Or, you might try observing a problem, and then proposing an innovative solution to fix it.

6. Passion & Enthusiasm

Many people in this world find themselves stuck doing things (often jobs) that they simply don't enjoy. So when scholarship judges come across applicants who truly love what they do, the judges sit up and take notice.

To convey this underlying passion and enthusiasm in an application, you need to describe your activities with a sense of excitement and wonder. For instance, in essays that asked

"Play up what you've done in terms of individual initiative. I had been in a math contest in elementary school, and I remembered how much I had enjoyed it. So I decided to recreate the experience for other elementary school kids."

Casey Cornwell
National Scholarship Winner

me to talk about my interests, I would often start with this sentence: "As far back as I can remember, a love for language and a passion for expressing ideas have been integral parts of who I am." I would then proceed to illustrate this passion by describing all of the activities I participated in that involved writing and communication.

Such an opening sentence helped demonstrate how all of the writing I did in high school was truly a labor of love. And phrases like "as far back as I can remember" communicated how this wasn't just a transitory interest that could change tomorrow, but something very important and deeply meaningful to me.

If you don't particularly exhibit some of these qualities, then perhaps this highlights some areas of personal development for you to work on...

7. Responsibility

The essence of responsibility is accountability—being accountable for your own actions and the consequences of those actions. Demonstrating responsibility is important to scholarship judging because it is a sign of maturity, self-confidence, and trustworthiness: It is a sign of maturity because it shows that we acknowledge and accept ownership for our actions and the effects these actions have upon others. It is a sign of self-confidence because taking responsibility for an outcome means being willing to put yourself on the line for its ultimate success or failure. Finally, it is a sign of trustworthiness when others (especially teachers, coaches, and parents) allow you to assume responsibility, illustrating their faith in your judgment and ability.

You can demonstrate your level of responsibility in many different settings—including your home, school, and community.

8. Civic Duty

In his Inaugural Address, President John F. Kennedy spoke these immortal words: "And so, my fellow Americans, ask not what your country can do for you—ask what you can do for your country." And in this call for sacrifice, Kennedy's oratory rejuvenated the notion of civic duty: Each of us, he stressed, has a duty to give something back to the nation that has given us so much.

"A man wrapped up in himself makes a very small bundle."

Benjamin Franklin

These days, however, people often forget or ignore their civic duties. That's why scholarship judges generally place substantial weight on such qualities. They want to leverage their scholarship dollars by granting college money to individuals who will pay back to society the amount of their scholarship may times over.

Successful scholarship applicants often demonstrate their sense of civic duty through participation in community service activities. In addition, applicants can also communicate this sense of civic duty through their expression of future goals that, regardless of the career area, are focused on making a big contribution to society.

9. Purpose

Perhaps the most challenging golden virtue for a young person to develop is purpose—the inner compass that helps one define goals, and gives life a sense of direction.

Now don't get me wrong—judges don't expect high school or college-aged students to have their lives already planned out. Indeed, even the best laid plans of a very focused individual occasionally get shaken up and rearranged. So when I talk about purpose, I'm not implying that you must devise a detailed road map for your entire life.

Rather, you will just want to demonstrate that you have taken the time to reflect on *where* you want to go and *how* you might get there. In my experience, the particular direction that your compass points at any one time does not really matter. The direction of your compass can indeed change (in fact, it almost always does), but just the fact that you are actually *aware* of your life compass, and can communicate its importance to you, speaks volumes to contest judges. By describing the dreams that currently motivate your efforts, you convey to judges that you are a person who is not afraid to voice your ambitions and set goals to reach them.

In many instances, conveying purpose in a scholarship application involves discussing a particular career interest (often in a personal essay). Purpose, however, is *not* limited to having a specific career goal in mind. Your purpose can be grounded in a desire to use your artistic ability and creativity in some exciting way. Or it can be to make a positive difference in the lives of your family and friends, as well as other people you come in contact with. In a nutshell, your individual purpose can be anything at all.

So if you want to convince scholarship judges that you're a person who will go places, remember that purpose is an important (and often overlooked) hidden judging criterion. Judges know that a student with a well-articulated purpose has a better chance than his or her counterparts of achieving goals and reaching dreams.

10. Character

Different people define personal "character" in different ways, but whatever your definition, the term deals with a person's core ethical and moral fabric. Character consists of qualities like integrity, honesty, loyalty, and courage. We often say that someone *possesses* strong character, as if it is a commodity that can be bought, sold, or stored in one's pocket. Character, however, is not so much a possession as it is a *state of being*. People with strong character don't possess it; they live it every day of their lives.

How do successful scholarship applicants typically demonstrate strong character in their applications? Often, applicants do this by including letters of recommendation that comment on their personal qualities. Generally, it's better to have someone else comment on your character than for you to do it yourself. You can, however, convey a sense of your character in an application by communicating your core values. Describing the qualities and values that you hold most dear can telegraph to a judge a great deal about your underlying character.

Employing the Virtues

Understanding the significance of these Ten Golden Virtues has two main implications for the scholarship application process.

First, it suggests that in determining the content of our scholarship applications, we should not only comb our records for activities that we have done, but also for instances in which we have exhibited outstanding personal qualities. Such qualities may be repeatedly exhibited in a given project or activity, or they may be associated with a particular memorable one-time event.

Second, we should try to communicate these personal qualities in our scholarship applications. One useful approach that I have employed is to try and convey each of these ten qualities somewhere in a contest application. Perhaps some of these qualities may be alluded to in an extracurricular activity list. Others could be mentioned in a personal essay. Recommendation writers could comment upon still other qualities in their letters of support.

Remember, these references need not be blatant. You don't have to explicitly say "I have this or that quality." It's usually more persuasive to demonstrate these personal qualities by describing them in a situational context. For example, you might communicate teamwork on an extracurricular activity form by emphasizing team dynamics in your descriptions of various activities. You can convey individual initiative in an essay by discussing some action you took on your own to help solve a problem. The ways to do this are endless.

Third, if you can't think of ways that you've demonstrated certain virtues, then try to find ways to exhibit them in future activities and endeavors. Perhaps you can't think of a time when you exhibited a strong sense of responsibility. Well, be on the lookout for future opportunities for you to assume responsibility and successfully fulfill your obligations. As an added bonus, this will also help you grow on a personal level.

GUERRILLA TACTIC #8

Try to convey each of the Ten Golden Virtues somewhere in your contest application.

COACH

In this dialogue, the Scholarship Coach answers questions about how younger students can prepare early for scholarship contests in later years.

Most scholarship winners (including myself) didn't start pursuing scholarships until college was right around the corner. Starting early gives you a big jump on the competition.

. . . About younger students

The following questions were submitted by Allotta Potential, a high school freshman from Fatchecks, New York.

Allotta: Are there any steps I can take right away to prepare myself for scholarship contests when I'm older?

Scholarship Coach: Yes! Younger students can employ what I call "positioning strategies." This means that you *position* yourself to win scholarships by building up the type of record that contest judges will look for. This will also position you to get into the college of your choice.

Allotta: What types of things should I do?

Scholarship Coach: Positioning yourself means building up a database of scholarship programs you will apply for in later years, and familiarizing yourself with the requirements of these contests. Once you know what to expect, you can work early to create the types of participation and experiences that contribute to impressive scholarship résumés. This will likely include participating in or designing your own community service programs; initiating your own creative, entrepreneurial, or academic research projects; and assuming leadership responsibilities in your school and community.

Allotta: Will this give me a big advantage?

Scholarship Coach: Most definitely. By starting early, you will be able to affect aspects of your record that others can't. You will be able to improve your essay writing and interviewing skills. You can take steps to accumulate a solid academic record and strong standardized tests scores. You will also be able to join organizations that sponsor scholarships in later years, and start building up a record with these groups right away. If you start early and work hard, nothing can stand in the way of scholarship success.

CHAPTER 6 SUMMARY

■ **Unseen Evaluators:** These hidden subcategories help scholarship judges compare scholarship applicants to one another. *Width evaluators* assess the range of an applicant's activities within a particular judging category; *depth evaluators*, assess the quality of those endeavors.

■ **Service to Others:** Width evaluators in this perennial judging category include school-based and community-based service, as well as self-initiated projects. Depth evaluators include the time commitment, impact, and responsibility level.

■ **Academic Achievement:** Besides schoolwork and standardized tests (with their associated grade point averages, class rankings, and test scores), other unseen evaluators affect the judging process. Width evaluators include academic clubs, individual study, and research projects. Depth evaluators include grade trend, class balance, class difficulty, and awards & honors.

■ **Extracurricular activities:** Most types of extracurricular participation can be classified in thirteen width evaluator subcategories. Depth evaluators for each of these subcategories include time commitment, leadership, and awards & honors.

■ **Leadership:** This judging category can be divided into four width evaluators: organization, issue-oriented, representative, and peer-directed leadership. Depth evaluators include positions held, impact, time commitment, organization size, as well as awards & honors.

■ **Implications:** The unseen evaluator framework emphasizes the many factors that influence an applicant's evaluation in each judging category. By treating these hidden evaluators explicitly, an applicant can better assess strengths and weaknesses. The framework also indicates how to compensate for poor performance in one evaluator subcategory by excelling in others.

■ **Ten Golden Virtues:** Most scholarship contests look for evidence of certain personal qualities in their scholarship winners—such qualities as hard work, overcoming obstacles, teamwork, perseverance, individual initiative, passion & enthusiasm, responsibility, civic duty, purpose, and character. Applicants should try to communicate and demonstrate these personal qualities.

Scoring Points

In this chapter, I'll show you how to enhance content in key areas and package your materials to increase your odds of winning.

CHAPTER CONTENTS

■ Content strategies
■ Packaging strategies
■ The "Contest Detective"
■ Putting it all together

CONTENT STRATEGIES

The term "content" refers to the raw ingredients of a scholarship application: all of the activities, awards, achievements, experiences, and credentials that are described in the application itself. **Content strategies**, therefore, encompass the tactical techniques we use to improve our records in key areas, thereby enhancing our overall scholarship résumés. In essence, content strategies help us expand upon what we've already done to increase our chances of taking home the money.

Of course, the extent to which we can enhance your record through content strategies depends upon the amount of time we have until a given scholarship application is due. If an application is due tomorrow, there's not a whole lot of content we can really add. But if a scholarship deadline is three to six months away, there's a great deal we can do to beef up your record in important ways. Indeed, even if you've only got a few weeks until a scholarship application deadline, there are still some powerful ways to use content strategies to enhance your record.

In the section that follows, I describe three main content strategies, and show how to implement these strategies based upon the time you have available.

Strategy #1

"I would ask myself 'What am I most interested in? What types of things am I good at? How can I make what I'm interested in and good at into a project?'"

Tom Kuo
National Scholarship Winner

Expand Upon Your Strong Points

At first glance, adding content in areas you're already good at may seem counterintuitive. If you already excel at something, why do we need to add to your record in that area? Well, the answer is that we want to take your strongest skills, and transform them into truly standout talents that get you noticed by contest judges.

This strategy, in fact, is closely related to the application themes we discussed in Chapter 5. Because a student's strong points are generally related to his or her application themes (we like things we're good at, and we're good at things we like), this strategy has the natural effect of further enhancing our self-portraits.

To illustrate this concept, I'd like to share with you a few examples from my own scholarship experience. As I alluded to earlier, one of the areas I tried to highlight in scholarship applications was my writing ability. Most of my writing experiences and achievements were centered around journalism—more specifically, newspaper writing. Consequently, I attempted to expand upon this obvious strength by showcasing my writing abilities in other arenas.

One way I did this was by approaching KLCC, the National Public Radio affiliate in my town, to write a series of radio commentaries on issues affecting young people. The radio station went for the idea, and in a matter of weeks, my voice hit the airwaves.

Another way I employed this strategy was by starting my own newsletter writing business. I approached the owners of the tennis club where I practiced, with an offer to write, design, and produce the club's monthly newsletter—thereby saving them significant money on contracting out the job to a local advertising agency. This project showcased a different side of my writing, and provided me with additional clips to include as supplementary materials in scholarship applications.

I also earned some money for doing this work, and so was able to communicate this activity as an entrepreneurial endeavor—further helping me in contests in which this type of self-initiative was important.

Now don't get me wrong: I didn't pursue these activities solely because they would enhance my scholarship (and college admission) chances. Writing was a field I loved, and these two projects were exciting opportunities. But the point I'm making is that the desire to enhance the content of my applications provided a spark that motivated me to find creative ways to express and improve my talents.

Adopting this strategy will help you enhance your skills in areas that are natural extensions of your interests and passions. You will be encouraged to dream up projects that you would have never considered, and to do things that you've always *wanted* to do, but never got around to doing.

If you don't have much time until a bunch of applications are due, adapt this strategy to fit the time available. Perhaps this means joining and participating in that after-school club you've been meaning to check out. Or maybe it means turning a class project into something that you can post on the Internet—informing and educating others. The possibilities are indeed endless.

In addition, even if you're applying for scholarships immediately, taking on long-term projects now will still have an impact. Consider my radio commentary project as an example: For scholarship applications that came up *before* I had actually delivered any commentaries, I would mention that I was currently "Writing a series of five on-air youth commentaries for a local National Public Radio affiliate." So even if you haven't had the chance to complete a substantial portion of a project, just the fact that you are *pursuing* the project can enhance your résumé.

Strategy #2

Shore Up Your Weak Areas

In addition to developing your strong points, it's also important to come across as well-rounded. Although your application spotlight should be shining on your primary and secondary themes, you will also want to include activities, achievements, and other credentials that demonstrate a wide range of exploration.

To implement this strategy, try to participate in activities that fill in glaring gaps in your record and help you become more well-rounded. To help you figure out the key areas in which you most need improvement (and we all could use a lot of improvement!), consult the sections on width and depth evaluators contained in Chapter 6. In a particular judging category, if you haven't addressed a substantial number of width and depth evaluators, try to participate in new extracurricular activities that extend your involvement into different areas.

GUERRILLA TACTIC #9

Find painless ways to fill in your résumé gaps.

For example, in my high school record, a high percentage of my most compelling achievements had clearly involved fields related to the arts and humanities. To emphasize that I wasn't just a one-dimensional student, not at all interested in math and science, I joined my high school's science club and competed on the Science Olympics and math teams. This participation demonstrated my

Participating in school clubs that extend the range of your involvement is a good way to shore up weak areas.

quantitative skills—a range of abilities that I didn't have the opportunity to exhibit in other extracurricular activities. Not only did this benefit my scholarship applications (and college applications, too), but I also improved my math and science skills on the side.

Strategy #3

Demonstrate the Golden Virtues

As we discussed in Chapter 6, scholarship judging is built around a set of golden virtues: things like hard work, overcoming obstacles, teamwork, perseverance, individual initiative, passion and enthusiasm, responsibility, civic duty, purpose, and character. To enhance what you present to the world in each of these areas, do the following exercise: List the ten virtues down the side of a page. To synchronize this list of virtues with your own value system, list additional traits that you find admirable—qualities such as creativity, curiosity, or open-mindedness. Next, write beneath each of the character traits you've listed, the activities and achievements in your record that demonstrate this character trait. If you aren't able to think of anything that demonstrates a particular virtue, then you've identified an area in which your content can be improved. Once again, find convenient ways—in the limited time you have—to participate in school- and community-related activities that demonstrate these qualities.

Remember, there's a reason why scholarship contests look for certain types of personal qualities in applicants: Such qualities are also important in life! Content strategies that enhance your golden virtues have the side benefit of honing undeveloped personal qualities (we all have them), to make you a more balanced, well-rounded, and successful person.

PACKAGING STRATEGIES

In the context of scholarship applications, "packaging" is the way in which you present yourself and put together your application materials so as to appeal to scholarship judges. In the last section, we discussed how content strategies help you enhance the raw ingredients of your application. Here, we'll see how **packaging strategies** can help you present these ingredients in their best light, maximizing your chances of winning.

In a broad sense, the first packaging strategy we discussed was the development of an application theme that paints a vivid self-portrait. This earlier discussion, however, didn't tackle how to package your application to best appeal to a particular contest's published and unseen judging criteria. How do you know which of your potential application themes you should employ for a given contest? Which recommendations should you include? What points should you drive home in the scholarship essay? The packaging techniques discussed in this section will help answer all of these questions by showing you how to assess a contest's main emphasis and underlying agenda. Enter "The Contest Detective."

The Contest Detective

Move over, Sherlock Holmes. Take a seat, Sam Spade. In this section, *you* become a "contest detective." Instead of investigating crime scenes, you'll be sifting through scholarship applications. You'll learn how to search for clues about the selection process, dust for judges' fingerprints, and establish the motives of scholarship sponsors. By applying these techniques, you'll gain a better understanding of each scholarship application, and will be able to custom-tailor your material to best fit the agenda—both the visible and the hidden parts—of each scholarship contest.

Get an Overall Impression

OK, so you're ready to become a contest detective? Well, like any good detective, one of the first things you'll want to do is to take in the big picture. The smart scholarship applicant knows the importance of taking a step back and assessing the overall tone of a contest. Asking yourself the following questions about each scholarship program can help you to better gauge the scholarship contest's central focus:

1. *What are the core values of the program?*

2. *Does the scholarship emphasize depth of involvement in a particular area, or breadth of involvement in many areas?*

3. *Do all extracurricular activities appear to be weighted evenly or are some emphasized over others?*

4. *Is the scholarship focused more on the future (what you want to do) or on the past (what you have done)?*

5. *Does the program emphasize traditional achievement metrics (GPA, standardized tests, etc.) or nontraditional measures?*

6. *Does the program group applicants in any special way (such as by career interest or geographic region)?*

7. *Does the program's sponsor have any type of social agenda or political leanings?*

8. *Does the scholarship stress any particular personal character traits?*

9. *Who are the contest judges? Do these judges have a similar perspective or view of the world?*

10. *What are the common threads among past winners of the scholarship contest?*

"When you're awarded a scholarship, the sponsor is accepting you as one of their own. Try to come across as someone they would find interesting and be proud of."

George Hicks
National Scholarship Winner

Asking yourself, and trying to answer questions such as these helps you understand the type of applicant the scholarship program is looking for. After posing these questions, you should be able to define, in a single sentence, what the scholarship contest is all about.

Pay Attention To The Details

The great Sherlock Holmes, of course, is renowned for his ability to notice, synthesize, and learn from seemingly insignificant details. Show good ol' Sherlock a lock of hair, a morsel of dried dough, and a pair of suspicious-looking oven mitts, and he'll show you the balding pastry chef who committed the crime.

Likewise, when investigating a scholarship contest application for clues, it's essential to pay attention to all the little details. Let me offer a case in point from my own scholarship quest: At first glance, the judging criteria for the *Milky Way/ AAU High-School All-American* scholarship appeared to be fairly straightforward. The application materials stated that judging would be based on "academic, athletic, and community service achievements." A closer examination of official rules (shown in minuscule type on the back of the application form), revealed additional details. More specifically, it stated the following:

> *"Academic excellence is not always reflected by such objective measures as grades, test scores, or class ranking. . . . School activities considered in this area [academic achievement] include such things as band, debate, and student government."*

What this passage told me was that the contest was employing a very broad definition of "academics." Participation in extracurricular activities was actually being included as part of academic achievement. This also suggested that the descriptions of extracurricular endeavors included in the application should highlight the academic value of the activity (because that was the fundamental criteria I was being judged upon). Because of this observation, I expanded my discussion of extracurricular activities, and emphasized the academic lessons being learned through them—something I wouldn't have done if I hadn't carefully read the fine print. Paying attention to these details helped me net a $10,000 scholarship from the contest.

This particular scholarship was recently phased out. Other contests, however—such as the ESPN SportsFigures Scholarship—are similar in scope.

Look for the Unusual

Another investigative technique you'll want to employ is the practice of looking for anything in an application that strikes you as out of the ordinary. Because most scholarship applications are created from a limited number of cookie-cutter molds, any deviations from the usual boilerplate requirements provides you with valuable information on the visible and hidden agendas of particular scholarship contests.

Start your detective work with the published judging criteria listed in any application. If a particular scholarship contains a judging criterion that seems especially personal, specific, or unconventional, you should take special notice: it can provide valuable insights about how the judging works.

For instance, in the Discover Card Tribute Awards, students are asked to have their applications address four out of five categories: special talents, leadership, obstacles overcome, community service, and unique endeavors. In the preceding list, the category that seems to stand out from the rest is "obstacles overcome." Although we've discussed overcoming obstacles in the "Ten Golden Virtues" section, it's unusual that a contest would single out this particular character trait as an entire judging category.

Whereas the other four categories deal with traditional areas such as extracurricular activities, hobbies, and individual projects, this out-of-the-ordinary category is much more personal and specific. Yet, Discover Card's decision to highlight this personal quality demonstrated its importance to the contest. And sure enough, when the national winners of the Discover Card awards were announced (of which I was one), nearly all of the winners had chosen to write about some obstacles they had overcome in their life.

Another place to look for the unusual is in the application requirements itself. In the Century III Leaders contest, for example, all applicants were required to take a school-administered examination on current events. Such a requirement highlighted the organization's emphasis on societal issues. Students who demonstrated a broad awareness of societal problems and then showed how, in their small way, they had tried to find solutions to such problems, generally did well in the overall competition.

An unusual essay question can also help you understand the type of winner a contest is looking for. On the application form of the National Honor Society Scholarship, for instance, I was asked to respond to a hypothetical situation in which I had observed a classmate cheating. The inclusion of such an unconventional essay question suggested the program's emphasis on character, integrity, and other personal qualities. As a result, I tried to emphasize these character traits in other portions of my application. When the dust settled, I had again taken home the scholarship money.

Customizing Your Materials

Using these "contest detective" techniques will help you define any scholarship contest's ideal applicant. Once you've come up with this definition, then it's simply a matter of packaging your record in such a way as to emphasize personal attributes consistent with this definition.

GUERRILLA TACTIC #10

Define each scholarship's ideal applicant, and emphasize personal attributes matching this definition.

By doing this, you'll be able to choose primary and secondary themes that fit the agenda of a particular contest. In all my applications put together, I employed five or six major themes; this process of analyzing each specific scholarship contest helped me choose which themes to use. The analysis also helped me to fine-tune reusable materials, drawing out aspects of my record that matched the emphasis of a particular contest. Finally, it helped me choose recommendation letters stressing character traits that judges would respond well to.

Keep in mind that the impact of such packaging strategies need not be limited to applications that evaluate your overall record. A recent first-place oration in the Voice of Democracy competition is a good example of this. Speaking on the topic of "My Service to America," the orator opened her speech with a vivid description of her grandfather's struggle for survival during World War II. Whether intentional or intuitive, the entrant's decision to define service in terms of wartime sacrifice makes good strategic sense in a contest sponsored by the Veterans of Foreign Wars.

This oration is shown in the Library of Sample Materials (Appendix B) on page B-3.

PUTTING IT ALL TOGETHER

The powerful thing about the strategies I've outlined in this chapter and prior chapters is that using them in con-junction with each other yields *synergy*—a result much greater than just the sum of the parts. And the best way to see these strategies in action is through an analysis of my winning entry in the Tylenol Scholarship program—a scholarship award that netted me a cool $10,000.

I started out the application by thinking about the best way to package it all. First, I noted that the program literature stated that the scholarship was designed to reward students who "demonstrate leadership in community activities." I also observed that judging was being conducted by the Citizens' Scholarship Foundation of America (CFSA)—a third-party organization that specializes in administering various scholarship contests. Because judging was being conducted by an organization unlikely to have a hidden agenda or unseen biases, I figured I could take the published judging criteria at face value: leadership in school and community activities (40 percent), clear statement of education and career goals (10 percent), and academic record (50 percent). Taking all these factors into account, I concluded that I should make leadership my *primary* application theme, with journalism and writing a *secondary* theme related to my career goals.

In applying this theme to my application, I first tackled the requested lists of school and community activities. To reinforce my theme, I made two activities dealing directly with leadership—participation in student government (as student body president) and service on the student court (as a

STORMIN' THE GATES: *Combining content and packaging strategies with a vivid application theme provides you with the optimal strategic approach for winning scholarship contests.*

justice)—as my first two items on the school activities list. On the community and volunteer service list, I led with the community service program I had founded, *The Homework Helpline*—a service activity that showcased my organizational leadership skills.

By thinking in terms of the unseen width evaluators, I also realized the importance of showing a wide range of leadership activities. So on my school activities lists, I followed up student government and student court (examples of representative leadership) with activities that demonstrated both issue-oriented and peer-directed leadership.

After leadership, the next items on my list depicted my secondary theme—journalism skills and writing ability. Because I had employed content strategies, I was able to list not only my newspaper-related endeavors, but also such activities as delivering radio commentaries, producing newsletters, and writing public service announcements for the local *Meals on Wheels* program.

Further down in my activities list, I mentioned activities that shored up weak areas in my record. This included brief descriptions of my involvement in science- and math-related clubs, competitions, and projects.

In addition to lists of activities, the contest materials also requested a 100-200 statement of my goals and aspirations. This was an occasion to reap the benefits of reusability: I dug out my old Discover Card Tribute Awards goals paragraph, and recycled it with very few changes. The alterations I did make were to highlight the leadership role journalists can take in educating the public on pressing issues.

Finally, the Tylenol application requested that I state, in a mere two or three sentences, "which experiences or persons have contributed to your achievements to date." In answering this question, I recognized that in discussing experiences or individuals who have helped shape me, I would really be revealing a lot about myself and the things I value. So I decided to single out people who have helped me develop skills and personal qualities directly related to the judging criteria, and to the "Ten Golden Virtues." I did this in the following way:

See page 146 for a description of the leadership width evaluators.

See page 120 for this essay excerpt.

Granted, these were three very long sentences. But I managed to pack a lot of compelling information into an application component with strict space limitations.

"My middle-school homeroom teacher helped me realize that leadership is the art of bringing out the best in others as well as myself, and that sharing my talents through community service is one of the most worthwhile and rewarding activities I can pursue. My high school journalism advisor not only helped me transform my writing skills, but also taught me how effective communication is our primary bulwark against the dangers of ignorance and intolerance. Growing up under my parents' umbrella of encouragement and guidance, I have learned how courage, faith, and perseverance—in combination with high ethical and moral values—can help me achieve my goals and realize my dreams."

In a nutshell, using all of these strategic techniques in conjunction with one another, helped me craft a scholarship submission that powerfully addressed the judging criteria, separated me from the pack, painted a vivid portrait of who I was, and thereby maximized my chances of winning.

ASK THE COACH

. . . About bad grades

The following questions were submitted by Rocky Graydz, a high school senior from Greenback, Arizona.

Rocky: My freshman and sophomore grades pretty much sucked. In contests that consider academics, should I tell judges about the reasons for my poor performance?

In this dialogue, the Scholarship Coach answers questions relevant to students who have had some rough spots in their academic records.

Scholarship Coach: Excuses don't come across well in scholarship essays. If you mention some of these reasons, don't treat them as "causes" of your bad grades. Instead, work them in as obstacles you have overcome or learning experiences you have worked through. Emphasize that you are a better, stronger person for having gone through these rough patches. In addition, remember that academic achievement has many width and depth evaluators. Consider participating in out-of-class activities and projects that involve academic areas. Have recommendation writers talk about your overall *grade trend*.

CHAPTER 7 SUMMARY

■ **Content Strategies:** Strategies to help scholarship seekers improve their records in key areas include (1) finding ways to highlight personal strong points in new arenas and activities, (2) shoring up weak areas by filling in résumé gaps with new types of participation, and (3) looking for new opportunities to demonstrate the "Ten Golden Virtues."

■ **Packaging Strategies:** Scholarship seekers can "package" their applications by presenting themselves and their materials in a way that meshes well with contest judging criteria.

■ **The "Contest Detective":** Analyze scholarship applications and materials for clues about the selection process. Ask questions that help define key characteristics about the contest. Pay attention to application details that provide hints about what judges will be looking for. Take note of unusual criteria, application requirements, and essay topics that suggest the emphasis of the scholarship program.

■ **Customizing Your Materials:** After defining a contest's ideal applicant, select application themes to use and materials to include that best fit this definition. Focus on personal credentials and choose recommendation letters that match the focus of a given contest.

■ **Synergy:** Combining the strategies described in Chapters 4 through 7 yields an overall effect much greater than the mere sum of the parts.

Creating Opportunities

Intermission

Have you ever wondered why some people who are very talented don't seem to reach their full potential? And why others—who don't appear to have any extraordinary abilities—rise to great heights? Perhaps the explanation for this paradox lies with an individual's ability to recognize, to seize, and even to create opportunity.

I've chosen this topic for *Intermission #3* because cultivating this skill—and it is a *skill*—pays especially large dividends in the scholarship game. Being able to create great opportunities leads to experiences and achievements that demonstrate your initiative and ingenuity, and help distinguish your applications from the crowd. In a larger sense, this is a skill that impacts virtually everything you do in life.

The Snowball Effect

What makes the ability to create opportunities such a powerful skill to have in your arsenal? Quite simply, it's the momentum of the snowball effect: Just as a snowball gathers speed and size as it rolls down a hill, each opportunity that you create leads to greater and greater possibilities for more opportunity creation.

Take my experience with the U.S. Senate Youth Program, for instance. In the spring of my senior year in high school, I won a $2,500 scholarship from the program, as well as a week's stay in Washington D.C. I could have just settled for enjoying an exciting trip, but I knew that it could be much more than this; it could be a springboard for a whole slew of new, exciting opportunities.

My first idea was to write a column about the experience for my hometown newspaper, *The Register-Guard*, of Eugene, Oregon. I didn't know if the newspaper's editors would go for the column, or even what the column would really be about, but I figured it was worth a shot. And because of my interest in government, I also came up with a plan to use some of my time in Washington D.C. as a vehicle to pursue the possibility of an internship with U.S. Senator Mark Hatfield (Oregon). I didn't know if either of these ideas would yield any results, but that didn't matter. The important thing was that I was actively searching for any possibilities to create new opportunities.

And the rest, as they say, is history. Upon returning from my trip, I pitched the finished article to my local newspaper, and they loved it. The article was published a few days later, and a teacher at a crosstown high school spotted it, and decided to use it as an instructional tool in his government class. This teacher, who I had never met before, would later write me a great scholarship recommendation letter. As for the internship, I convinced Senator Hatfield's Chief of Staff to interview me for an internship position during my stay in Washington. Shortly after returning home, I was thrilled to find out that I had got the job.

It gets better yet! Writing the article and interning in Washington had rejuvenated my interest in political journalism. Upon enrolling at Harvard, I learned that syndicated columnist George Will was guest teaching a class for the term.

"A wise man will make more opportunities than he finds."

Francis Bacon

I took the class, told him of my interests, and he agreed to meet with me each week to critique my articles.

This experience also proved important when 1996 rolled in. I thought it would be interesting to attend the Democratic and Republican National Conventions, and so I came up with an idea to write a series of columns on the conventions from the youth perspective. *The Oregonian* newspaper sent me to the conventions, covered my expenses, and printed my columns on the Op-Ed page. *The Boston Globe* also printed some of my commentary as well.

Finally, all of these experiences helped me get articles on winning scholarships for college printed in *The New York Times* and *U.S. News & World Report*, among other publications. It was these articles that lead to the book you are now reading. And, of course, the snowball continues to gather speed. . . .

More Than Luck

As I experienced this remarkable chain of events, I began to fully appreciate the importance of preparing myself to seize other opportunities as their "open windows" passed before me—and to go one step further by actually creating those windows myself.

We have all known or heard of someone who spends his entire life waiting for an opportunity to fall into his lap. Occasionally, one might—but when a person takes this attitude, there is a good chance that he won't even be able to recognize it, should one hit him squarely between the eyes.

Undoubtedly, good fortune played a role in my successes. But it was more than just luck. By constantly creating opportunities for myself, I put myself in the position to benefit enormously from any lucky breaks that came my way. If you can master the art of opportunity creation (I'm still working on improving my skill at it), an abundance of college scholarships will show up on your doorstep. And that will only be the beginning. . .

Participating & Observing

How exactly does one create an opportunity? You can start by playing the roles of both the participant and the observer. First, it is important to be active in a lot of different areas in which you are interested. For example, you'll be hard pressed to anticipate opportunities in journalism unless you immerse yourself in the field. I would have never come up with the idea to write a column on the Democratic and Republican conventions if I hadn't first worked on the school newspaper and built up a portfolio of my work.

As a participant, you will be in the heart of the action, and all sorts of peripheral projects may come your way. So always give activities a try before judging whether or not they are worthwhile. In addition, place a greater emphasis on all activities in which you can assume, or later assume, some type of leadership roles.

And even while you are a participant, maintain an observer's frame of mind. This means keeping your eyes and ears peeled for anything out of the ordinary. Evaluate the special circumstances of every project with which you are involved. Use each activity as a catalyst to set in motion future opportunities.

Stacking the Odds

Winning scholarships can lead to many future opportunities. Some organizations recruit winners of prominent scholarship contests for special programs. Other scholarship winners have landed internships with groups affiliated with the scholarship sponsor.

Furthermore, never leave events solely up to chance. Do everything in your power to make things turn out the way you want them to. If you are unable to get an appointment with certain influential people you want to speak with, don't just accept it. Instead, go to their office early in the morning, wait until they show up, and set an appointment in person. I've had to do this. Believe me—it works!

Last, remember to take advantage of all of the special resources around you. If you live in a college town, look into special university programs or possible internships with professors. If you are especially enjoying a subject in school, talk to the teacher about how you can pursue it in more depth.

Additionally, try approaching the most successful students in your school—even recent graduates—and find out what activities have been the most beneficial to them. In general, always go out of your way to talk to those who might be able to direct you toward intriguing future projects. With this type of inquisitive mindset, you will undoubtedly find an abundance of exciting possibilities awaiting you.

PART IV

When the Whistle Blows

Essay Excellence

In this chapter, I'll show you how to write essays that stand out from the crowd and bring home the big bucks.

CHAPTER CONTENTS

- Principles of winning essays
- Recycling essays
- Conquering writer's block
- Refining your essay
- Tips for specific topics
- Short-answer questions

PRINCIPLES OF WINNING ESSAYS

Essays are critical components of many scholarship applications because they represent an applicant's best opportunity to directly communicate interests, passions, beliefs, and values. In essence, essays may be the part of your application in which you have the greatest opportunity to paint a wonderfully vivid self-portrait.

One misconception about the scholarship essay is that you need to be a naturally gifted writer to craft a strong one. While writing skill can prove useful, you don't have to be a prolific writer to create an effective essay. More than writing ability, the key is understanding and properly applying a few simple, strategic principles.

The vast majority of winning scholarship essays follow the principles outlined below. As is the nature of any set of rules, there are times when it may be appropriate to break them. But before we can even consider breaking these rules, we first need to thoroughly understand and be able to effectively apply them.

Principle #1

Show, Don't Tell

One of the most prevalent mistakes committed in weak scholarship essays is that applicants *tell* rather than *show*. What's the distinction? Well, *telling* occurs when the applicant makes broad (often self-congratulatory) statements without backing them up with specific examples. *Showing*, on the other hand, involves describing a situation or activity, or telling a story that illustrates the statement.

So don't just *tell* contest judges that your are "exceptionally trustworthy and responsible." Instead, *show* them your trustworthiness and sense of responsibility by describing an activity or event in which you demonstrated these admirable personal qualities. Don't just *tell* judges that a particular reform will improve the educational system. *Show* them by describing the dramatic educational benefits of a pilot project you helped initiate. Taking this approach captures the reader's attention and adds credibility to what you say.

Principle #2 | Keep Things Personal

Regardless of the specific question posed, most scholarship essays are designed to provide judges with a better sense of who you are, what you believe in, and how you think. As a result, relating the essay question to your unique experiences and perspectives makes your composition more compelling.

Such a strategy is not limited to essay questions that are personal in nature. Some of the best essays I've seen on issue-oriented topics, still relate the subject matter to personal experiences. An essay discussing the issue of homelessness was related to an applicant's eye-opening experience of working in a homeless shelter. I connected one of my own essays on reforming the educational system to my experiences in setting up a telephone-based peer-tutoring system called the *Homework Helpline*.

If the essay question deals with a topic in which you don't have direct experience, try relating the topic to someone you know—such as a relative or family friend. For instance, if an essay question asks you what it means to be a patriot, perhaps you could discuss personal experiences your grandfather had on the beaches of Normandy during World War II. To frame the story in terms of your *own* experience, you could describe a memorable conversation you've had with your grandfather about the war.

Taking this approach also enhances the credibility and believability of your application. As mentioned in Chapter 5, contest judges view applications with a skeptical eye: They recognize that applicants have strong incentives to tell them what they want to hear. But essays rooted in personal experience seem less likely to be contrived by the writer simply for the sake of appearances.

"In my essays, I would include personal details that showed why I'm special, why I'm unique, why I'm an individual— unlike anyone else in the application pool."

William Moss
National Scholarship Winner

Principle #3 | Use Effective Organization

Effective organization provides judges with a detailed road map that helps them follow the points in your essay. Organization demonstrates the thought you put into the essay, and enhances the underlying logic of the main ideas you are trying to drive home.

A standard organizational framework for a scholarship essay—or any essay for that matter—is a three-part format. In the first part of the essay, the *introduction*, you frame the subject matter to be covered in the piece. In the introduction, you are trying to achieve two main goals. First, you want to give the reader some idea of where you're headed. This can be done formally with a thesis statement that summarizes the main point of the essay, or more casually by giving the reader a general sense of the terrain the essay will cover.

Second, your essay should draw readers into the subject matter by grabbing their attention in an interesting way. Many scholarship winners have done this by telling an interesting story or anecdote, or by vivid description. Whether the focus of your introduction should be more on summarizing the argument in the essay or grabbing the reader's attention depends upon the subject matter and tone of your essay. Many issue-oriented essays focus more on summarizing the main argument, while many personal essays focus more on engaging the reader. Some of the best scholarship essays I've seen, however, emphasize both of these elements in equal doses via a two-paragraph introduction—with the first paragraph "hooking" the reader, and the second providing a blueprint for the remainder of the essay.

The body of the essay is where the action happens: the place where you develop your main points and ideas. The body structure itself can vary significantly. The main effect you should be aiming for, however, is a logical development of your points, and a natural progression of thought—as if your ideas were moving along a clear path. To do this, it's often convenient to organize the body of your essay into a series of paragraphs, with each paragraph developing a major idea, and building upon the prior one.

You will hear from many people that the conclusion is the place where you restate and summarize the main points developed in an essay. For me, however, merely revisiting ground you've already covered is a bit boring—and a waste of space in applications where each word is a precious commodity. I prefer to think of the conclusion as an opportunity to reference key points in an essay in an original way—one that extends the concepts even further. In a personal essay, for instance, you may want to comment upon how the personal qualities you've described will help you in your future career. In an essay focused on a societal problem, you may want to project your vision for what the world will look like once the problem is solved. If you've opened with a story, consider revisiting that story, and extending the connections between the significance of the anecdote and the points you've covered.

This basic structure I've outlined, of course, is just one approach. I've seen many other organizational structures that work well too. If you're struggling to come up with a good organizational format for your essay, however, the basic format described here is a proven way to go.

Principle #4

Always adhere to the word limits. This demonstrates that you are capable of following directions. Besides, you don't want to give judges any reason to disqualify you! In fact, keep your essays a few words below the limit just in case a judge or contest administrator makes a mistake when tallying up your word count.

Make Each Sentence Count

Because of word limits and space limitations, a big part of writing a strong scholarship essay is learning how to explain and fully develop all of your points, ideas, and concepts in a restricted amount of space. To do this, it's essential to make each sentence count toward the development of your main idea. You should be able to explain to yourself the purpose of every sentence you write. Furthermore, avoid long transitional phrases and sentences that eat up space without accomplishing anything. Don't be redundant. (Did I say don't be redundant?) Make your point and move on.

To keep your essay tight and eliminate spots that drag, try the following technique: Write the first draft of your essay long—perhaps 25 percent longer than the word limit—then force yourself to pare down the verbiage. The only way to create concise, powerful writing is through careful editing.

Principle #5

Make Your Essay Unique and Memorable

For a moment, pretend you are judging a large scholarship contest. As a judge, you may be responsible for reviewing hundreds of essays, and, you're supposed to keep all of the applicants clear in your mind, and rank them according to some objective criteria. A thick stack of applications sit on the desk in front of you, and because the pile addresses the same set of questions over and over and over and over again (often in a similar manner to one another), it can indeed be a monotonous task.

To avoid having a judge just skim through your essay, you need to make it unique and memorable. The first way to do this is by taking to heart Principle #2. By adding vivid personal details to an essay, you make the essay uniquely yours. And by choosing details and stories that engage the reader, you make your essay memorable.

Second, you can make your essay unique and memorable through content. Redefine the question in an interesting way. For instance, if the question asks you the importance of democracy, turn the question on its head by vividly describing a world completely devoid of democracy. You can also do this by including some interesting research, references, or facts that teaches the judges something they didn't already know or fully appreciate.

Third, you can express your ideas in novel ways. One effective technique I've employed on several occasions is the use of an *extended metaphor*—a metaphor that permeates your entire essay. The use of metaphors is a powerful technique because it allows you to take well-tread concepts and express them in novel and insightful ways.

Metaphors also allow you to simplify complex ideas, and often paint vivid imagery in a judge's mind. Furthermore, a well-developed, extended metaphor brings a sense of cohesion to a scholarship essay, and can contribute to an attention-grabbing introduction and conclusion.

The types of metaphors are endless. One scholarship winner wrote an essay looking back at different points in American history as if they were different rooms in a house. In one of my own winning essays, I used a clipper ship to describe the importance of freedom to our nation:

> *"As a proud vessel of freedom, America has been crafted from the resilient planks of democracy. Our heritage of justice provides a firm rudder—holding this Yankee clipper on a steady course, while allowing for necessary corrections at critical way points on our voyage. . . . But no matter how seaworthy the craft, how adept the captain, or how friendly the waters, even a great sailing ship can become paralyzed: Without the winds of freedom to drive her forward, America would find herself shackled 'in irons.'"*

RECYCLING ESSAYS

In Chapter 4, we discussed the importance of recycling your application materials whenever possible. In this section, we revisit the topic of recycling in a bit more depth, and explore how scholarship essays can be reused.

As you'll recall, recycling elements of your application not only saves you time and energy, but also improves the quality of the work as you repeatedly rework and rethink the same passages. When you get good at recycling it's amazing what results you can achieve in minimum time: A nip here, a tuck there, a bit more reworking, and then presto. . . your old essay has been magically recycled into a new shiny one.

The most important aspect of recycling essays is realizing in advance how one topic can bridge multiple applications and seemingly unrelated questions. For instance, suppose a scholarship application asks you to do the following:

> *"Name an individual who has had a significant impact on your life, and discuss what you've learned from that person."*

Let's also suppose that another scholarship essay, for an entirely different scholarship contest, presents you with this topic:

> *"Describe an important conversation you've had in the past year."*

Even though these two questions are very different, they offer considerable opportunities for recycling essays. Why not write an essay about an important conversation you've had in the past year with someone who has had a profound impact on your life? Recycling the same essay to fit each of these contests would thus be a simple task. Perhaps all that would be needed would be small changes in the introduction to emphasize the person in one case, and the conversation in the other.

Let's look at another example. Suppose a scholarship contest you're planning on applying to poses the following essay question to applicants:

> *"Discuss and describe an extracurricular activity that has special meaning to you."*

Another scholarship program asks you an entirely different question:

> *"What do you hope to get out of college?"*

Even in this setting, there are potential benefits to be gained from recycling. When asked to describe an extracurricular activity important to you, pick something that you plan to continue with in college—say, a certain type of community service work. In the essay on the extracurricular activity, you could include a discussion of how the activity has been so important to your life that you plan to explore it even further as a college student. For the essay on your college hopes, you could work in a paragraph or two on how college will help you to continue to pursue and develop your interest in the particular extracurricular area.

Another powerful way to recycle essays is to combine elements of two or more essays you've already written to create an essay that combines the best parts of both. To illustrate this technique, let me first introduce you to an excerpt of an essay I wrote for a scholarship in Oregon sponsored by the Portland Trailblazers basketball team:

For the full text of this essay, see page B-12 in Appendix B.

"As a sapling pushes its limbs skyward, its roots burrow deeper into the dark, moist sanctuary of soil. It is here, where the foundation lies—at the source of stability and strength—where probing tentacles soak up the very sustenance of life. And just as the young tree draws its strength from this underlying foundation, a college education empowers its graduates with the strong roots of lifelong learning: the impetus for intellectual growth, work-skills enhancement, and personality development.

Through this solid educational base, youth is instilled with the discipline and perseverance to stand tall in a world permeated with the winds of challenge and storms of adversity. Providing both stability and nourishment, a college education excites the mind and spirit—drawing out the inner faculties, as personality, convictions, perspectives, and attitudes blossom. To educate, after all, is to develop from within. . . ."

In addition, recall an excerpt of an essay I wrote for the Discover Card Tribute Awards, which I first showed you when discussing theme development in Chapter 5. To refresh your memory I've reprinted the excerpt below:

"Because of a strong interest in writing and communication, an aptitude for analysis and problem-solving, and a fascination with the inner workings of government, I plan to pursue a career in print and broadcast journalism, as a political columnist and commentator. A well-rounded education will unlock the gates of opportunity—not only helping to clarify complex issues and providing skills for becoming a more persuasive writer and effective speaker, but also preparing me to be a responsible contributor in this world of infinite possibilities. . . . As a well-educated journalist, I will strive to broaden minds and uncover truth—thus doing my part to make a difference in the world."

Finally, let's examine an essay I wrote for the Georgia-Pacific Foundation Community Scholarship that combined elements of both. I found it useful to draw upon both of the prior essays because this contest wanted me to discuss the benefits of college to all undergraduates, as well as show what I hoped to gain from the experience as an individual. The contest also requested that I comment upon my career plans after graduating college.

You can see that I've changed some words around and reduced the flowery content, but this essay is still essentially a recycled combination of my prior two entries.

I won $5,000 in this contest, and a judge later told me that out of all the students who won scholarships through the program, my application stood out the most because of the care and thought that went into it.

> *"A college education empowers one with the robust skills of lifelong learning: the impetus for intellectual growth, work-skills enhancement, and personality development. Through this solid educational base, I expect to be instilled with the discipline and perseverance to stand tall in a world permeated with the winds of challenge and storms of adversity. Providing both stability and nourishment, my college education will, I hope, excite both mind and spirit—drawing out my inner faculties, as personality, convictions, perspectives, and attitudes blossom. To educate, after all, is to develop from <u>within</u>.*
>
> *The well-rounded college education that I am seeking should unlock the gates of opportunity—helping me become a more persuasive writer and effective speaker, as well as an adept analyst and problem-solver. . . .*
>
> *Because of a strong interest in communication, an aptitude for analysis and problem solving, and a fascination with the inner workings of government, I plan to pursue a career in print and broadcast journalism, as a political columnist and commentator. As a well-educated journalist, I will strive to broaden minds and uncover truth—thus doing my part to make a difference in the world. . . ."*

To reread this essay, flip back to page 187.

Recycling essays, however, doesn't just have to be limited to the *content* of your essay. Recycling might also involve a particular way you express ideas, such as through a vivid metaphor. To illustrate this point, recall the essay I excerpted a few pages ago in which I used a clipper ship to describe the nation, with freedom representing the winds driving us forward.

I was able to successfully recycle this metaphor in several scholarship essays on a variety of diverse subjects. Here's an example from an essay on an entirely different topic—the importance of stock markets:

> *"Stock markets harness winds of capital to help propel our nation's most promising—and often most fragile—entrepreneurial vessels. But more than passive sails that just capture these powerful winds, stock markets actually help summon them.... While the companies themselves must provide product and know-how—the hull and rudder of any corporate vessel—markets transform the raw power of investment capital into propulsion for our nation's best business ventures. After all, no matter how seaworthy the craft, how adept the captain, or how friendly the waters, even a great sailing ship becomes paralyzed without this driving force."*

If you've come up with a good metaphor or a particularly poignant or creative way of expressing an idea, try to reuse it in different settings.

The one thing to keep in the back of your mind as you recycle, however, is that you don't want to force something to be recycled when it really isn't a good fit for the question. Furthermore, through the process of revising, rethinking, and reworking a passage, it's possible to lose the focus of the essay. To avoid this, constantly ask yourself if the recycled passage is truly answering the question posed.

GETTING IN THE FLOW

For many scholarship applicants, the hardest thing about writing an essay is the blank page. The intimidation of starting from scratch can cause even the most talented writers to feel paralyzed. In this section, however, I describe some techniques I've found useful to jump-start the writing process, and cure even the nastiest case of writer's block.

Technique #1: The Free Write

A lot of times, what stops us from moving along with our writing is that we're afraid to put something on the page that doesn't already sound good. What we should be trying to do, however, is to get as much as we can down on the page, so that we can edit and re-edit it later. Here's one way to form this new habit: Set a timer for 20 minutes, and force yourself to sit down and write nonstop for the entire time about anything that happens to jump in your head—even something barely related to the essay topic. The key here is just to keep writing, and keep the ideas flowing freely.

Technique #2: Consult Other Essays

Sometimes to get us going, all we need is a little bit of inspiration. Often you can get this inspiration by rereading other scholarship essays you've written, or by reading winning essays written by others (such as the ones contained in Appendix B). Just immersing yourself in language for awhile can spark a whole new range of ideas.

Technique #3: Talk It Over

Sometimes the cause of writer's block is the difficulty in organizing the jumble of thoughts running through our heads. A simple solution to this is just to talk over your essay topic with someone else—such as a parent, sibling, or friend. Just having this dialogue often helps you make sense of abstract concepts and see patterns that you had missed before.

Technique #4: Record Yourself

There are times when the very act of writing can get in the way of idea creation. If you happen to be a particularly verbal person, try tape recording yourself as you talk about the topic. Sometimes when I've done this, I merely transcribe what I say, and wind up with part of a first draft.

Technique #5: Move Locations

If one place seems to be sucking your creative juices dry, go somewhere else. If you've been writing on the computer, grab a pen and paper and go write somewhere else. Try writing in parks, coffee shops, or anywhere else you're at ease. If you need to clear your mind, try going for a walk or drive.

Technique #6: Zoom In

There have been occasions when I felt overwhelmed by the topic, and didn't have the faintest idea how to organize all the thoughts running through my head. At such times, I zoom in—trying to focus on some detail, description, or point that I do feel comfortable writing about. There's no law saying you have to write an essay in any particular sequence, so pick some aspect of the essay that you have a firmer grasp on and start writing.

HONING YOUR ESSAY

There's a saying that some of the best writers are, in fact, not particularly great at writing—they're just good at *rewriting*. Likewise, a good scholarship essay usually is drawn out from a process of reevaluating your concepts and ideas, and reassessing how you communicate those points. To show how this occurs in a actual scholarship contest, I've included below, an excerpt from an intermediate draft of an essay I wrote for the Century III Leaders program. The application had asked me to propose a solution to a problem facing America. I chose the topic of education:

This excerpt is from the middle of the essay. I've focused on this section to make the rewriting analysis easier to follow. For the winning entry in its entirety, see page B-8 in Appendix B.

"Current solutions often throw money at problems in education, but don't look to harness already-present resources. In looking to the future, we must find solutions to this educational crisis in three steps. First, we need to make a strong commitment to deliver a quality product. School must make sure that basic areas are covered before expanding the curriculum. We first need to improve the building blocks of learning—reading, writing, and math. Next, we must motivate and inspire students to go

far beyond minimum expectations. America was built on the principle that with hard work and perseverance, anything is possible. We need to reaffirm this belief by encouraging students to pursue learning outside what is spoon-fed in class. Last, we must find new ways to customize education to help students adapt to the rapidly changing world of the future. We need to train students how to maximize resources, share information, and work cooperatively. These abilities will be the new measure of success."

This draft wasn't bad, but the passage still had some glaring weaknesses. First, it mentioned some important reform concepts, but didn't really take the time to fully develop the ideas. As a result, it seemed to be more a conglomeration of catch phrases for educational reform than something that had a lot of real substance. Second, the passage only made passing reference to alternatives to my point of view. Failing to recognize and make my case against differing views was a big omission.

The passage also lacked a sound organizational structure; all of these ideas had been lumped into one big paragraph, even though each idea merited its own organizational unit. Furthermore, I wasn't making every sentence count. The second sentence of the passage was largely a transitional one that didn't accomplish much of anything. The sentence beginning "America was built on the principle" was tangential to the topic at hand. In short, both my ideas and my expression of those ideas had to be fleshed out further. I tried to address these weak points in a subsequent version:

"Lowering standards so as to get more high school students through the system and into college each year is <u>not</u> the panacea for this debilitation in learning. Today, businesses rightly complain that they must reeducate even <u>college</u> graduates in basic academic skills. Some policy makers would have us believe that simply bolstering programs with more money will solve our problems. Unfortunately, money isn't the panacea either: Positive change

BULL'S-EYE:
The process of rewriting your essay helps you to home in on your core message until your ideas can't miss the target.

demands wisdom and discipline, and a lack of money often becomes a convenient scapegoat for failure. In fact, as an active student government member, I've learned how workable solutions are achievable without always allocating new funds—by harnessing underutilized resources, such as the students themselves.

Educators must make the commitment to deliver a quality product. Schools must refocus their energies to ensure that basic core subjects are adequately covered before expanding content. By minimizing distractions, we can increase the critical time allotted to developing the building blocks of learning—reading, writing, and math.

Next, we must motivate and inspire students to go far beyond minimum expectations. And in the process, we must <u>raise</u> the expectations of students as well as their parents. Furthermore, we need to emphasize and teach <u>how</u> to learn, not merely <u>what</u> to learn. We should encourage students to pursue learning outside of what is covered in class.

Last, we must find new ways to customize education to help students better prepare for the 21st century. The communications and computer revolutions have forever changed our lives. We need to train students and teachers to maximize resources by sharing information over electronic networks. We should create lower-tech programs that will act as supplementary "training wheels" for the interactive, multimedia resources of tomorrow. The difference between present practicalities and future possibilities is only a matter of the technological level of the networking links."

In this revision, I developed each of my points more fully, and revised my organizational structure to put each point in its own paragraph. The passage begins by addressing two alternative ways of addressing the problem, and showing why such "solutions" won't work.

I would have liked to revise the passage further, but alas, I ran out of time. It didn't seem to matter, however, as I was the national winner in the competition.

At the end of the first paragraph, I've even made the essay more personal by referencing a lesson learned from my own student government experience. The phrase I used at the end of the paragraph—"the students themselves"—was meant to foreshadow a discussion of a service program I created called "The Homework Helpline." I fully described this project in a later section of the essay. Notice too, how I was more careful with my word choice and sentence structure. Overall, the persuasiveness of this essay has been enhanced significantly.

Tips for Revising Essays

Before revising an essay, try to distance yourself somewhat from the material. If possible, take a day or two off from working on the essay, and allow the material to simmer in the back of your mind. You'll come back to the essay after your brief sabbatical with a fresher perspective.

When revising your own work, get in the habit of reading your essay out loud. Essay writers frequently skip over trouble spots and mistakes when reading silently because their minds fill in gaps in the text, and read more into the words than what's actually there. Reading aloud, however, gives your ears a chance to catch what your eyes miss. If something is awkwardly phrased or out of place, you'll hear it right away. As an added precaution, you can tape record yourself reading the essay, so that you can play back the tape and focus exclusively on listening to words.

Or better yet, have a friend or family member read your essay out loud. Keep a notepad in front of you, and listen for places where phrases are out of sequence, confusing, or poorly worded. Take note of where the reader fumbles over words, has to reread things, or seem to get lost, as these are indicators of passages that might need more work.

In general, never craft your scholarship essays in a vacuum. Instead, ask teachers and peers whose opinions you value to analyze the strengths and weaknesses of what you've

GUERRILLA TACTIC #11

Get others to read your essay out loud, and listen for trouble areas.

Always "spell check" your essays, but don't rely on this process; it won't be able to detect words that are spelled correctly, but used improperly.

written. Ask family members to contribute their ideas. Spending numerous hours revising the same essay can cloud your eyes to mistakes that others won't miss. Listen to what they say and heed their advice as best you can. Recognize that even though your editors might not know how to *solve* a problem in your essay, they will likely be able to "red flag" areas that are problematic or confusing. And remember—never take criticism personally.

TIPS FOR SPECIFIC TOPICS

In scholarship applications, a handful of essay topics are perennial favorites. In this section, I describe some common strategies and tactics scholarship winners use to nail these types of essays.

Future Career Aspirations

In these types of essays, you should seek to demonstrate four main points. First, you want to show *why* you're interested in a particular career. For the most part, it doesn't matter which career you choose; scholarship judges want to know what is motivating you to follow this path. Next, you want to demonstrate that you've taken the time to consider how you're going to reach this career goal. Building a successful career takes patience and hard work. Judges want to see that you understand what's involved in accomplishing your goals.

A nice touch in career aspiration essays is to discuss how you plan to contribute to society through your career.

Third, you should demonstrate any steps you've already taken to pursue the particular career. This gives added credibility to your career aspirations, and shows that the interest is more than just a passing fad. Finally, you want to illustrate your potential to excel in the field. Demonstrating this potential often involves showing that you have already begun to exhibit the skills and abilities necessary to succeed in the field.

Your Greatest Achievement

When scholarship judges ask you to discuss something you've accomplished, the particulars of the accomplishment are only *half* the story they are interested in. They also want to know how *you* view your own achievements, and what types of accomplishments are important to you.

Seek to explain not only *what* you did, but *why* you did it. As most of us are good at things we enjoy, show judges your passion for the area of achievement, and illustrate how this fueled your impressive results. Be proud of your accomplishment, but keep the focus on your accomplishment, not on merely gratifying your ego.

A Person You Admire

Contrary to popular belief, this type of essay is really *not* about the person you happen to admire. It's actually about *you*. The type of person you choose to admire is really a mirror reflection of the personal qualities and characteristics that you value most.

So don't just give a report on the person. Explain why you think this individual's contributions are important. Discuss the qualities of the person that make him or her admirable, and show how you've tried to emulate these qualities in your own life.

Be aware that historical figures like Gandhi, Martin Luther King, Jr., and Abraham Lincoln make popular choices. So if you choose a well-known figure, try to approach the essay in a creative way. Otherwise, pick someone specific to your own life who you know others won't choose.

Solving a Pressing Issue

These types of issue-oriented questions often center around current events, policy debates, and ethical questions. In general, write about an issue you care about. It's much easier to be persuasive when you're passionate about the topic.

Do outside research in newspapers, magazines, books, and Web sites, and demonstrate that you are knowledgeable about the subject and have more than just a superficial understanding of the issue. In making your argument, don't oversimplify the debate. Even if you advocate one position, discuss the other viewpoint, then show why your perspective makes more sense. Such issues are rarely black and white, so be sure to discuss the grey areas too.

If you have the option of choosing an issue, try to find subjects that you have some personal experience with. This will provide you with more ammunition for your argument. Avoid controversial issues (such as abortion) that could alienate a scholarship judge.

Some well-placed quotes and citations on a given issue can be effective, but don't overdo it. Excessive quoting makes you sound like a parrot who is merely repeating the opinions of others. Use quotes to reinforce your points, not to make them for you.

Growth Experiences

Essay questions focused on growth experiences ask you to write about an episode or event that has had a significant influence on the type of person you've become. The experience itself can be either positive or negative, but the key factor is describing what you've learned from the situation.

A particular experience need not be overly dramatic to be an effective growth experience. Don't make the mistake of trying to attach some huge symbolic significance to everyday events that seem pretty mundane. Growth experiences, by their very nature, deal with personal qualities and characteristics, so try to work in references to some of the Ten Golden Virtues if possible.

The Ten Golden Virtues were described in Chapter 6.

If your growth experience is an obstacle you've overcome, don't dwell on the obstacle itself for too long. The focus should not be on the problem you faced, but on the steps you took to overcome it.

SHORT-ANSWER QUESTIONS

In addition to full-fledged essays, scholarship applications may also pose short-answer questions. Such questions demand brief responses—usually 150 words or less. Our techniques for answering essay questions need to be modified to take into account the very compact space we have to make our case. Although our general principles of showing rather than telling, and focusing on personal details still apply, we have to employ these principles in a modified organizational format.

Your responses to short-answer questions should reinforce your primary and secondary application themes. As a unit, your short-answer responses should provide a sense of cohesion and reflect a clear pattern of thought.

When writing responses to short answer questions, there is rarely enough space to develop an adequate introduction, as you would in a normal essay. So try to make your opening sentence more of a thesis statement that declares the main point of your response. Don't try to overload your response to a short-answer question with too many major points; prioritize your potential points, stick to one or two of the most important, and try to develop them adequately.

After presenting your main point, try to back it up with a couple of examples. You won't have space for an actual conclusion, but try to end on a poignant thought that backs up or extends your main point. To give you an idea of what a solid organizational structure for a short-answer question looks like, I've included one of my winning responses from the semifinalist round of the Coca-Cola Scholars Program.

Question: Coca-Cola Scholars have been representative of the diverse economic, ethnic, and occupational backgrounds of families in the United States. Please describe any personal characteristics about yourself or your family that have been important to your development.

"Growing up as a child of mixed descent, with an American father and Thai mother, I have learned that this difference is more significant than its "face value." Given the privilege of seeing life through this dual-focus lens, I have been exposed to views and am able to formulate ideas from two distinct perspectives. Because Western and Asian cultures have different things to offer me—for example, the patience, perseverance, and strong work ethic from the East, and the creativity, pioneering attitude, and spirit of volunteerism from the West—I have tried hard to combine the best from both worlds. My parents have demonstrated to me the benefits of this special East-West synergy when analyzing complex situations, solving problems, and exchanging ideas. I have been taught how courage, faith, concentration, and determination—in combination with high ethical and moral values—can help me achieve my goals and realize my dreams."

This final sentence was recycled from my Tylenol Scholarship application materials (see page 171).

CHAPTER 8 SUMMARY

■ **Show, Don't Tell:** Instead of merely *telling* judges how good you are, *show* them with stories and anecdotes. This makes your essays more credible and memorable.

■ **Personal Details:** Relate the essay question to personal experiences and unique perspectives. Choose appropriate topics that facilitate this.

■ **Organization:** Structure essays for clarity and logic. If needed, fall back on the standard three-part format (introduction, body, and conclusion).

■ **Conciseness:** Each sentence in an essay should serve an important purpose. Eliminate long transitional phrases and redundancy. Write first drafts 25 percent over the word limit, then pare down the verbiage while keeping main ideas intact.

■ **Unique & Memorable:** Craft each essay to stand out by including personal details and notable content, or by expressing ideas in novel ways (such as the use of an extended metaphor).

■ **Recycling essays:** Pick essay topics that bridge multiple essay questions. Try combining elements from two or more essays to create a new essay. Recycle metaphors and other creative expressions of your ideas.

■ **Writer's Block:** Don't let a blank page intimidate you. To get yourself in the flow, try free writing, consulting other essays, conversing with a friend, recording yourself, moving locations, or focusing on manageable details.

■ **Honing Your Essay:** *Rewriting* is even more important than writing. Reassess ideas, and reevaluate how you communicate these points. Taking some time off after writing a first draft is helpful. Read essays out loud, and get others to do so. Ask friends, family, and teachers for critiques.

■ **Specific Tips:** Scholarship winners often employ common strategies for essays dealing with career aspirations, outstanding achievements, people admired, solving problems, and growth experiences. Learn from what others have done.

■ **Short-Answer Questions:** When required to respond in "150 words or less," follow a compact organizational format. Focus on one or two main points.

Glowing
Support
Letters

*In this chapter,
I'll show you how to
get glowing letters of
recommendation
that fit the demands
of each scholarship
contest.*

CHAPTER CONTENTS

- Developing a menu of recommendations
- Cultivating strong support letters
- Working with recommenders
- Qualities of a great letter

STAR WITNESSES

Think of your letter of recommendation writers as your star witnesses—not unlike those in a courtroom trial. They are the ones who corroborate your story, testify on behalf of your character, and offer supporting evidence to why you are worthy of the scholarship award.

Trying to obtain letters from these star witnesses can be either an extremely satisfying or totally frustrating experience. It's a positive experience when recommenders say such glowing things about you that the words seem to radiate right off the page. When you're handed recommendations that don't put you in such a good light, or weren't crafted with much thought or care, you can wind up in a foul mood.

At the crux of the problem lies the fact that letters of recommendation are the one element of your application that *you* don't control. You're dependent on others—people who may or may not have the time, energy, or skills to craft the support letters you need.

And make no mistake about it, the quality of your letters of recommendation can make or break your chances of winning. This is because they provide other insights into your personality, skills, and character. It's not that judges don't trust what you say. They just want added evidence that you are really as wonderful as you say you are.

Although you don't have *direct* control over what people write, I've found that there are indeed some powerful strategies you can employ to insure that you receive recommendations that put you in the best possible light.

Strategy #1:

Develop a Menu of Recommendation Writers

For a variety of reasons, any given recommendation letter may not be as strong as you expected. The recommender could have been juggling many other projects, and not have devoted the time it takes to craft a quality letter. Or maybe your recommender was in a bad mood when he sat down to write your letter. In other instances, the recommender who thinks very highly of you may not possess the writing skills to effectively communicate this on paper.

GUERRILLA TACTIC #12

Obtain more recommendation letters than you need, then pick and choose the best letters to include with each application.

"I had something like 30 recommendation letters, and would choose the ones to use based on the criteria of the scholarship I was applying for. For some scholarships, I used science-focused recommendations, while for others I picked ones that stressed community service."

Will Carson
National Scholarship Winner

For these reasons, it's important to obtain as many recommendation letters as possible. Procuring more than enough recommendations provides insurance against those that are less glowing than anticipated. And because most scholarship applications have you include recommendation letters *with* your other application materials, you'll be able to read the letters (and evaluate their strengths) before sending them off to contests.

In this way, getting plenty of letters provides you with a virtual menu of recommendations to choose from. People who know you in different contexts will often have different perspectives, and the more perspectives you can accumulate, the better. This menu also gives you the ability to choose the most appropriate recommendation letter when custom-tailoring each scholarship application. You will be able to select recommendations that best address a particular contest's judging criteria, best complement the other materials you've prepared for the contest, and best reinforce your major application themes. When choosing from this menu, I used certain recommendations repeatedly, while others I included only on specific types of contests. Remember, it's always better to first request a recommendation letter, and then decide at a later date whether you want to submit it with a particular application. By doing this, you'll be able to choose which letters are best to include with different scholarship packages.

To develop a menu of recommendation letters, build on the strategies outlined in Chapter 4. As you'll recall, as part of our winning game plan, I suggested that you make a broad list of potential recommendation writers who know you from both school- and non-school-related contexts. We'll now it's time to convert this list into as many recommendation letters as possible.

We should note that developing this menu has other advantages for students who have not yet applied to college. Unlike the format for most scholarship recommendation letters, many college applications specify that recommendations be mailed separately by the recommender (thereby decreasing your chances of reading it before it's sent off). Because your scholarship recommendation letters will likely become your college recommendation letters, however, developing a menu of scholarship recommendations provides you with the ability to pick and choose between letters you might not otherwise see.

Strategy #2 | **Cultivate relationships with potential recommenders**

You'll be able to request a recommendation letter right away from people who have known you in multiple contexts. For potential recommendation writers who don't know you as intimately, you will want to get to know them better before you ask them for a letter.

I call this strategy *cultivating* a recommendation, and it's important for several reasons: First, there's a big difference between a passable recommendation and a great one. As we'll discuss later in this chapter, great recommendations can only be written by people who know you well. Because of this, cultivating a great recommendation is well worth the wait.

Second, once a recommender writes you a recommendation, it's more difficult to get him or her to update or enhance it. So you don't want to have someone write it too soon—before he or she has a chance to learn all of the wonderful things about you. Of course, if you need a recommendation for an application right away, you won't have time to cultivate a letter. But once again, if you try to develop a menu of recommendation letters, your scholarship fate won't hang in the balance of any given letter.

This strategy is especially important if you aren't able to list bunches of people who you're certain would write you strong recommendations. By following some cultivation guidelines, you'll be able to transform mediocre recommendations into glowing ones.

So how does one cultivate a great recommendation letter? You do it by getting to know a potential recommender in a more in-depth context. If you're seeking a letter from a particular teacher, you might, for instance, participate in the extracurricular activities he or she advises. Or you could serve as a teaching assistant (which usually means helping grade papers) or lab aide for the teacher. Or perhaps it's as simple as regularly asking questions and meeting with the teacher after class or during office hours. The possibilities are endless.

For others in your school—such as principals, counselors, or deans—make a point of getting to know them. Regularly ask for advice and sign up for appointments. Remember, these individuals are powerful allies to have in your quest for scholarship money.

For recommenders outside the school environment, the strategy is much the same. If you hope to get a recommendation letter from the coordinator of a community service program you volunteer for, perhaps you want to first take on some added responsibilities for the program. If you plan to get a recommendation from an employer, go the extra mile to make sure that you perform your job above and beyond the call of duty.

Cultivating a recommendation isn't about putting on a show so someone will write nice things about you. Rather, it's about giving someone the opportunity to learn more about you—thus gaining a better understanding of your personality, talents, skills, and character.

Sometimes a scholarship contest will give you the option of submitting additional recommendation letters. Assuming you have enough strong recommendations, always submit these extra letters. Doing this provides you with added opportunity to make your case to scholarship judges. Cultivating an arsenal of recommendations will insure that you have the necessary firepower in reserve.

Strategy #3 | Communicate Effectively with Recommenders

For a moment, pretend you are a trial lawyer in the midst of a big case. You're ace in the hole—a star witness—is scheduled to take the stand. Would you put this witness on the stand without prepping him first? Of course, not.

And just like the courtroom example, you wouldn't want your letter of recommendation writers to "testify" without preparing them first. So the best applicants prepare their recommenders by providing them with written summaries of their activities, achievements, awards and honors, and goals.

Communicating to your recommenders the application theme we developed in Chapter 5 is critical. By conveying this information, they can mention things in their letters that will reinforce and enhance your theme.

A lot of this information can simply be copied from other components of the application, or from other applications you've completed. In your summaries, only include résumé material that you want recommenders to address, as they may quote information directly from these sheets. Don't overwhelm your recommenders with pages and pages of information. As a rule, I always tried to keep these summaries to a maximum of three pages. Any more than this, and the recommender might opt not to read it thoroughly.

To the front of this summary, attach a cover letter. This letter is your opportunity to tell the recommender about the focus of the scholarship contest, the application theme you've tried to develop (which you would like her to help reinforce), and any specific points you hope she will mention.

The key is to do all of this *tactfully*. Express your deep gratitude for the help. Don't make it seem like you're *telling* someone what to write. Instead, you're just trying to provide your recommendation writer with enough information to make the job easier and less time-consuming.

All of the recommendation writers I have encountered were appreciative of the cover letters and summaries, as the items helped jog their memories of what I had done, informed them of achievements they hadn't been aware of, gave them a better idea of what type of letters the scholarship judges were looking for, and made the process of writing a personalized recommendation much easier.

Taking the time to write good cover letters demonstrates to your recommendation writers that you're putting a lot of time and care into your applications. And if you treat your own materials with care, they will feel a responsibility to do the same with their part of your submission.

You should also include information on how to address the letter (if it's not simply, "To whom it may concern"); when you need to receive the letter by; and any directions specified by the contest (such as when a contest requests that the writer comment on your ability to work with others).

To give you an idea of what this letter should look like, I've included a sample recommendation cover letter on the adjacent page. If you're short on time, you can simply substitute your own personal information and contest-specific facts into this template.

To make sure that your recommendation writer hasn't forgotten about your letter, employ the following tactic: About a week or so after you've submitted the cover letter, go up to your recommender and ask if he or she needs any additional information, or has any questions for you.

Dear Ms. Thompson,

Thank you again for agreeing to write me a recommendation letter. As I mentioned in our conversation, your recommendation letter is part of a scholarship application I'm submitting to the National Scholarship Foundation's Student Excellence Awards program. The contest awards scholarships to students who exhibit excellence in extracurricular activities.

In my application materials, one of the important areas I'm trying to highlight is my leadership responsibilities and skills. As my student government adviser, I thought you would be an excellent person to comment on these aspects of my extracurricular involvement. Of special interest to the Student Excellence Awards program would be activities like the food and clothing drive I helped organize last year, the student government fundraising efforts I recently initiated, as well as my representation of our school on the district youth violence task force. The application materials also request that you comment upon the personal qualities I have exhibited through such projects.

As additional background information, I've attached a list of my extracurricular projects, with the ones related to student government in bold face. Since the deadline for postmarking materials is December 5th, it would be great if I could pick up your recommendation letter (for inclusion with the rest of my application) two weeks from this Wednesday. Your letter can be addressed to the "Student Excellence Awards judging committee."

Once again, thank you so much for all your time and energy in writing me this recommendation. I really appreciate it and am grateful for all of your help during the year. If you have any questions, feel free to call me at home at 555-5431.

Many thanks,

Joe Student

Communicating effectively with your recommendation writers also enables you to take advantage of a loophole in the requirements of many scholarship applications. Letters of recommendation, unlike essays or extracurricular activity lists, rarely have length limitations. So if there wasn't any room elsewhere in an application to mention an activity or award, I would ask my recommendation writers to include these "selling points" in their letters. This allowed me to side-step contest space limitations, and sneak in an extra plug or two.

Strategy #4 **Minimize the Work for Recommendation Writers**

When you're applying for bunches of scholarship contests, this can create a lot of extra work for your recommendation writers. Let's say, for instance, that throughout the year you will be using a particular recommendation letter in about 10 to 15 different applications. This implies that you're going to need to get 10 to 15 copies printed, with slight modifications made to each version to meet the specific demands and requirements of each contest. Furthermore, if specific references are made to the scholarship's name in the header or body of the letter, you'll need to get those changed too. Finally, all of this needs to get done by each contest's deadline.

As you can see, all of these tasks implies a lot of repetitive work to ask of your recommendation writers. To minimize work for them, suggest to your recommenders that they give you an electronic copy of their letter on disk (and provide you with some letterhead or stationary if they use it). This way, *you* can be the one to print out each copy and make sure that references to the scholarship's name are correct. Once you've done this, you'll be able to hand the

GUERRILLA TACTIC #13

Get electronic copies of recommendation letters on disk to reduce the burden on recommendation writers and gain better control over obtaining additional copies.

recommendation writer a printout of the customized letter, ready for a final check and signing. Doing this not only helps out your recommendation writers, but also serves the added function of giving *you* control over making sure that new copies of letters are done properly and completed on time.

Try to anticipate in advance which applications are suitable for the reuse of a particular recommendation letter. This way, you can request in your cover letter some additional information that may not be needed for immediate contests, but that will be necessary for later ones.

When this isn't possible, you will need to get your recommendation writers to make small changes, additions, and adaptations to their basic letter to fit each contest. To do this, write another cover letter and ask them to add comments on a particular area requested by the new scholarship contest. To make things even easier on your recommenders, attach a copy of their prior recommendation letter, and suggest that they make changes and additions in red pen. Then, you can be the one to type the changes into the letter, obtain a printout, and bring it to them for a signature.

There may be times, however, when you need changes on such short notice that you may need to employ other strategies. On one contest, for instance, I only found out about a particular contest the night before the application was due. I was scrambling to put together an application, and I wanted to use a particular recommendation letter, except that it didn't comment upon on a few key areas specifically requested by the application materials. So I called up the recommendation writer, and politely informed him of the situation. He suggested that I ask him over the phone any additional questions the application posed, take down his responses, add them to recommendation letter myself, and then bring a copy for him to look over and sign in the morning.

I took him up on the offer, and ended up winning the scholarship; I subsequently employed this technique when rushing to meet impending deadlines of other contests. Quite a few other scholarship winners I've interviewed have related similar stories and techniques.

Making small changes and additions to a recommendation letter to fit new contests actually helps improve and refine the letter—almost as if you were editing it. I discovered that after a few of these small alterations were made, good recommendation letters could become great ones.

If an upcoming contest requires a short nomination statement (generally 150 words or less), approach someone who has already written you a strong recommendation, and ask him if you can assemble this statement by stringing together key passages from his letter.

Mounting a major scholarship campaign means that you will need the help of your recommendation writers over and over again. The best way to insure this help is to be courteous and appreciative. Try to plan ahead and give your recommenders at least two to three weeks notice before you need their letters. Write thank-you notes regularly.

So if you're rushing to meet a deadline, and need modifications made to a recommendation letter on short notice, tactfully suggest to the recommendation writer that you interview him or her in person or over the phone. Explain that you could take down his or her answers verbatim, and then insert the comments in appropriate places in the prior letter. The recommendation writer, of course, will have the opportunity to read the changes and make any additional modifications, before signing off on the copy.

This strategy works whether or not your recommendation writers decide to go along with this interview method. Since you've tactfully informed them of the impending deadline—while being considerate of the burden this places on their time—they may very well offer to make the necessary modifications themselves.

QUALITIES OF A GREAT LETTER

Understanding what makes an outstanding letter of recommendation helps you make better decisions about which letter to include with a particular application. It also helps you better cultivate your recommendations, and communicate effectively with your recommenders.

Too many students include recommendations in scholarship applications from individuals who don't know them well enough to comment beyond a very limited setting. When a letter of recommendation is a form letter, judges can smell this a mile away. Statements like "Bob is a valued member of the class," or "Mary shows great promise"—without any specifics to back up these statements—come across as empty words.

Great recommendation letters, on the other hand, are so specific, detailed, and personal that they could only be meant for you. Often they include revealing stories or anecdotes that illustrate how you've exhibited certain positive qualities. References to specific incidents and occasions make your recommendations seem more genuine and memorable. To illustrate this point, let's examine an excerpt from a recommendation by my journalism advisor:

> *"As a reporter and editor Ben continually took complicated, difficult issues, researched them thoroughly, interviewed numerous sources, and wrote clear articles appropriate for his readership. For example, Ben covered the school reorganization that has been mandated on the state level by House Bill 3565. Even educators had trouble understanding and analyzing the complex information and how it should be applied to their respective schools. Ben, after reading numerous documents most students would resist digging into, attended faculty information sessions after school, interviewed key people in the school and the district, and wrote a series of clear, comprehensive articles."*

Merely stating that I was a good reporter would have limited effect on contest judges. But my adviser backed up this statement by citing a specific example that illustrated the point.

So you can appreciate the power of anecdotes in another style of letter, I've reprinted below part of a letter written by my longtime tennis coach, discussing an event that occurred when I first started playing tennis at age 10:

> *"Ben had only been playing tennis for three months when he entered his first tournament. My employer warned me that Ben would lose handily in the tournament and advised me to prepare him for the worst. Throughout the tournament, I watched Ben run down hundreds of balls with unwavering concentration. When the smoke cleared, Ben took home the Championship trophy. This accomplishment was incredible, but the thing that astonished me most was how this victory caused Ben to work harder, instead of being satisfied with his great accomplishment."*

My tennis coach could have simply said that I have a strong work ethic on the court. This anecdote, however, illustrated the point in much more vivid terms. Furthermore, it showed that this is a character trait I've had from a young age.

Finally, great recommendation letters distinguish themselves by making bold statements that contest judges know are not just written for everyone. For instance, my student government advisor wrote the following in a recommendation letter for a leadership-related scholarship program:

> *"I have taught in Oregon's schools for more than thirty years and served a couple of terms in the Oregon legislature, and I can say unequivocally to you that I've not seen a better candidate for this type of scholarship."*

Famous Isn't Always Better

Some scholarship applicants make the mistake of going out of their way to include recommendations from famous or well-known people. One scholarship applicant I know, for instance, pulled some strings to get a recommendation letter from the Governor of his state. The letter he received, however, lacked specifics, wasn't particularly glowing, and spent a lot of time making political statements. This was understandable: the Governor didn't know him at all.

So don't fall into the trap of submitting impersonal recommendation letters. These types of letters don't help your scholarship cause. Your best bet for strong recommendation letters will be people who know you well.

Of course, you can always request these "big-name" recommendations just to see how they turn out. But don't count on a great result.

CHAPTER 9 SUMMARY

■ **A Menu of Letters:** Obtain as many letters of recommendation as possible. Use this menu of letters to custom-tailor application support materials.

■ **Cultivate Relationships:** Cultivate deeper relationships with potential recommendation writers. Allow them to learn more about your personality, talents, skills, and character.

■ **Communicate Effectively:** Provide a recommender with a written summary of your activities, achievements, awards and honors, and goals. Attach a tactful cover letter that explains the focus of the scholarship contest, your thematic approach, and any special points that should be mentioned.

■ **Multiplicity:** Obtain copies of recommendation letters on disk. Print out copies and obtain signatures as needed.

■ **Modifications:** To fit the demands of particular contests, ask your best recommenders for small modifications to their standard letters. Do whatever is necessary to minimize their added work.

■ **Great Letters:** The best recommendation letters include stories, anecdotes, bold statements, and other compelling details. Seek out such letters.

CHAPTER 10

Filling in the Blanks

In this chapter, we dissect the scholarship application form, and reveal plenty of strategies and guerrilla tactics for submitting extracurricular activity lists, awards & honors summaries, transcripts, and other key components.

CHAPTER CONTENTS

- Tips for the application form
- Extracurricular activity lists
- Awards & honors lists
- Transcripts
- Supplementary materials

PAPERWORK PROWESS

We've researched. We've strategized. And we've got killer essays and glowing recommendation letters up our sleeves, too. Now it's time to actually fill out those pesky scholarship application forms. The goal of this section is to show you how to whip all of those questions, lines, boxes, and blanks into tiptop shape. In the section below, we discuss some practical considerations of filling out forms; in later sections you'll learn strategies and guerrilla tactics for submitting stat sheets, extracurricular activity lists, awards & honors summaries, transcripts, and supplementary materials.

Make Plenty of Copies

As a rule, always make multiple copies of the original scholarship application form. You'll want at least one copy to do a practice run, in which you will fill in all the blanks in pencil, planning what you're going to write. Additional copies should be kept as backups for the inevitable tears, typos, smudging, and last-minute editing that always seems to occur. This is definitely not the time to skimp on those seven-cent photocopies.

You'll be spending some quality time at the local Kinko's.

Type Your Application

Scholarship applications should be typed—whether on a computer or a typewriter. No matter how many times you practiced your penmanship in elementary school, it still looks tacky and is hard to read.

For many scholarship applications, you'll have to fit at least some of the requested information in blanks on the pre-printed application form itself, so you may want to drag that old typewriter out of the closet. If you decide to get a little high-tech, you can scan the form into the computer and then "type" in the blanks. Otherwise, enter your responses on a computer in your favorite word processing program, print them out, and then cut and paste them by hand into the proper spaces. Then make a photocopy of the completed form to make it look neat (and so that the glued responses don't fall off in the mail).

Try to keep things neat on the application form. After reviewing large numbers of applications, contest judges with tired eyes have little tolerance for entries that are hard to read. Avoid minuscule type, close spacing, and tiny margins.

Attach Additional Sheets Whenever Possible

Many scholarship contests allow you to attach additional sheets of paper to the scholarship application form if the space provided is not adequate. If this is allowed, take them up on the offer.

Attaching additional sheets allows you to bypass the limits and constraints of the form itself. Furthermore, because you complete these additional sheets on your own computer in a format that *you* (not the contest administrators) specify, you will be able to reuse and adapt old submissions from other contests with minimal work. For lengthy application components like extracurricular activity lists or awards summaries, I would simply write "Please see attached sheets" in the space provided on the application form itself. Then, the lists or summaries would be included exclusively on my own self-attached sheets.

When you complete work on attached sheets, try to retain the general look and format of the original application form. For instance, if the application places extracurricular lists in a multi-column format, then adopt a similar style on your own sheets. Also, be sure to include all requested information on your self-made forms.

Don't Leave Spaces Blank

On applications that require you to use the forms provided, you'll be prompted to include lists of extracurricular activities, awards and honors, and other data in pre-formatted spaces. As a general rule, try to avoid leaving any of these spaces blank. Leaving such spaces blank gives the impression that you don't have enough credentials to even meet the demands of the form. Instead, you want to leave the impression that you have many more credentials than could possibly fit in the space provided. So what do you do if a form has spaces for a listing of ten activities, but you can only think of seven? Try the following guerrilla tactic: Add more detail and description to each activity you list. By doing this, you can get rid of the extra white space, and expand upon your strongest areas.

GUERRILLA TACTIC #14

If you don't have enough credentials to fill up a form, expand the descriptions of what you do have.

Trimming Out the Fat

Sometimes on a very compact application form, you have the opposite problem: If you're only given very limited space, it's hard to fit in a lot of compelling information. To combat this problem, you'll need to eliminate information that isn't 100 percent essential. You can do this by getting right to the meat of the information, and getting rid of the fat. On an application with unlimited space, you might have written:

> *As vice president of the Service Club, I was in charge of running a special benefit auction to raise funds for the local Meals on Wheels program.*

But on a compact application, instead write:

> *Service Club (Vice President). Organized charity auction.*

For especially compact spaces, try separating items in a list with semicolons, and using parentheses to briefly mention important details:

> *Service Club (VP); JV Basketball (Captain); Science Olympics (physics bowl); school newspaper (sports editor).*

Save Each Draft and Revision

Always save every draft and revision that you complete. When you're revising something on the computer, don't save on top of the old version. Instead, create a new file with a slightly modified name (such as "essay_revised"). Likewise, file away old printouts, notes, and other printed or written material in an accessible place.

Taking these steps serves two important purposes. First, it provides a safety net in case you accidentally delete material, or decide that you actually prefer an old revision of a piece to a rewritten version. Second, keeping all of your intermediary work aids in your reusability and recycling efforts. Some early draft that didn't work for a particular application might be a good starting point for a different contest.

THE STAT SHEET

The "Stat Sheet" is the part of the application where you fill in basic information such as your name, address, graduation date, information about your school, names of recommendation writers, career interests, etc. For applications that take into account academics, you may also be asked to supply your GPA, class rank, or test scores.

Stat sheets are fairly self-explanatory, but I'll offer two quick tips from someone who has filled out dozens of them. First, scan the stat sheet right away for any signatures that are required. Some applications require signatures of recommendation writers, nominating teachers, or principals; I can remember overlooking such details, and having to run around trying to track down people the day before an application was due. Second, make sure all the information on the Stat Sheet matches what is contained in any other of the other application components (especially things like your career interest or grade point average). This sounds simple enough, but it can get confusing when you're filling out multiple applications simultaneously.

ACTIVITY LISTS

Compiling extracurricular activity lists represents a prime opportunity to reap the benefits of reusability and recycling. Because most scholarships generally expect these lists in the same type of format, you'll be able to customize lists you've already submitted to fit the demands of new contests.

You can do this in one of two ways. First, you can choose the extracurricular list format of an upcoming scholarship contest, and after completing this submission, modify it to fit the requirements of subsequent contests. The method that will save time in the long run, however, is to create your own master extracurricular activities list that contains the full range of information any contest is likely to request.

To create your own master list, I suggest developing a format that includes the following categories: activity name, brief activity description (including your specific contribution to the activity), activity-related awards & honors, offices

Activity Name	Activity Description	Awards & Honors	Offices Held	Hours per week

A full-size, electronic version of this standard extracurricular activity form is available for your use in the Reader's Resource Room at the winscholarships.com Web site.

or positions held in the activity, and hours per week spent on the extracurricular endeavor. A recommended format for this master list is shown above. You can format this type of list in a word processor like Microsoft Word, or in a graphics layout program like Adobe Pagemaker.

After creating the basic format, it's time to start filling in the information. To do this, begin by pulling out information from the personal inventory lists we created in Chapter 4. When we created these lists, however, the goal was just to keep track of all of your potential scholarship résumé items. To add them to our master extracurricular activity list, we want to convert these notes into "résumé speak." To do this, you want to use words that convey action, responsibility, and leadership—words like "organized," "managed," "coordinated," "led," "founded," "recruited," "achieved," and "represented." You don't want to say something that isn't true, but like any résumé, you want to put your record in the best possible light.

As I mentioned before, keep a broad definition of what constitutes an extracurricular activity. For example, it's perfectly acceptable to include endeavors that seem more like events than ongoing activities. Be sure to include, for instance, any educational or community-oriented workshops, conferences, and camps you have participated in.

If you've accumulated a long string of extracurricular activities on your master list, you may want to group particular types of extracurricular activities together to make it easier for the judges to make sense of all the information. To group the listings, you can use the width evaluators for extracurricular activities described in Chapter 6, or you can come up with your own categories.

On my own extracurricular activity lists, I would group together, in separate categories, the types of activities I wanted to emphasize most: the ones related to journalism, leadership, and community service. I would create a bold heading to identify the particular category.

Ranking Your Activities

The spot of highest visibility in an extracurricular activities list is at the top of the list. With contests judges reviewing numerous applications, there is no guarantee that they'll thoroughly read all of your listings. They will, however, read the items that come first.

Because of this, you should rank your activities in order of importance, with the top of the list reserved for activities you definitely want judges to notice. What criteria should you use to determine what's most important? Here are several characteristics of activities that should be highlighted near the top of your list:

■ Activities that are directly related to application themes you frequently use.

■ Activities that you initiated or founded.

■ Activities in which you hold a title or position of responsibility.

■ Activities in which you made a special contribution (note this contribution in a few words).

Keep in mind that this ranking on your master list is not an absolute one—just your best guess of where your activities stack up against one another. We'll modify the order of extracurricular activities to fit the strategic considerations of each contest.

Customizing Your Master List

Once you've created your master list of extracurricular activities, your ongoing task will be to customize this list to fit each new contest. This means re-ranking and reordering the listings, modifying the format to fit each contest's guidelines, and eliminating some listings to fit the space limitations.

First, you will want to take into account your application theme, and place activities that mesh well with this theme at or near the top of your extracurricular list. Second, after using the "contest detective" packaging techniques described in Chapter 7, you will want to place certain activities higher in your list—activities that seem to fit the scholarship's definition of the ideal applicant. Finally, make a decision to highlight or eliminate any category of information that isn't specifically requested by the contest. For instance, if a contest doesn't request information on how many hours per week you devoted to an activity, only include it if it helps your cause.

If you need to trim your list to fit space requirements, start by eliminating activities near the bottom of your master list. Be sure, however, to leave in enough variety of activities to illustrate your well-roundedness.

As discussed in Chapter 6, internships, jobs, and other work experiences can be included as part of your extracurricular activities.

AWARDS & HONORS LISTS

Any scholarship contests you've already won should be listed in this section. Such credentials show judges that others have deemed you a worthy applicant. It's generally best, however, to highlight what the award was given for (such as leadership or artistic achievement) rather than focus on the scholarship money or dollar amounts.

In putting together awards & honors lists, many of the same strategies we used in compiling extracurricular activities also apply. Start out by using the personal inventory information you've been collecting to create a master list. Some of these items can be culled from the awards and honors segment of your master extracurricular activity list. We should note, however, that when awards and honors are treated as a separate component, you should also include those awards and honors that aren't associated with any particular activity (such as if you're selected for the Honor Roll).

To rank your awards and honors, first list those that are most impressive. How do you decide what's most impressive? Just try to imagine which awards and honors your mom or grandmother would be likely to brag about to their friends. Typically, these prestigious awards would be ones that involve any national or state recognition. Follow that up with any local or regional awards that are prized in your community. If you're short on awards you can cite, try thinking of recognition in broader terms—such as if your fellow Investment Club

members "honored" you by selecting you to be vice president. Likewise, just being *nominated* for an award or scholarship can be considered an honor. Even if you didn't win a U.S. Senate Youth Program Scholarship, for instance, you could write that you were nominated by your school as a candidate for the award.

Include added details about the selectivity and significance of the award if it puts the award in a more impressive context. For instance, if your school selects only one individual to receive its "outstanding student award," make the most of it. However, if practically everyone with a pulse gets the award, keep this information to yourself. You should also add explanations for any awards and honors that will not be clearly understood from the titles alone.

Once again, when customizing this information for particular contests, take into account any packaging considerations when deciding what awards and honors to highlight. Any awards in areas dealing directly with judging criteria should be placed at or near the top of your list.

If a scholarship requests both an extracurricular activity list and an awards and honors list, there are a few additional considerations. To sidestep any space limitations in the awards and honors section, you could include activity-related awards with your extracurricular activity list. You should avoid a lot of redundancy between the two lists, except in those areas that you want to stress (such as areas dealing with your theme).

THE TRANSCRIPT

Many scholarship seekers assume that school transcripts are application components that they can't affect or shape—short of getting better grades. I've discovered, however, that this is far from the truth. You *can* impact your transcript because transcripts contain—or can potentially contain—more than just a record of your grades.

Here's how to do it: At some high schools, students are allowed to include lists of their awards and honors within the official transcript. (Sometimes a brief extracurricular activity summary can be included too.) Usually, this information is

Always keep several official transcripts (the ones stamped with the school seal) in a file so that you have ready-to-go transcripts for last-minute scholarship entries. If your school also releases unofficial transcripts, keep these on file as well (some contests don't require official ones).

included on a secondary page of the transcript, apart from the standard course and grades summary. In most cases, however, this information doesn't just get automatically listed there like your grades do; you typically have to submit the information yourself. Most students, however, aren't aware that this is possible. So inquire with your registrar about whether there's anything like this included in your school's transcript. Request a sample official transcript to see for yourself.

Even if this isn't standard policy at your school (it wasn't at mine), you can still employ this strategy—you just need to get permission to include this extra information from the powers that be. My principal game me permission to have listed as part of my official transcript, a special two-page addendum describing honors and awards I had received in both school-and non-school related activities. Moreover, I was allowed to format my own list of awards and honors, print out a copy, and simply provide a copy to the registrar. As the year progressed, and I accumulated more awards and honors (including the scholarships I won), I would update my awards list and submit the latest version for inclusion with my transcript.

The inclusion of this addendum allows you to circumvent space limitations imposed on the rest of the application, and places special emphasis on your most compelling achievements. Even in contests that don't specifically request this kind of information, you can't be faulted for including it, because it's part of your school's official transcript. Likewise, in contests that limit you to compact spaces for awards and honors information, you can't be faulted for your addendum's length or detail because each school has its own unique transcript format. Furthermore, having it included in your transcript, reinforces the credibility of what you say because the entire transcript is authenticated with the school seal.

GUERRILLA TACTIC #15

To sidestep space limitations and highlight your most compelling achievements, include an awards & honors addendum as part of your school transcript.

So take the initiative to ask your principal or registrar about the possibility of including some support information as an addendum to your transcript. Explain in a tactful way that students at some schools are allowed to do this, and it gives them a strategic advantage. Remember, you are one of *their* students; they want to do what they can to help your scholarship cause.

Are Test Scores Included?

Another aspect of your transcript that you can exert some influence over is the inclusion of any standardized test scores you've taken. This information is usually kept as part of your transcript, but is often segmented into a separate section that may or may not be included when you request a transcript for scholarship organizations or colleges. So find out whether your school specifically includes these types of test scores on a secondary page of your transcript.

Such test scores aren't limited to just PSATs, SATs, or ACTs. Schools generally keep records of how you have performed on SAT II subject tests, Advanced Placement (AP) exams, and state assessment tests. My school automatically included all of these scores on page two of my transcript.

Build a good rapport with the person in charge of printing and authenticating transcripts (typically the registrar). You might need his or her help in the future.

Once you know whether test information is included, you can lobby your principal or registrar to include or not include this information in your transcripts for scholarships. If you received stellar scores, you'll obviously want this information included. This way, even when scholarships don't request test score information, the judges will still see your high marks.

On the other hand, if your scores aren't too impressive, you'll want this information kept hidden. Be aware that some schools have more rigid policies when transcripts are mailed directly to colleges. You can, of course, argue that a scholarship organization requesting a transcript is only after grade information, and isn't entitled to see your test scores. So if you explain the particular situation, school officials will often give you more leeway.

ADDITIONAL MATERIALS

If a scholarship application gives you the option of sending additional supplementary materials, then take them up on this offer—assuming you have something worthwhile to send. Many students can substantially strengthen their applications by including writing samples, artwork portfolios, music recordings, and other examples of their work. This is especially useful if your application theme specifically deals with your talent in one of these areas.

If you do submit something, however, make sure that it is indeed impressive and relevant to the scholarship you're applying for. Talk to your teachers, coaches, or instructors in specific areas to help you pick which samples to include, and don't go overboard with pages and pages of extra stuff. Instead, pick a few exemplary samples of your work. In general, refrain from including things like photocopies of award certificates. These only take up space and can annoy some contest judges.

Some scholarship contests—especially smaller, local ones—might not specifically state that you can submit samples of your work, but if you call and ask, they'll permit you to do so. If a scholarship form exhibits flexible rules and formatting guidelines, then it may even be acceptable to include a few pages of supplementary material, even without specifically asking permission.

MAILING YOUR APPLICATION

If you have enough time to mail out your scholarship application well in advance of the deadline, you can send it regular U.S. mail, and follow up to check that it was received. If you are short on time, or there's no other way to verify the package's arrival before the deadline is passed, you may want to send your materials with built-in verification that it arrived safe and sound. When you sink a lot of work into an application, it's often worth a couple of extra bucks to make sure that your materials have arrived at their destination.

In this case, opt for delivery by U.S. Postal Service "Certified Mail" with a Return Receipt Requested card, or "Priority Mail with an Acknowledgment Receipt." If your deadline

For local scholarships, you may also have the option of delivering your application materials in person. Doing this may allow you to meet and make a good impression on scholarship judges and administrators.

only requires that you *postmark* it by a particular date, then it's usually not necessary to use an overnight or second-day delivery service. If the scholarship application has to be *received* by the following day (or two), you might have to depend on familiar overnight services such as Express Mail, FedEx, UPS NextDay, or other couriers. Remember too, that if you're mailing to a Post Office Box, you're required to "go postal"—that means using the good ol' U.S. Postal Service.

COACH

In this dialogue, the Scholarship Coach answers questions relevant to already-enrolled college students who are seeking scholarship dollars.

. . . About older applicants

The following questions were submitted by Ima Incollege, a college junior from Needcash, Florida.

Ima: In scholarship contests, are there differences between what's expected of college and high school students?

Scholarship Coach: There are a couple of major differences. First, because college students are considerably older and more experienced than their high school counterparts, they're expected to have a clearer picture of fields and careers they want to pursue. Second, judges recognize that extracurricular activities at the college level are considerably more time consuming. You're not expected to participate in as many types of extracurricular activities. You are, however, expected to have more notable accomplishments and achievements in these activities.

Ima: Do all of the strategies in this book still apply?

Scholarship Coach: Yes, yes, yes! The strategies in this book work for scholarship applications at *all* levels. One potential difference you may find, however, is more institutional rigidity and red tape at the college level. It might be harder, for instance, to influence the supplementary contents of your transcript. Cultivating recommendations is even more critical for undergrads because at many schools, professors have less individual contact with students.

CHAPTER 10 SUMMARY

■ **Paperwork:** Make multiple copies of original application forms, and type your application. Attaching additional sheets (if allowed) is preferable to cramming information on the form. Save all intermediate work—both on the computer and as printed copies.

■ **No Blanks:** Fill in all blanks when contests forms request lists of activities or awards. If necessary, expand the descriptions of your credentials to fill up the space.

■ **The Stat Sheet:** Scan forms for required signatures. Make sure that information on the stat sheet matches the rest of the application.

■ **Activity Lists:** Create a master extracurricular activities list that includes the following categories: activity name, brief activity description, related awards & honors, offices or positions held, and time commitment. Rank activities on the list in a systematic fashion—with activities of great strategic importance at the top of the list. Customize this master list to fit the strategic considerations of each contest.

■ **Awards & Honors Lists:** Create a master list, rank your most impressive awards first, and customize this ranking to fit each scholarship contest. Include added details about the selectivity and significance of the award if it helps your cause.

■ **The Transcript:** Obtain permission to include an awards and honors addendum as part of your school transcript. Find out if standardized test scores are included, and lobby your school if this policy isn't optimal for you.

■ **Additional Materials:** Send samples or portfolios of your work if permitted by contest guidelines. Don't pad applications with excess material; pick and choose your highest quality work.

■ **Mail Service:** For added peace of mind, send completed scholarship applications using a mail service that verifies its safe arrival.

CHAPTER 11

Acing the Interview

*In this chapter,
I'll show you some
powerful techniques
for making a great
impression in a
scholarship interview.*

CHAPTER CONTENTS

- Preparing points and anecdotes
- Refining your interview skills
- Staying relaxed and focused

INTERVIEW MASTERY

Ever wonder how certain entertainers, journalists, and politicians seem so relaxed and well-spoken in television interviews? Well, here's a little secret: It's not because they've got natural talent coming out of their ears. Rather, it's that they all have prepared and practiced enough to appear this way.

In this chapter, I'll illustrate some proven strategies and tips that will help you achieve similar results in your scholarship interviews. You'll discover that an interview need not be a dreaded event. In fact, scholarship interviews can actually be *fun*.

Before we begin, I should note that most scholarship applications do *not* include interviews. This doesn't mean, however, that knowing how to handle yourself in interviews isn't important: When judges do conduct interviews, your performance in them usually carries considerable weight in the overall evaluation process.

Because of this significance, take the time to learn and employ the techniques outlined in this chapter. Besides, strong skills in this area will serve you well during your entire life—whether you're applying to college or graduate school, trying to land that dream job, or undergoing the informal "interviewing" of a first date.

PREPARING FOR THE INTERVIEW

What you do *before* you even show up for an interview contributes to more than 50 percent of your overall performance. Put another way, preparation and practice are the keys to feeling comfortable and natural in the interview setting. So how do you prepare for a scholarship interview? Try the following steps:

Ideally, you should start preparing for an interview three to five days before the main event.

1. Do your homework. An important aspect of performing well in an interview is understanding the perspective of the interviewer. If you understand where the interviewer is coming from, you'll be able to anticipate where he or she will go with questions—allowing you to formulate answers that are likely to get a good response.

To prepare, research the organization sponsoring the contest. If you've already employed the "contest detective" and packaging strategies outlined in Chapter 7, a lot of this work will have been already completed.

Find out what you can about the person or people who will be interviewing you. Are they affiliated with the sponsoring or administering organization? Are they educators? Or are they members of the Fraternal Brotherhood of Aardvark Lovers? Uncovering snippets of background information gives you some idea about what types of questions to expect, and what types of preferences your interviewers might have.

If your interview will be conducted by phone, prepare notes that you can read at a glance. Before the interviewer calls, lay out these notes on a table near the phone so that you can easily read them during the interview.

2. Prepare a few key points. Don't just respond to whatever an interviewer throws at you. Go into an interview already prepared to make a few key points of your own— selling points that demonstrate you are deserving of the scholarship award. At least one of these points should emphasize your application theme. Communicate your theme with passion and enthusiasm, and never assume that an interviewer has read your application word for word.

At the same time, don't dwell on your theme to the exclusion of everything else. Interviews allow judges to discover more dimensions of you than they can on the written page, so also be sure to communicate your "well-roundedness." You may also want to reinforce some of the Ten Golden Virtues discussed in Chapter 6.

3. Prepare anecdotes to illustrate your points. What's the cure for a dull interview? Quite simply, *an anecdote is the antidote.* Telling stories and giving examples keeps the interviewer interested and engaged. For instance, if your application theme centers on community service, don't just recite a laundry list of all the service activities you've done. Talk about a specific community service project, and a particularly memorable occasion when you felt your efforts made a big difference. Tell an interesting story about a person you helped and how that made you feel. In the end, this conveys much more about your service efforts than just reciting a list of facts.

4. Anticipate interview questions. What constitutes interview questions is no big secret. In fact, you can generally predict at least some of them. So take the time to come up with a list of potential questions. Don't just review these questions in your mind; write them down on index cards.

The specific questions, of course, depend upon the emphasis of the particular scholarship. For instance, if the scholarship is aimed at students interested in a certain field of study, expect questions about your career goals and your experience with the subject matter. If the scholarship contest is sponsored by an organization that highly values patriotism, expect questions asking about your citizenship duties as an American. To get you started, I've listed below some common interview questions:

It's no surprise that many of these questions are similar to standard essay questions.

- Where do you see yourself in 20 years?
- Who is someone that you admire, and why?
- What are your greatest strengths and weaknesses?
- What is your favorite book, and why do you like it?
- How would you like to be remembered?
- What has been your greatest accomplishment?
- What kind of activities have you participated in?
- Why do you want to go to college?
- Why should we award you this scholarship?
- Is there anything else you'd like to add?

5. Prepare answers. Once you've come up with a pile of questions on index cards, write out answers to these questions on the reverse side of these cards. Don't bother writing out actual sentences, just jot down a few notes that will remind you about what you want to talk about. Never try to memorize actual responses verbatim. After all, you want to seem relaxed and natural.

6. "Pepper" yourself. Put these index cards in a box or favorite hat, and draw out random questions to practice your interview responses. To see yourself from the interviewer's perspective, try videotaping your responses.

Conduct these practice sessions as if they are a rehearsal or a scrimmage. When you feel comfortable with your responses, do a mock interview with a friend, family member, teacher, or school counselor. Provide them with your list of questions, but also allow them to ad lib as well.

Incidentally, all of these tips are good advice for college admissions interviews.

7. **Prepare questions to ask the interviewer.** At the conclusion of an interview, I've often been asked if there's anything I'd like to ask the interviewer. Be prepared for this type of reverse question. A well-thought out and articulate question can tell the interviewer a lot about you. Questions are also an opportunity to convey your knowledge of the sponsoring organization. In addition, it's nice to be able to give the interviewer a chance to talk as well.

8. **Prepare samples of your work.** Samples and portfolios that illustrate your talents can make a strong impression on interviewers. Bring copies of your sample work that you can leave behind with the interviewer. The sample work will emphasize your strengths, and will remind the interviewer to consider you when it's time to decide who wins the scholarship money. This strategy is especially important if a focal point of your application is your artistic or writing ability—talents that are best demonstrated through sample work.

In addition, it never hurts to bring informative material that was not contained in the written application. If, for example, the written application only provided you with limited space to list and discuss your extracurricular activities, bring expanded listings and descriptions to leave with the interviewer.

GUERRILLA TACTIC #16

Leave sample work with interviewers to highlight your talents and remind them to consider you when it's time to award the money.

9. **Reread and review your written application.** Given the time it takes to evaluate scholarship candidates, your interview may take place weeks or months after you have

submitted the written application. Because of this, it's important to refresh your memory about everything that was contained in the written form. During interviews, judges often ask you specific questions about things you've included on the form. So review your application, and be prepared to talk intelligently about any information you have submitted.

THE BIG DAY

As the old adage (and shampoo tagline) goes, "You never get a second chance to make a first impression."

It's the morning of the big interview. To do your best, you will want everything to be in order the moment you walk into the interview room. To ensure this result, employ the following suggestions:

1. Dress for success. Make an impression on the judges by wearing a lime green jumpsuit. . . just kidding. In general, you should make a bold statement with what you say, *not* with how you dress. Men should wear either a business suit or else a dress shirt, nice sports coat, and tie. For women, go with a dress, pants suit, or dressy skirt/pants and blouse.

2. Avoid stress. Before your interview, stay away from people or activities that easily irritate you.

3. Pack grooming supplies. Pack a hair brush, makeup, deodorant, mouthwash, or any other last-minute supplies you may need.

4. Refresh your memory. An hour or so before your interview, review your key points, anecdotes, and practice questions and answers.

5. Arrive at least 15 minutes early. It's always better to arrive early and get settled. In addition, the interviewers could be ahead of schedule, and you don't want to make them wait. If you're unfamiliar with the location of the interview, make sure that you know how to get there ahead of time.

THE MAIN EVENT

Finally, it's time for the main event: the interview itself. The following tips are a few tricks of the trade scholarship winners have employed to win interviewers over to their corner. Practice these techniques in your mock interviews until they are second nature.

1. Use a firm handshake and make eye contact. It's old fashioned, but it still works. Make a mental note of the interviewer's name when he or she tells it to you. Burn it into your brain cells.

2. Listen. No one likes to be ignored. Look attentive when the interviewer is talking to you—even if he's reciting the history of broccoli. Resist the temptation to "tune-out" the interviewer in preparation for what you want to say next. Failing to show attentive listening is like communicating to interviewers that they don't matter. Remember—attentive listening is one of the highest compliments we can pay anyone. Show genuine interest in what the interviewer is saying, and you'll create a strong impression.

3. Don't perform a monologue. It's easy in an interview to start reciting your opinions and accomplishments to the point that the interviewer doesn't get a word in edgewise. Resist the urge to start talking and never stop. Also be careful of not getting lost in the minutia of every activity so that you wind up giving a ten-minute discourse on all the finer points of your city dump cleanup project.

To the extent that you can, strive to create a two-way dialogue. If your interviewer comments on something you say by talking about his or her own experiences and background, ask a follow-up question. Most people enjoy talking about themselves, and will appreciate the attention.

4. Find common ground. Each interviewer will respond to your various activities, experiences, credentials, and goals differently. This is understandable. Interviewers are viewing *your* life from the perspective of their own. For this

---

If you are interviewed by a panel of judges (two or more people), be sure to make eye contact with and divide your attention between each interviewer—even if only one does most of the talking.

"No one likes to interview someone who looks really uncomfortable. So you want to look calm and relaxed and make the interviewer feel at ease."

Mattias Geise
National Scholarship Winner

PLAY IT COOL:
*Scholarship interviews
need not be an intimi-
dating, frightening,
or nerve-wracking
experience. Just
pretend that you're
sitting in the comfort
of your own living
room, having a pleas-
ant conversation with
someone who happens
to be really interested
in your life.*

*It's natural to second-
guess yourself after an
interview. But don't
beat yourself up over
something you didn't
say or do. You did your
best at the time, and
that's what counts.
Besides, you probably
did much better than
you think.*

reason, observe when interviewers are especially interested in something you say, and talk about it in more depth; don't forget to ask them questions too.

If you're talking about how much you love painting, for instance, and the interviewer comments, "Oh, I enjoy painting as well," seize the opportunity to ask him a question such as "What type of painting do you do?" I know of one scholarship applicant who spent nearly an entire interview conversing with the interviewer about their shared interest in volleyball. He won the scholarship.

5. Make your points. . . but don't force them. Try to communicate the points and anecdotes you prepared by working them into your answers. But if you aren't asked about something you wanted to talk about, don't attempt to force it

At the end of an interview, express your thanks and repeat the interviewer's name. To that person, his or her name is the sweetest sound in the world.

into the conversation so as to completely digress from the interviewer's questions.

6. Leave your annoying habits at home. We all have our share of annoying habits, but in an interview you want to look mature and composed. Avoid tapping your foot, shaking your leg, or any type of fidgeting. Try to cut down on using "um," "like," and "you know" when you talk.

7. Be enthusiastic, smile, and have fun. During the interview, try to be enthusiastic and cheerful (remember passion & enthusiasm comprise one of the Ten Golden Virtues). Also, don't be afraid to show off your pearly whites. A smile puts the interviewer at ease, dissipates the tension inside of you, and conveys confidence. Besides, interviews should be fun. If you've practiced enough, all of the other points I've mentioned should already be second nature to you, and you'll be able to relax and go with the flow.

If possible, send your interviewers handwritten thank-you notes to express your gratitude for their time.

CHAPTER 11 SUMMARY

■ **Early Preparation:** Find out what you can about the person or people who will be interviewing you. Prepare some key points and anecdotes to illustrate those points. Anticipate potential interview questions, and jot down notes about how to answer them.

Practice your responses by yourself, with a friend, or in front of a video camera. Brainstorm some questions to ask your interviewer. Prepare samples of your work to bring to the interview, and re-read your written application.

■ **Before the Interview:** Dress appropriately for the occasion. Avoid stressful activities before the interview, and bring needed grooming supplies. Review key points, anecdotes, and practice questions. Arrive at the interview early to allow for some time to get settled.

■ **Face to Face:** Upon meeting the interviewer, give a firm handshake and make eye contact. Be attentive when the interviewer talks and listen carefully. Refrain from talking endlessly; give the interviewer a chance to comment on what you say. Seek to find common ground and shared experiences with the interviewer. Make your prepared points and anecdotes when appropriate, but don't force the issue.

Act mature and composed, and leave your annoying habits at home. Remember to be enthusiastic, smile frequently, and enjoy the experience.

Being Smart About Your Studies

Intermission

For most of this book, we've treated the grades on your transcript as being set in stone—a factor to be emphasized if your grades are strong, or downplayed otherwise. In this *Intermission*, however, I'll illustrate some simple principles and powerful techniques that can dramatically raise your grade point average. If you already receive good grades, these methods will help you optimize your learning and minimize the time it takes to maintain these grades.

Of course, the subject of how to do better in school could be a separate book in its own right. So I've decided to focus on a few areas that can provide you with the most "bang for your buck"—simple, painless methods that can help you raise your performance in classes right away. In the following section, I describe five important actions to enhance your performance in school.

Action #1: Ask Questions and Question Everything

In the traditional school format, material is spoon-fed to you in different forms—including lectures, textbooks, and class assignments. But the problem with this approach is that *no one else but you knows how you learn best.* And since the material probably isn't tailored to your optimal learning style, it's likely to be presented in a way that isn't right for you.

Asking questions, however, leads to ownership of the subject matter. Questions allow you to translate the material into a framework that fits your style of learning. Not only does this help you understand the material better, but it improves your ability to recall information. On many occasions, I've remembered an important concept during an exam by thinking back to the questions I asked when trying to learn it.

Asking questions doesn't just mean raising your hand in class. Even more important is developing an internal dialogue with the material you're studying. This dialogue means that you are continually questioning everything you read, and asking questions *even when you think you understand the material.* Especially powerful is the "what if" question. With this type of questioning, you test the margins of your understanding by applying your knowledge to a hypothetical situation. For instance, if you are studying economics (my college major) you might ask yourself, "What would happen to a market economy if supply didn't equal demand?" I've found that by constantly feeding myself these "what if" questions, I am able to predict and prepare for questions that actually end up on the exam.

Remember, the point of a question is *not* simply to answer it, but to get you to think. In fact, *knowing what questions to ask is more important than knowing the answers.*

Action #2: Focus on the Most Important Material

It's important to recognize that not everything you are asked to read or do is of equal importance. Some assignments will contain meaty information requiring several read-throughs to marinate the concepts in your mind. Other assignments may only necessitate a quick skim-read to pick out key themes.

Make a good impression on your teacher in the first few weeks of a class. Once you establish a reputation for good work, this can positively impact how your later assignments are graded.

"It's what you learn after you know it all that counts."

John Wooden

Try to do the assigned reading ahead of time. But if you haven't gotten around to it, try the following tactic: As class begins, take the first opportunity to raise your hand and say something. Teachers are eager to have multiple students participate in class, and if you speak up early on, you'll lessen the chance of being called on later.

Out of all of the Actions, this one took me the longest to perfect. If I wasn't doing well in a class, I'd try to sit down and go line by line through all the material. But by taking this approach, I would end up spending *too much* time on things that were not particularly important, and *too little* time on the really critical subject matter. As a result, even though I had put in a lot of extra effort, I didn't see any substantial improvement in my school performance.

Then, by learning to devote adequate time to the most important areas, I witnessed impressive results. By focusing my energy on the most important aspects of a course, I avoided getting bogged down in the minutia. So how do you figure out what is the most important material? Well, that's where Actions 3 & 4 come into play.

Action #3: Put Yourself in the Teacher's Shoes

Everything that's assigned in a class is assigned to students for a reason. Clever students recognize this and approach each assignment as if they themselves were teaching the class. Why was this reading passage assigned? What's the big picture here? How does this fit in with the rest of the course? These are the questions that clever students ask themselves. By doing this, they are able to identify which materials and assignments are the most important to review and study, and which ones they can breeze through.

If you're unsure about the answer to a test question, try asking the teacher to clarify the question or tell you about the kind of answer expected. Sometimes having a teacher rephrase a question is enough to jog your memory. Teachers often provide additional clues if you pay close attention.

Thinking from the teacher's perspective is also a useful technique to employ when you're taking a test. I've often found that even though I don't know the answer to a test question, by thinking about the possible concepts that the teacher must be trying to test, I can narrow down the possibilities until I figure out what the teacher is trying to get at.

Because grades are important, it's also worthwhile to get to know the personal likes, dislikes, and biases of your teacher. Use quizzes and little assignments to test out grading standards. Ascertain how much detail is required to get full credit on a question, so that you can estimate the amount of time you'll need to spend on a given answer before moving on.

Action #4: Procure Course Overview Materials

In every course, there is a set of concepts and skills that students are supposed to master. Unfortunately, while we're in the midst of learning the material, we often don't have a good sense of the kind of things we'll be tested on at the conclusion of the course. If only we could take the course *twice*, then the second time around we'd already know which are the key concepts and skills to learn.

So how can we get a feel for where the course is headed without actually repeating the course? Try a technique that clever students have used. Simply obtain unit and final exams from prior terms that the course has been offered—preferably when it was still being taught by the same teacher. This way, as you're learning the material, you'll have a good idea about how you'll eventually be tested upon it. You can obtain old exams from students who have already taken the class, or else can request them from your teacher directly. At some schools (such as Harvard), old exams are filed away in student-accessible binders or posted online.

Don't wait until the night before the final exam to do this. It would defeat the whole purpose. By having these exam references at the *beginning* of a course, you can figure out as you go along which is the critical material you must learn. In addition, I've often found that many teachers don't write entirely new exams from prior years. Because of this, you may have already prepared for specific questions (with only minor changes) that appear on your current exams.

Teachers may modify a course from year to year, so keep in mind that tests from prior years should only be used as study guides— not as a substitute for paying attention in class.

Action #5: Be Resourceful

Sometimes you'll have to deal with a difficult teacher, a boring textbook, or a confusing assignment. But it's still up to you to find resourceful ways to learn the material.

So if your assigned textbook "doesn't make the grade," stop by a library or bookstore to pick up a supplementary book or two. If your teacher isn't the easiest to understand, organize a study group (making sure to invite students who seem to know what they're doing). To get a slightly different perspective on the material, try trading notes with classmates.

"I never let schooling interfere with my education."

Mark Twain

PART V

When the
Buzzer
Sounds

Parting Shots

In this final chapter, I discuss some tips for managing your scholarship dollars, describe a little-used technique for reducing your tuition bill, and conclude with some thoughts on the game we've played.

CHAPTER CONTENTS

- Tracking your scholarship winnings
- Tuition reductions through AP testing
- What we've learned

THE HOME STRETCH

Well, you've made it! You now know the hidden rules, proven strategies, insider secrets, and guerrilla tactics of winning the scholarship game. If you've internalized the information in this book and have invested the necessary time and energy into applying these principles, I'd wager that you've already started winning the big bucks, or are well on your way to staking your scholarship claim. Before we call this a done deal, however, there are a few issues to consider in the game's aftermath. In this chapter, I'll describe some key tips for managing your winnings, a powerful method for reducing your tuition bill, as well as reflect on what winning scholarships is *really* about.

KEEPING TRACK OF YOUR WINNINGS

When you get that congratulatory letter or phone call informing you of your latest scholarship triumph, I suggest doing one of three things: scream at the top of your lungs, scarf down a mountainous ice cream sundae, or run 3.6 miles. . . buck naked. Once you've gotten that out of your system, you can then begin to ponder the nitty-gritty details of how you actually get paid your scholarship money. (**Hint:** Don't expect a brightly-painted sweepstakes van to roll up to your door with a big fat check.)

Scholarship Payment Plans

Through the process of managing my own scholarship funds, I've encountered several distinct variations of scholarship payment plans. To give you an idea of what to expect, I've described them below:

- a one-time, lump-sum payment to you
- a one-time, lump-sum payment to your school
- term-by-term fixed payments to you
- unscheduled variable-sum payments to you
- unscheduled variable-sum payments to your school

To make all of this even more confusing, the sponsors and administrators of scholarship awards often specify limited time frames in which you must use the funds. Common variations of these time frame limitations include:

These variations in payment plans arise, in part, because the scholarship sponsors and administrators of the funds have standardized logistical systems for transferring money, disbursement it to the student, and accounting for all of these transactions.

- 4 years from time of your high school graduation
- 4 years from time of your first college enrollment
- 6 years from time of your high school graduation
- 12 years from time you receive the award

Finally, we should note that some scholarships may be restricted for use at two- and four-year colleges, while others allow funds to also be used at trade and technical schools and for the pursuit of graduate-level studies.

In nutshell, you want to clearly understand who gets paid the scholarship check (you or your college), how this payment is made (in one big lump or in multiple installments), when you must use the funds (in 4 years or a longer time frame), and what schooling it covers (two- and four-year colleges, trade and technical schools, or graduate school).

Staying Flexible

As pointed out earlier in the book, the government doesn't tax scholarship money you spend on tuition, or on bona fide school-related books and fees. Expenses like room and board, however, are taxable.

The best scholarship payment plans provide you with choice, and offer maximum flexibility in each of the above key areas. Such flexibility is important because it enables you to choose payment schedules that take into account changes in your family's income, college-funded financial aid allotments, and any potential tax consequences. The best payment plans I've encountered allow you to draw upon the scholarship money in any size chunks you wish, whenever you so choose.

Your Friendly Scholarship Administrator

The scholarship administrator is the person who is in charge of handling the logistics of paying out your scholarship money. I've found it very helpful to start a dialogue with the administrator for each scholarship, and to discuss payment options and procedures with these individuals.

First, you want to be aware up-front of any possible limitations, requirements, or restrictions on receiving the funds. For instance, some scholarships require that you submit an annual proof of registration form, official transcript, or fund request letter. Other scholarships, such as the Coca-Cola Scholars program, require that you submit a brief statement of your major activities and projects. Some of the more academically-focused scholarships require that you maintain a minimum grade point average of, say, 2.5.

Second, you want to be aware of the procedure for getting funds transferred to you. For scholarships administered by an organization different than the one putting up the money, the funds aren't just sitting in an account waiting for you. The administrator has to request funds from the sponsor, and there is often a rigid procedure for doing so. This becomes important when you need scholarship payments immediately (often so that you can register for classes), but it takes weeks for the money transfers to be processed.

Most importantly, the scholarship administrator often has the power to make special exceptions to payment rules to meet your needs. For instance, several scholarship administrators allowed me to determine withdrawal amounts, come up with my own payment schedule, and defer the balance of my winnings until later years—even though the official regulations didn't specifically permit this. In other instances, when I missed request deadlines or forget to submit required documentation, these administrators helped me figure out a way around the red tape. Starting a friendly dialogue with your scholarship administrator is thus very advantageous, and puts a powerful ally in your corner.

Tracking the Details

If you don't have time to take care of all of these details, having a parent who can help you manage your winnings is very useful.

My parents and I discovered that the more scholarships and money I won, the more we had to pay attention to all the different requirements and compliance forms for each organization administering the funds. Keeping all of this straight will also be important for institutional financial aid and tax considerations that may be pertinent to your situation.

To stay organized, the first thing you'll want to do is to make a list of everything you've won, and then set up a summary chart of key information. On this chart, you will want to include:

See the Reader's Resource Room on the winscholarships.com *Web site for a ready-to-go form you can use.*

- the name of the scholarship
- the administrator's name & contact information
- the total amount of award
- the payment schedule
- the expiration date for final payout
- any reporting and maintenance requirements
- the allowed use of funds

Pay special attention to the reporting and maintenance requirements portion of the chart. This information tells you about how frequently you must communicate with scholarship administrators (each term, annually, etc.), and what paperwork you must submit before receiving your money. If you neglect these simple tasks, you might not be able to get your scholarship money when you need it.

Some Additional Tips

I've learned from experience the importance of making sure that your scholarship checks actually do make it to your school's billing office *and* get entered into your account. In some cases, checks sent directly to your school's billing office might just sit there without anyone contacting you, waiting for you to come in and sign your name, endorsing them over to the school. There might also be cases where a scholarship administrator has dropped the ball, and has not sent out your check to your school when you requested it. So in the end, it's really going to be your responsibility of tracking the money from point A to point B.

If you are planning to take time off from college, you will need to check with each scholarship administrator to inquire about the usage rules and make special provisions if possible. If you're involved in a study-abroad program, for instance, some administrators will allow you to forward the checks to the foreign school. In other cases, you're allowed to postpone payment until you enroll again (if, for example, you're taking time off to pursue an internship opportunity). All of this depends on the rules and flexibility of each scholarship's payout plan.

SLASHING YOUR COLLEGE COSTS

Some colleges may also offer tuition reduction possibilities for students who pass International Baccalaureate (IB) exams.

The AP test program is run by The College Board. Although substantial fees are charged to take the exams, these are minor expenses compared to the potential savings.

One of the most underutilized methods for reducing the cost of college is the Advanced Placement (AP) testing program. Many students have encountered the term "AP" somewhere along their high school careers, but relatively few recognize the dramatic savings that can be realized by students who know how to employ the potential benefits of the program. What are these benefits? Quite simply, for achieving passing scores on a certain (not too demanding) number of tests, most colleges will grant you up to one year's worth of college credit—thereby saving you 25 percent off the total cost of your four-year college education!

Here's the basics of how AP testing works. Throughout the country, in May of each year, students can take special subject exams (after pre-registering and paying the fees). These exams are given in a wide variety of subjects including American history, economics, physics, biology, government, calculus, chemistry, music theory, computer science, and psychology. The tests are supposed to be equivalent to introductory college-level courses, but in actuality, passing many of these tests is considerably easier. A large percentage of U.S. high schools offer AP classes that prepare you to take these exams.

Colleges typically grant credit for passing individual AP tests, and considerably more credit for passing several of them. The latter is where the dramatic college savings can occur. At most colleges, if you achieve solid scores on a specified number of AP tests, you're granted sophomore standing! This means that when you first set foot on campus to register for classes, you already have the credits of a sophomore. Because you can graduate in three academic years (six semesters), the cost of your college diploma is reduced by one-fourth!

If you've heard that AP classes are only for "brainiacs" you're mistaken. Any student willing to invest the time and energy into learning the material, can score well on them.

In addition, the standard set by most colleges to receive one year's worth of credit is not particularly tough. At Harvard, where I applied this strategy, students are granted one year's worth of credit if they receive scores of 4 or 5 (passing is 3 on a 5-point scale) on only four AP exams. In the scheme of things, achieving those scores on four AP exams is not particularly tough if you're willing to put in the effort to prepare for them. For instance, if you take two AP exams your junior year in high school and two more your senior year—a manageable number for any student—you've already made it.

So if you're going to be in high school taking classes anyway, why not use the opportunity to take AP classes that prepare you to take AP tests that can ultimately save you a ton of money. Because these classes are more demanding that your average high school course, you may want to arrange your schedule or pick classes so that you can devote the majority of your homework time to these courses. Even if your high school doesn't offer AP classes, you still have several options. Talk to your principal about arranging to take or sit in on AP classes at other schools in your area. Some students (including yours truly) have studied for these exams on their own by using a variety of special "test-prep" books available in libraries and bookstores.

As a side benefit, college admissions officers and scholarship judges alike look very favorably on applicant transcripts that are sprinkled with these more-challenging classes.

I should also note that just because you use AP tests to gain sophomore standing, *doesn't* mean that you have to graduate in three years. Many students choose to spread out their three academic years over four calendar years so that they graduate with their regular class (in fact, that's what I did). This is an especially good strategy if you're interested in taking a term or two off to study abroad, travel, work, take an internship, or conduct thesis research. By starting with sophomore standing, you can take a year off from classwork, not receive course credit for that year, and still graduate with your class. Some students who choose to stay in the area during their time off, even live on campus—allowing them to partake in college life without having to go to classes. Furthermore, most colleges give you the option of staying for a fourth academic year if you so choose.

Of course, if you choose to work for that year off, the money earned can go a long way to paying for the rest of your education.

For all of these reasons, AP testing is a powerful way to potentially slash 25 percent off the total cost of attending college. In this way, using AP tests to gain a year of credit is like winning a scholarship that provides for an entire year of college credit. For students attending some of the country's most expensive private colleges, this can mean more than $30,000 in savings!

WHAT WE'VE LEARNED

Well, every book has to come to an end. And I suppose the best books do this sooner rather than later. So before I've worn out my welcome, I'd just like to offer a few reflections on what playing the scholarship game is *really* all about.

Although the need for money has motivated our quest, the scholarship game is not solely about winning money for college. The game is also about setting a goal, and being willing to do what it takes to reach it. It's about not letting current financial circumstances dictate our destinies. It's about accepting risk and having faith: the risk of putting yourself on the line and the faith that comes with believing in yourself.

To succeed in this game, we've had to expand our skills, talents, and abilities. We've had to think strategically. We've had to learn how to effectively promote ourselves. We've had to become more well-rounded. We've even had to reflect on our own lives, and in the midst of the chaos, try to paint vivid portraits of who we really are.

And therein lies the beauty of it all: To win the scholarship money, we've had to become *worthy* of winning it. And win or lose, as corny as it may sound, this may be the grandest prize of all.

In conclusion, I'd just like to thank you for sticking it out with me to the end. Best of luck with your scholarship quest, and I hope that all of your educational dreams come true. Until the next time...

I'd love to hear from you. . .

How did your scholarship quest turn out? Was this book helpful to you? Any suggestions for future editions? Got any interesting scholarship stories and tips to share with others? Just want to say hello?

In case I haven't already made it abundantly clear, I want to hear from you! So don't leave me hanging by my inbox and mailbox with nothing to do. When you get a free moment, jot me a quick note. I promise I'll do my best to write back just as soon as I can.

I might even take some of your comments and include them in future editions of this book, or post them on the book's companion Web pages. (If you don't want me to include your name, just say so.)

The preferred way to contact me is via e-mail at:

benkaplan@winscholarships.com

Or, if you're so inclined, you can snail mail me at:

Benjamin Kaplan
c/o Waggle Dancer Books
P.O. Box 860
Gleneden Beach, OR 97388

I look forward to hearing from you!

One more thing. . .

I also conduct lectures, seminars, and workshops; write articles for various publications; and consult with organizations desiring to set up scholarship programs. If you'd like to discuss any of this with me, please contact me at the addresses listed above.

APPENDIX A

Directory of Scholarships

A selection of scholarship contests excerpted from *The Scholarship Sleuth*™

ABOUT THE DIRECTORY

This directory of scholarships features profiles of several dozen scholarship contests. These profiles have been excerpted from *The Scholarship Sleuth*—my comprehensive directory of top scholarship opportunities (also available from Waggle Dancer Books).

Each listing includes the amount of scholarship money available; a description of entry requirements, judging criteria, application components, and deadlines; and detailed contact information (including addresses of contest Web sites if available). In a special "Sleuth Says" section, I offer advice and insider tips derived from my own experiences and from interviews with contest administrators and past winners of the scholarship. Start by browsing each page of the directory, paying special attention to the eligibility rules listed under the header "Target Recipient."

As contact information and entry deadlines for each scholarship contest can change, be sure to regularly visit the Reader's Resource Room at **winscholarships.com** for the latest directory updates. If you're interested in obtaining a copy of the complete *Scholarship Sleuth* directory, you can do so at the publisher's Internet site located at **waggledancer.com** on the World Wide Web.

ALL-USA ACADEMIC TEAMS

Target Recipient

USA-Today sponsors separate competitions for high school and college students. The *All-USA High School Academic Team* competition is open to high school students who are nominated by principals or teachers at U.S. high schools. *The All-USA College Academic Team* competition is open to college students at any accredited 4-year institution in the U.S. who are nominated by college presidents or faculty members.

Money Matters

20 first-team winners in both the high school and college competitions receive $2,500 scholarships. Biographies of the winners are published in *USA-Today*.

Entry Requirements

Nominees write a 250-word essay describing their most outstanding intellectual endeavor. The independent endeavor can be in art, music, literature, poetry, scientific or scholarly research, history, community service, or public affairs. The nominating teacher/professor includes a 250-word description of why the intellectual endeavor is outstanding. Applicants also submit a written application that includes a transcript, lists of school and community activities, standardized test scores, and up to three supporting letters of recommendation. Judging is based on a nominee's academic record, creativity, leadership, and independent scholarly or artistic work.

Application Deadlines
Early February (high school)
Early November (college)

Contact Information
USA Today
c/o Carol Skalski
1000 Wilson Boulevard, 22nd Fl.
Arlington, VA 22229

Phone: (703) 276-5890

Sleuth Says:

The *high school* contest is a high-powered academic competition in which most winners have near-perfect SAT scores and stellar grades. As for the winners' most outstanding intellectual endeavors, independent research projects related to math and science tend to dominate. The smattering of winners without impeccable academic credentials typically have some special project or unusual talent going for them.

The *college* competition appears less focused on pure academic achievement than its high school counterpart. The diverse group of winners come from a wide variety of colleges spread across the country. The common thread often found among winning students is a devotion to community service or social action.

AMERICAN LEGION ORATORICAL CONTEST

Target Recipient

Contestants must be in grades 9 through 12 and under the age of 20. They must also be citizens or lawful permanent residents of the United States.

Money Matters

The top three national winners receive $18,000, $16,000, and $14,000 college scholarships, respectively. Six students who advance to the second round of the national competition receive $3,000 scholarships. 54 state winners receive $1,500 scholarships. In addition to the national awards, several hundred scholarships are awarded at the local level.

Entry Requirements

Orations are delivered live to a panel of five judges at each stage of the competition. The contest is composed of two speeches: the prepared oration (8-10 minutes) and the assigned discourse (3-5 minutes). The subject to be used for the prepared oration must be on "some phase of the Constitution of the United States which will give emphasis to the attendant duties and obligations of a citizen to our government." The assigned discourse is a speech concerning a specific passage of the Constitution, assigned by contest administrators. Contestants must be prepared to speak on any one of four assigned passages (which vary from year to year).

Application Deadline

Early December
(varies on the local level)

Contact Information

The Americanism and Children & Youth Division
The American Legion
P.O. Box 1055
Indianapolis, IN 46206

Phone: (317) 630-1249
Fax: (317) 630-1223
E-mail: mbuss@legion.org
Web site: www.legion.org/orator.htm

Note: Interested students should also contact their local American Legion post.

Sleuth Says:

You don't have to be Sherlock Holmes to realize that the group putting on this scholarship contest has strong feelings about patriotism and the brilliance of the U.S. Constitution. In recent years, winners have spoken about the importance of the right to vote, the Constitution as a nurturing force for our nation, and how exercising our freedom of speech actually protects our Constitution. One common approach among winners is to open with imagery taken from a historical event or context.

AMERICA'S JUNIOR MISS

Target Recipient

High school senior girls are eligible if they are U.S. citizens and have never been married. (Prospective contestants are advised to contact their state's program during the summer between their sophomore and junior years or as soon into the junior year as possible. Some programs on the local level may occur during junior year).

Money Matters

At the local and state levels, the program awards more than $4.9 million in scholarships and other awards each year. At the national level, students compete for $115,000 in scholarship money. The student selected as America's Junior Miss receives a $40,000 scholarship. The first and second runners-up receive $15,000 and $10,000, respectively. In addition, monetary awards totaling $50,000 are given to leading scorers in each of several events (such as $5,000 for Scholastic Achievement).

Entry Requirements

The contest is a pageant of sorts (although there is no swimsuit competition). Selection is based on judges' interview (25 percent), creative and performing arts (25 percent), scholastic achievement (20 percent), presence and composure (15 percent), and fitness (15 percent). Behind-the-scenes screenings are used to evaluate scholastic achievement and to conduct the judges' interviews. The other three events are scored on stage.

Application Deadline

Varies at the local level
(generally in the fall)

Contact Information

America's Junior Miss
P.O. Box 2786
Mobile, AL 36652-2786

Phone: (334) 438-3621
E-mail: ajmiss@aol.com
Web site: www.ajm.org

Note: Contact information for programs in your state can be found at the Web address listed above.

Sleuth Says:

To get an idea of how the contest works, watch the national competition on the TNN country cable channel in early July. This competition tries hard to be much more than a beauty pageant. Contestants who reach the national level generally have strong academic credentials (in recent years the 50 state winners have averaged a GPA of 3.8 on a 4.0 scale).

Unlike some traditional beauty pageants, interviews are conducted entirely behind-the-scenes. It's important to anticipate and prepare for potential questions (see Chapter 11) so as to avoid the standard pageant answer in which you superficially proclaim your love of world peace or some other lofty ideal.

ARTS RECOGNITION & TALENT SEARCH (ARTS)

Target Recipient

Applicants enrolled in high school must be graduating seniors. Applicants not enrolled in school must be 17-18 years old (as of 12/1). Entrants must be U.S. citizens or permanent residents (unless applying in jazz).

Money Matters

Nearly $300,000 in cash awards have been earmarked for ARTS applicants whose work has been judged outstanding. 125 finalists (20 in dance, 20 in music, 5 in jazz music, 10 in voice, 10 in photography, 25 in visual arts, and 20 in writing) receive cash awards of $3,000, $1,500, $1,000, or $500. An unlimited number of $100 honorable mention awards are also granted.

Entry Requirements

Applicants compete in eight artistic disciplines: dance, music, jazz music, photography, theater, the visual arts, voice, and writing. Entry requirements vary with each discipline, but generally involve the submission of videotapes, audio tapes, portfolios, or other sample work. 125 finalists perform final auditions live in Miami (all expenses are covered by the NFAA). Students are permitted to apply in multiple disciplines, but only one financial award will be given to any individual. Entry requires a substantial application fee ($25 per discipline for early registration, $35 otherwise), but a limited number of fee waivers are available.

Application Deadline

Early June (early registration)
Early October (final registration)

Contact Information

National Foundation for
Advancement in the Arts (NFAA)
800 Brickell Avenue, Suite 500
Miami, FL 33131

Phone: (800) 970-ARTS
  or (305) 377-1147
Fax: (305) 377-1149
E-mail: nfaa@nfaa.org
Web site: www.nfaa.org/arts.html

Sleuth Says:

Even if your artistic work doesn't exactly fit an entry category, don't let that deter your from applying. In this contest, judges tend to take a much broader view of an artistic category than you might initially think. The visual arts discipline, for instance, includes such fields as costume design, film and video production, and jewelry making. The writing discipline not only includes fiction writing and poetry, but also expository writing, plays, and movie scripts.

Judging is conducted by professionals in each discipline— two panels of high-powered leaders in an applicant's field. To receive an award, you generally have to be in the top 5 percent of the applicant pool.

AYN RAND ESSAY CONTESTS

Target Recipient

The Ayn Rand Institute sponsors three separate essay writing contests: one for 9th and 10th graders, one for 11th and 12th graders, and one for business undergraduate and graduate students.

Money Matters

The 9th and 10th grade contest awards one first prize ($1,000), 10 second prizes ($200 each), and 20 third prizes ($100 each). The 11th and 12th grade contest awards one first prize ($10,000), 5 second prizes ($2,000 each), and 10 third prizes ($1,000 each). Undergraduate business students are awarded one first prize ($5,000), one second prize ($3,000), and one third prize ($1,000). Graduate business students compete for one first prize ($7,500), one second prize ($5,000), and one third prize ($2,500). All awards are cash.

Entry Requirements

9th and 10th graders write an essay (600-1200 words) on Ayn Rand's novelette *Anthem*. 11th and 12th graders write an essay (800-1600 words) on Ayn Rand's *The Fountainhead*. Business undergraduates and graduates write an essay on Ayn Rand's *Atlas Shrugged*. Essays are judged on the basis of clear writing, logical organization, and the outstanding grasp of philosophic meaning. Entrants choose to answer one of several questions.

Application Deadlines

Mid February (undergrad & grad),
Early to Mid April (high school)

Contact Information

9th & 10th grade contest:
Anthem Essay Contest, Dept. W
The Ayn Rand Institute
P.O. Box 6099
Inglewood, CA 90312

11th & 12th grade contest:
Fountainhead Essay Contest,
    Dept. W
The Ayn Rand Institute
P.O. Box 6004
Inglewood, CA 90312

Undergrad & grad contest:
Atlas Shrugged Contest,
    Dept. W
The Ayn Rand Institute
4640 Admiralty Way, Suite 406
Marina del Rey, CA 90292

Phone: (310) 306-9232
E-mail: essay@aynrand.org
Web site: www.aynrand.org/
    contests/index.html

Sleuth Says:

This type of contest is so heavily identified with the ideas of its sponsor, that it makes good strategic sense to visit the sponsor's Web site to learn all about "objectivism." Having your essay inadvertently oppose any of the tenets of this philosophy is probably not a wise move.

BMI STUDENT COMPOSER AWARDS

Target Recipient

The contest is open to applicants under 26 years of age (as of 12/31) who are citizens or permanent residents of Western Hemisphere nations.

Money Matters

Broadcast Music, Inc. (BMI) awards nine cash awards ($500-$3,000) totaling $20,000 (the number and amount varies each year).

Entry Requirements

Contestants submit an original musical composition in manuscript form. Exceptions may be made for electronic music or other works that cannot be adequately presented in score. (Such works can be submitted on reel-to-reel tape or cassettes.) Contest rules do not specify any restrictions regarding musical style, instrumentation, or length of the manuscript. Jointly written compositions may also be submitted if all composers meet the eligibility criteria. Each submission is reviewed by a panel of at least three judges, with the identity of each contestant kept anonymous. Selection of winners is based upon formal content of the composition; melodic, harmonic, and rhythmic idioms; instrumentation and orchestration; and the age of the composer. When two compositions are judged to be of equal merit, but there is an age difference between composers, preference will be given to the younger contestant.

Contact Information

Ralph N. Jackson
BMI Awards to Student
   Composers
Broadcast Music, Inc.
320 West 57th Street
New York, NY 10019

Phone: (212) 586-2000
Web site: www.bmi.com

Sleuth Says:

In recent contests, more than 400 young people have submitted compositions. While a substantial number of winners study at music conservatories, other winners study privately. Above all, judges are looking for evidence of genuine creative talent. An additional benefit of the BMI competition is the program's assistance in helping the winners secure commercial publication and recording of their work. Winners of these awards tend to be very serious and well-trained musicians—so it's probably safe to say that a new cover of "Chopsticks" just won't cut it. . .

Application Deadline

Mid February

COCA-COLA SCHOLARS PROGRAM

Target Recipient

Applicants must be high school seniors who are U.S. citizens.

Money Matters

The Coca-Cola Scholars Foundations grants 50 four-year $20,000 scholarships and 200 four-year $4,000 scholarships.

Entry Requirements

The selection process has three phases. First, students submit a "Scantron" electronic questionnaire in which they bubble-in answers to questions that assess both the quantity and quality of their school and community involvement, as well as their academic and employment records. Next, 1,500 to 2,500 semifinalists are sent an expanded application in mid-December that requires detailed biographical data, an essay, a school transcript, and personal recommendations (due by early February). Students are asked to comment on books or articles they have read, their involvement in community leadership, their most remarkable accomplishment, and their major social concerns. Finally, 250 finalists attend the National Competition in Atlanta, Georgia, and participate in an interview with a panel of judges. Applicants only compete with others from their geographic region, with each region awarded a specified quota of scholarships (based on demographics and participation of regional bottlers).

Application Deadline

Late October

Contact Information

Coca-Cola Scholars Foundation
P.O. Box 442
Atlanta, GA 30301-0442

Phone: (800) 306-COKE
  or (404) 733-5420
Fax: (404) 733-5439
E-mail: scholars@coca-cola.com
Web site:
www.thecoca-colacompany.com/
  scholars/index.html

Note: Applications are available from school guidance counselors.

Sleuth Says:

Coca-Cola places an extremely strong emphasis on selecting a group of winners that come from diverse economic, ethnic, and occupational backgrounds. Winners in this competition typically end up attending a wide variety of colleges and universities—not just the most competitive or prestigious ones. Compared to other big national programs in which academic achievement is considered, Coca-Cola seems to place much less emphasis on the numbers game. In fact, many winners of this scholarship have had less-than-stellar GPAs and SAT scores.

DISCOVER CARD TRIBUTE AWARDS

Target Recipient

Entrants must be high school juniors with at least a 2.75 cumulative grade point average for the previous two academic years (9th and 10th grade). Applicants must also be enrolled in a public or registered private school in the U.S. or U.S. territories, or be a U.S. citizen enrolled in an American school abroad.

Money Matters

The Tribute Award program makes available more than 470 awards annually. On the national level, the program awards three $20,000 gold awards, three $15,000 silver awards, and three $10,000 bronze awards. In each state, the program awards three $2,500 gold awards, three $1,750 silver awards, and three $1,250 bronze awards. Each state gold winner is automatically considered for national awards. Selected states also award $1,000 merit awards.

Entry Requirements

The Tribute Awards are based upon the idea that "not every student's achievements can be measured in grade points alone." Entrants must demonstrate accomplishments in four out of five categories: special talents, leadership, obstacles overcome, community service, and unique endeavors. Students address these categories in a two-page criteria statement. Students also submit a 200-word description of career goals, three letters of recommendation, and a school transcript.

Application Deadline

Mid January

Contact Information

Discover Card Tribute Awards
c/o American Association of
   School Administrators
P.O. Box 9338
Arlington, VA 22219

Phone: (703) 875-0708
Web site: www.aasa.org/
   discover.htm

Sleuth Says:

One thing they don't tell you on the application is that based on your specified career choice, you are automatically grouped into one of three judging categories: (1) Trade & Technical studies, (2) Arts & Humanities studies, and (3) Science, Business & Technical studies. Because you are only judged against applicants in your category, if you are unsure about your career choice, pick one in a category where you are most competitive.

Looking at recent winners, a high proportion of them have shared compelling stories based on the obstacles they have overcome. Because entrants select four out of five areas to address, pick your four best, then informally discuss the fifth somewhere in your application. This way, you get to address more of the criteria without being formally judged on your weakest area.

THE DUPONT CHALLENGE

Target Recipient

Entrants must be enrolled in grades 7 through 12 in the U.S., U.S. territories, or Canada. Applicants are divided into the Junior Division (grades 7-9) and the Senior Division (grades 10-12).

Money Matters

DuPont awards two first-place cash prizes ($1,500 each), two second-place prizes ($750 each), two third-place prizes ($500), and 96 honorable mentions ($50 each). First-prize winners (along with one parent and their sponsoring science teacher) receive all expense-paid trips to Houston's NASA Space Center.

Entry Requirements

Entrants write an essay (700-1,000 words) discussing a scientific or technological development, event, or theory. Students are advised to discuss the significance of the subject matter, how the subject captured their interest, any relevant background information, and differing views on the topic (including their own point of view). Quotes and ideas that are not their own should be attributed in the body copy of the essay (do not use footnotes or endnotes). Essays should have a title, as well as be typed and double-spaced (with one-inch margins). A bibliography should be included on a separate page at the end of the essay.

Application Deadline

Late January

Contact Information

The DuPont Challenge
Science Essay Awards Program
c/o General Learning
   Communications
900 Skokie Boulevard, Suite 200
Northbrook, IL 60062-4028

Phone: (847) 205-3000
Web site: www.glcomm.com/
   dupont/

Sleuth Says:

Unlike other science-oriented contests that may involve years of research, this one specifies a much more manageable task—an essay that you can research and write (without doing field work) in a relatively short period of time. In recent contests, winning essayists have written on such topics as nuclear waste disposal, the war on cancer, black holes, and computer graphics, to name a few. Judges have noted that winning essays generally contain the following:

(1) an appropriate choice of subject matter

(2) thorough research using a variety of resource materials

(3) careful consideration of how the subject matter affects you and humankind

DURACELL/NSTA INVENTION CHALLENGE

Target Recipient

Entrants must be students in grades 6 through 12 who are U.S. citizens. Entrants may submit project entries as individuals or as teams of two. Students are grouped into two categories: grades 6-9 and grades 10-12.

Money Matters

In each grade level category, Duracell awards 1 first-place award ($20,000 savings bond), 2 second-place awards ($10,000 savings bonds), 5 third-place awards ($3,000 savings bonds), 12 fourth-place awards ($1,000 savings bonds), and 30 fifth-place awards ($500 savings bonds). If a winning entry is submitted by a pair of students, the prize money is divided evenly between the two.

Entry Requirements

Entrants design and build a device that runs on Duracell batteries. Applicants also submit a two-page description of the device and its uses, a schematic (wiring diagram), a photograph of the device, and a brief entry form. Entrants first submit the above materials without sending along the actual device. Students who want feedback on ideas for potential projects can submit optional "First Step" papers. Students write one-page essays describing their device, and receive letters containing a general critique (including a recommendation on whether they should proceed with the project). First step submissions are due by mid-November.

Application Deadline

Mid January

Contact Information

Duracell/NSTA Invention
    Challenge
National Science Teachers Assoc.
1840 Wilson Blvd.
Arlington, VA 22201-3000

Phone: (888) 255-4242 (toll-free)
Fax: (703) 243-7177
E-mail: duracell@nsta.org

Sleuth Says:

If you don't know much about electronics, don't worry: A Starter Kit is available for students who need some help with the basics of electronics. Two electronics professionals are also available to discuss technical questions with entrants via e-mail: Mark Yeary (mbyeary@gte.net) and Gordon Isleib (dfzm70a@prodigy.com). And if you have multiple ideas for projects, it's a good idea to submit multiple "First Step" submissions (see left) to help you decide upon one to pursue. Last year's first-place winners submitted a moving map and teaching tool that shows continental drift (grade 8), and an alarm that automatically arms itself to protect against laptop computer theft (grade 12). See photographs of these inventions in the Library of Sample Materials (Appendix B).

ESPN SportsFigures Scholarship

Target Recipient

Applicants must be high school seniors who have participated in interscholastic sports, have a 3.0 GPA, and are U.S. citizens or legal residents.

Money Matters

Eight awards of $2,500 are given each year. ESPN selects one male and one female winner in each of four regions (west, midwest, northeast, and southeast.

Entry Requirements

Judging is based upon three categories: academic achievement, service to school and community, and leadership in interscholastic sports. Applications include a 250-word essay describing how the three judging categories (both separately and together) have enhanced the student's high school experience. Personal interviews may also be required (ESPN covers travel expenses).

Application Deadline

Mid March

Contact Information

ESPN SportsFigures Scholarship
P.O. Box 630
Hartford, CT 06142

Phone: (860) 766-2000
or (860) 585-2000

Sleuth Says:

Be aware that these types of sports-related scholarship contests are never solely about athletic ability. If the contest didn't emphasize other criteria, it could inadvertently jeopardize the NCAA eligibility of its winners.

In general, the winners of such contests tend to be solid athletic performers at the high school level, but not superstars. A powerful strategy for a contest like this is to focus on the lessons learned and character traits developed from your athletic participation. See "The Athlete" theme in Chapter 5.

GUIDEPOSTS' YOUNG WRITERS CONTEST

Target Recipient

Entrants must be high school juniors or seniors. Students who are in equivalent grades in other countries may also enter.

Money Matters

The program awards eight scholarships: First prize ($8,000), second prize ($7,000), third prize ($6,000), and fourth through eighth prizes ($1,000 each). 17 entrants selected as honorable mention recipients receive portable electronic typewriters (the eight scholarship winners also receive typewriters).

Entry Requirements

Entrants submit a first-person story about a memorable or deeply moving experience, and how their faith in God related to, or was affected by the experience. Each story must be a true personal account of the author. Manuscripts should be a maximum of 1,200 words (typed, double-spaced). Contest announcement and rules are published in the October issue of *Guideposts*, a monthly inspirational interfaith magazine. Scholarship winners are announced, and have their stories published in the June issue of *Guideposts* magazine.

Application Deadline

Late November

Contact Information

Young Writers Contest
Guideposts Magazine
16 East 34th Street
New York, NY 10016

Phone: (212) 251-8100
Fax: (212) 684-0679

Sleuth Says:

Winning stories in this contest often follow a standard formula: they are centered around a personal or family crisis, and describe how faith in God helped the writer through the crisis. In addition, some writers go one step further by emphasizing how the crisis itself was actually "a blessing in disguise."

By reading *Guideposts* magazine (especially the June issue where the winning stories are published), you get a feel for what types of stories do well in this contest. Don't forget to ask your English teacher for permission to start on your story as a class project or writing assignment. One winner did this and turned class time into an $8,000 prize.

INTEL SCIENCE TALENT SEARCH

Target Recipient

Entrants must be high school seniors at public, private, or parochial schools in the United States or U.S. territories. American students attending foreign schools are also eligible to apply.

Money Matters

The first-prize winner receives a $50,000 scholarship. The second- and third-place winners receive scholarships of $30,000 and $20,000, respectively. Fourth through sixth place receive $20,000 each. Seventh through tenth place each receive $15,000. The other 30 finalists each receive a $4,000 scholarship award. All scholarships may be applied toward study in the sciences.

Entry Requirements

Each student must submit an independent research project in the physical sciences, behavioral and social sciences, engineering, mathematics, or biological sciences (excluding live vertebrate experimentation). The research report, including all appendices, tables, and charts may not exceed 20 double-spaced, typewritten pages. Students also complete a lengthy entry form designed to evaluate their promise as scientist (the criteria includes scientific attitude, curiosity, inventiveness, initiative, and work habits). Students must also submit an official transcript and include available standardized test scores. All 40 finalists are selected and interviewed in person.

Application Deadline

Early December

Contact Information

Science Service
1719 N Street, NW
Washington, DC 20036

Phone: (202) 785-2255
E-mail: sciedu@sciserv.org
Web site: www.sciserv.org

Sleuth Says:

The Intel Science Talent Search (formerly known as the "Westinghouse Science Talent Search") is a Nobel Prize of sorts for high school seniors. In fact, five past winners have gone on to win real Nobel prizes!

A common thread among winning students is the selection of a good mentor. High school students, on their own, simply don't have the resources or knowledge-base to carry out many of these research-intensive projects. Intel winners typically work closely with college professors or research scientists, or participate in summer research programs like the MIT-affiliated Research Science Institute (RSI). So perhaps the best advice is to search out colleges, universities, or laboratories in your region for a suitable project mentor to help guide your work.

LUCENT GLOBAL SCIENCE SCHOLARS

Target Recipient

The scholarship program is open to all high school seniors in the United States. College freshman at selected universities in Brazil, Canada, China, Germany, Japan, Mexico, The Netherlands, Thailand, and the United Kingdom are also eligible to apply.

Money Matters

A total of 50 $5,000 scholarships will be awarded to U.S. applicants. International students compete for 30 $5,000 college scholarships. In addition to the monetary awards, all 80 winners gather at a week-long, all-expense-paid Global Science Summit.

Entry Requirements

Students submit written applications in which they demonstrate their exceptional abilities in the sciences and communication-related academic areas. The program is administered in the U.S. by the National Alliance for Excellence, and internationally by the Institute for International Education (IIE). The program seeks to identify and assist future leaders in the field of communications technologies. Past winners tend to be extremely well-rounded with outstanding academic credentials. Internships may be offered to winners following their first year of college if appropriate assignments can be found.

Application Deadlines

Early February (in the U.S.)
Varies by country (international)

Contact Information

U.S. students:
National Alliance for Excellence
63 Riverside Avenue
Red Bank, NJ 07701

Phone: (732) 747-0028
E-mail: info@excellence.org
Web site: www.excellence.org

International students:
Institute of International Education
809 United Nations Plaza
New York, NY 10017-3580

E-mail: info@iie.org
Web site: www.iie.org/pgms/
    lucent/

Sleuth Says:

According to Linda Paras, president of the National Alliance for Excellence, students who are successful in the contest are extremely multidimensional. Not only are the students gifted in science-related fields, she says, but "40 out of our 48 winners from last year play music at a very competitive level." This is another high powered science contest with a heavy focus on independent scientific research.

NATIONAL ALLIANCE FOR EXCELLENCE SCHOLARSHIPS

Target Recipient

Applicants must be U.S. citizens planning to attend or already attending a full-time institution of higher education in the U.S. (or an approved foreign study program). The competition is open to high school seniors, college students, graduate students, and returning students.

Money Matters

The program awards various merit-based scholarships that range in value from $1,000 to $5,000.

Entry Requirements

Interested students apply in one of four contest categories: academic, technological innovation, visual arts, or performing arts. Each category has separate entry requirements. Students entering in the academic category must have a minimum SAT score of 1300 (or 30 on the ACT) and a 3.7 GPA (graduate students may submit scores from the GRE, LSAT, or other appropriate tests). Applicants in the technological innovation, visual arts, or performing arts categories submit samples of their work (such as slides, photos, videotapes, portfolios, etc.), as well as two teacher recommendation letters. All entrants may also submit a resume with a list of awards and honors received in their field of specialization. Students may enter more than one contest category, but must fulfill the separate requirements for each.

Application Deadline

Students may apply year-round.

Contact Information

National Alliance for Excellence
20 Thomas Ave.
Shrewsbury, NJ 07702

Phone: (732) 747-0028
E-mail: info@excellence.org
Web site: www.excellence.org

Note: Entrants must submit a one-time processing fee of $5.00 with their completed application.

Sleuth Says:

One of the unusual things about this contest is that there are no application deadlines. Students may submit application materials year-round, with scholarships handed out on a continuous basis to qualified applicants. Before becoming a winner in this contest, students must advance through the semifinalist and finalist stages of the competition (which may involve the submission of additional materials). Applicants will be notified within 90 days if they have advanced to the semifinalist round. This is clearly an achievement-oriented competition, but due to the year-round application policy, there's probably less head-to-head competition than other contests of this type.

NATIONAL HISTORY DAY CONTEST

Target Recipient

Entrants must be students in grades 6-12. Students are divided into two separate grade level divisions: Junior division (grades 6-8) and Senior division (grades 9-12). A student may participate as an individual or as part of a group of two to five students.

Money Matters

The program doles out 14 first-place awards ($1000), 14 second-place awards ($500), and 14 third-place awards ($250). The *History Channel* also sponsors three $5,000 awards to senior students. There are also additional special cash awards whose numbers and amounts vary.

Entry Requirements

Applicants submit entries in seven contest categories: Individual Paper (1,500-2,500 words), Individual Exhibit, Group Exhibit, Individual Performance, Group Performance, Individual Documentary, and Group Documentary. Each year, the competition focuses on a particular theme (such as "Turning Points in History: People, Ideas, Events"). Judging is conducted on the district, state, and national levels (the top two state winners in each event advance to nationals). Selection of winners is based on historical quality (60 percent), clarity of presentation (20 percent), and relationship to theme (20 percent). Educators and historians serve as judges at each level of the competition.

Application Deadline

March or April (varies on district level)

Contact Information

National History Day
0119 Cecil Hall
University of Maryland
College Park, MD 20740

Phone: (301) 314-9739
E-mail: hstryday@aol.com
Web site:
www.thehistorynet.com/
NationalHistoryDay/

Sleuth Says:

This is the type of contest where going the extra mile really counts. You can often predict winners in such contests by the time they've invested into their project.

Because this is a history competition, pay special attention to footnotes, bibliographies, endnotes and other forms of documentation—giving credit to the work of others.

To leverage your time, you might want to suggest to your history teacher that your class do a National History Day project instead of another assignment (or as an alternative to an assigned paper). Or if you're allowed to pick your own topic for a paper, pick one that fits the National History Day guidelines.

NATIONAL HONOR SOCIETY SCHOLARSHIPS

Target Recipient

Applicants must be high school seniors who are members of the National Honor Society (NHS). Each school (NHS chapter) may nominate two chapter members who demonstrate outstanding leadership, scholarship, character, and service.

Money Matters

The program grants 250 scholarships of $1,000. Scholarships are paid to the winner's college during the freshman year.

Entry Requirements

Nominees complete a written application form comprised primarily of lists of student activities, awards and honors, work experience, and community service. Applicants also submit a school transcript, SAT or ACT scores, and brief recommendation paragraphs from the school principal and another school official. Each applicant also writes a brief essay (250-300 words) dealing with a hypothetical scenario involving character and leadership. Each chapter is free to follow its own procedures to select two nominees. The national guidelines recommend, however, that a scholarship review committee (composed of students, faculty members, and administrators) be formed to judge written applications. Chapter nominees compete only with other nominees from the same state. The total number of awards given to students in each state is proportional to NHS chapters and members in that state.

Application Deadline

Early February

Contact Information

Attn: Dep. of Student Activities
National Association of
     Secondary School Principals
1904 Association Drive
Reston, VA 20191-1537

Phone: (800) 253-7746, ext. 324
    or (703) 860-0200, ext. 324
Fax: (703) 476-5432
E-mail: dsa@nassp.org
Web site: www.nassp.org/
    scholarships/index.html

Sleuth Says:

Be prepared to answer tough questions dealing with honor and ethical dilemmas. Because the NHS has four tenets for selection into the organization—character, leadership, service, and scholarship—showcase these virtues in all components of your application.

This contest is similar in many ways to the Principal's Leadership Award (also profiled in this directory). In fact, both are administered by the National Association of Secondary School Principals. So if you do a good job on one of these applications, you've got a strong chance of winning both contests.

NATIONAL PEACE ESSAY CONTEST

Target Recipient

Students are eligible if they are in grades 9-12, and attending school in the U.S. or U.S. territories. U.S. citizens attending school overseas may also apply.

Money Matters

The top three essay writers in the nation receive scholarships of $10,000, $5,000, and $2,500, respectively. The top essay writer in each state receives a $1,000 scholarship. All state winners are invited to attend an all-expense-paid awards program in Washington D.C.

Entry Requirements

Entrants write an essay of no more than 1,500 words on a pre-specified question related to international peace and conflict resolution. Essays are judged according to the following criteria: the quality of background research; the quality of the analysis; and the form, style, and mechanics of the essay. Each of the three judging categories carry equal weight. Essays that do not have citations and a bibliography are disqualified. Judging is first conducted at the state level by experts selected by the Institute of Peace. National winners are selected from the state winners by the Institute's Board of Directors.

Application Deadline

Late January

Contact Information

United States Institute of Peace
1200 17th St., NW, Suite 200
Washington, DC 20036-3011

Phone: (202) 457-1700
   or (202) 429-3854
Fax: (202) 429-6063
E-mail: usip_requests@usip.org
Web site: www.usip.org/ed.html

Sleuth Says:

A big part of doing well in this essay contest is to think hard about what conflicts and international crises best illustrate your main points. Many winners have chosen to describe two contrasting examples—one that shows how effective diplomacy works and another that shows what happens when it doesn't. National first-place winner Jeanmarie Hicks, for instance, used the Venezuelan Border dispute and the Iraq-Kuwait dispute to frame her discussion of preventative diplomacy—with the Venezuelan conflict cited as a positive example and Iraq-Kuwait used as a negative one. See Appendix B (page B-10) for a sample winning essay by another first-place winner.

OPTIMIST INTERNATIONAL ESSAY & ORATORICAL CONTESTS

Target Recipient

Essay Contest: Optimist International sponsors a contest for students who are high school sophomores, juniors, or seniors. The contest is open to U.S., Canadian, and Jamaican students. *Oratorical Contest:* The speech contest is open to students under 16 years old (as of 12/31).

Money Matters

Essay: The first-place winner receives a $5,000 scholarship. The second- and third-place winners receive $3,000 and $2,000, respectively. The 54 district winners receive all-expense-paid trips to participate in a 4-day conference on freedom and leadership. *Oratorical:* Two winners in each state (one boy and one girl) receive $1,500 scholarships. Smaller prizes are awarded at the local level.

Entry Requirements

Essay: Students write essays of 400-500 words on the selected topic (such as "Freedom, Our Most Precious Heritage"). Judging is based on material organization (40 points); vocabulary and style (30 points); grammar, punctuation, and spelling (20 points); neatness (5 points); and adherence to contest rules (5 points). *Oratorical:* Students prepare and deliver a 4-5 minute original speech on a selected topic related to civic responsibility. There is no national contest for oratorical participants, and boys and girls compete separately. Judging is based on poise, content, delivery and presentation, and overall effectiveness.

Application Deadlines

December, January & February
(varies on local level)

Contact Information

Optimist International
Attn: Program & Youth Clubs Dep.
4494 Lindell Boulevard
St. Louis, MO 63108

Phone: (314) 371-6000
Fax: (314) 371-6006

Sleuth Says:

At each level of the *essay* competition, submissions are evaluated by a panel of three judges. Each judge individually ranks the entries, and then the ratings are combined to determine the winners. In the past, this contest has been open to many different approaches and styles of essays. Study the contrasting approaches of two winning essays reprinted in Appendix B (pages B-11 and B-12).

Each year, a different topic is chosen for the *oratorical* contest (such as "Growing Up in Today's World" and "Optimism in My Life"). The formal evaluation sheet used by contest judges reveals that entrants must follow directions to the letter. Severe penalties are levied for even the slightest infractions—such as time violations, self-identification, forgetting to announce the official topic, or failure to cite non-original material verbally. The bottom line: Pay close attention to the rules.

PRINCIPAL'S LEADERSHIP AWARD

Target Recipient

Entrants must be high school seniors who are nominated by their schools on the basis of outstanding leadership. Each school may nominate only one senior.

Money Matters

150 awards of $1,000 are handed out each year. The awards are administered by the National Association of Secondary School Principals.

Entry Requirements

Students complete a written application which includes grade point average and class rank, standardized test scores, a list of extracurricular activities, a list of awards and honors, and a list of community involvement. Responses are limited to the space provided, making most responses quite brief. Applicants write a short essay (250-300 words) describing a situation in which they've used their leadership skills to handle a personal or school crisis. The application also requests brief recommendations (less than 150 words) from the school principal and a counselor or club adviser. Each nominating school is assessed a $4 application fee. The method of selecting the principal's nominee is a local decision left up to each school. National winners are announced in April.

Application Deadline

Early December

Contact Information

Attn: Dep. of Student Activities
National Association of
    Secondary School Principals
1904 Association Drive
Reston, VA 22091-1537

Completed Applications:
Principal's Leadership Award
P.O. Box 6317
Princeton, NJ 08541-6317

Phone: (800) 253-7746, ext. 324
    or (703) 860-0200, ext. 324
Fax: (703) 476-5432
E-mail: dsa@nassp.org
Web site: www.nassp.org/
    scholarships/index.html

Sleuth Says:

In this type of contest, your ability to fit credentials and describe activities in very small, preassigned spaces is critical. So be sure to read up on the techniques for doing this in Chapter 10's "Filling in the Blanks."

Even your recommendations must fit on the form and be under 150 words. Past winners have accomplished this by dissecting their full-length recommendation letters, and then piecing together some of the best sentences—with the recommenders approving the abridged compilations.

PRUDENTIAL SPIRIT OF COMMUNITY AWARDS

Target Recipient

Applicants must be 11- to 19-years old or in grades 5 through 12 at the time of the application deadline, and must also have initiated a volunteer community service activity. Each school may submit one nomination for each 1,000 students. Girl Scout councils and 4-H organizations may also nominate students.

Money Matters

104 state winners (two in each state plus D.C. and Puerto Rico) receive $1,000 and an all-expense-paid trip to Washington D.C. 10 national winners (selected from the state winners) each receive an additional award of $5,000.

Entry Requirements

Entrants describe an individual community service activity, or their significant leadership role in a group activity, that has taken place during the prior school year. Applicants discuss (in a written application) the inspiration behind the service idea, how the activity was created, the amount of effort devoted to the activity, the impact of the work, as well as reflect on their own personal growth. Applications are submitted to the state selection committee chairperson in each state. Competition is separated between high school and middle school students: In each state, one high school student and one middle-level student are named state winners. State winners are allowed to reapply in subsequent years (national winners are no longer eligible).

Application Deadline
Late October

Contact Information

Prudential Spirit of Community
CSFA
1505 Riverview Road
P.O. Box 297
St. Peter, MN 56082

Phone: (800) 253-7746, ext. 324
  _or_ (703) 860-0200, ext. 324
  _or_ (800) THE-ROCK, ext. 1143
Fax: (703) 476-5432
E-mail: spirit@nassp.org
Web Sites:
1) www.prudential.com/
      community/spirit
2) www.nassp.org/scholarships/
      index.html

Sleuth Says:

The common thread among top winners is a self-initiated service effort that is often inspired by a personal experience. Here are some examples:

Allison Wignall,18, has been an outspoken activist on AIDS prevention since age 12.
  Pettus Randall,17, founded a program partnering high school and grade school students to help improve reading skills.
  Andrew Allshouse,16, launched community book drives to create libraries for needy kids.
  Lauren Detrich,14, personally raised $50,000 as part of a Cystic Fibrosis Foundation walk-a-thon.

ROBERT C. BYRD HONORS SCHOLARSHIP

Target Recipient

Applicants must be high school seniors who are U.S. citizens (or certain eligible noncitizens). Each state establishes its own academic requirements. Typically, states require students to have GPAs that rank in the upper 25 percent of their class and SAT scores above 1150 (or above 27 on the ACT).

Money Matters

The amount each student receives from the Byrd scholarship program depends upon the annual appropriations by Congress each year. In recent years, the typical award has been between $1,000 and $1,500 annually. Awards are renewable for four years (contingent on available federal funds) bringing the monetary value of the award to between $4,000 and $6,000. Each state is allotted a number of Byrd scholarships proportional to its population, with a substantial number of awards handed out in each U.S. Congressional District.

Entry Requirements

Specific entry requirements and judging criteria vary from state to state. Students apply through a written application, which generally includes a grade transcript, the submission of standardized test scores, a list of extracurricular activities, and essay questions.

Application Deadline

Early March

Contact Information

For the agency in your state administering the Byrd program, see Appendix C (pages C-1 to C-4).

Federal contact:
Department of Education
Attn: Federal Student Aid
    Information Center
P.O. Box 84
Washington, DC 20044-0084

Phone: (800) 4-FED-AID
Web Site: www.ed.gov

Sleuth Says:

Because every state administers the scholarship program differently, your best strategy is to contact past winners in your area and question them about how they approached the application materials. There is a pre-specified number of winners in each Congressional district, so you will be able to find past winners in your immediate vicinity.

THE SCHOLASTIC ART & WRITING AWARDS

Target Recipient

All students in grades 7-12 who attend school in the U.S., U.S. territories, U.S.-sponsored schools abroad, and Canada are eligible.

Money Matters

Over 1,000 cash awards are presented annually, ranging in value from $100 to $1,000 each. Graduating seniors compete for 10 Portfolio Awards of $5,000 each (5 in art and 5 in writing). One additional Artistic Portfolio winner receives a $20,000 prize.

Entry Requirements

Students submit entries in the visual arts or writing. In the visual arts there are 16 distinct categories: painting; drawing; mixed media; printmaking; sculpture; photography; computer graphics; video, film, and animation; environmental design; graphic design; product design; ceramics; jewelry and metalsmithing; textile and fiber design; art portfolio; and photography portfolio. In writing there are 9 categories: short story; short short story; poetry; essay/nonfiction/opinion; dramatic script; humor; science fiction/fantasy; general writing portfolio; and nonfiction portfolio. Each artistic or literary work may be submitted in only one category (with the exception of portfolios). Of the 250,000 works of art and writing that are reviewed on the local level each year, 30,000 works are forwarded to New York for the national judging.

Application Deadline

November to January (varies by state)

Contact Information

The Scholastic Art &
  Writing Awards
555 Broadway
New York, NY 10012

Phone: (212) 343-6892
E-mail:
GeneralInfo@Scholastic.com
Web site: scholastic.com/
  artandwriting/

Sleuth Says:

The Scholastic Art & Writing Awards, established in 1923, is the longest-running program of its kind in the United States. Judging is conducted by artists, writers, educators, museum professionals, and gallery owners appropriate to each field. According to program manager, Evelyn Guzman, although the specified criteria is based upon technical competence, originality, and personal voice or style, how such criteria is judged can be quite subjective. "It's so varied what we select from year to year, and that's the beauty of it," says Guzman. "Our panelists of judges are a real cross-section, some with very traditional styles, others more experimental." So for younger applicants, perhaps the best advice is to keep submitting entries year after year.

SIEMENS WESTINGHOUSE SCIENCE AND TECHNOLOGY COMPETITION

Target Recipient

Students submitting individual projects must be high school seniors who are legal or permanent residents of the United States. Team projects may involve younger students as members of the team, but the team leader must be a high school senior.

Money Matters

The top individual entrant receives a $120,000 college scholarship. The top team in the nation receives $90,000 (to be divided among two or three team members). Scholarships of $20,000 are awarded to the top individual in each of six regions. Scholarships of $30,000 are awarded to the top team in each of six regions (to be divided among the team members). Scholarships may be used for both undergraduate and graduate level studies.

Entry Requirements

Students may enter as individuals or as members of two- to three-person teams. Each individual/team first submit a detail research report (20 pages or less) that describes an original scientific research project. Each project must have a teacher/advisor who will supervise the research effort. Applicants must also provide a school transcript, and a teacher/advisor recommendation that confirms their contributions to the project. Only projects related to mathematics or the biological or physical sciences will be considered.

Application Deadline

Late September

Contact Information

Siemens Westinghouse Science
   and Technology Competition
Educational Testing Service
Rosedale Road, Conant Hall
P.O. Box 6730
Princeton, NJ 08541

Phone: (877) 822-5233
E-mail:
foundation@sc.siemens.com
Web site:
www.siemens-foundation.org

Sleuth Says:

This contest is a new scholarship program, and is quite similar to the Intel Science Talent Search in its focus on original scientific research.

One unique feature of this contest, however, is that students are allowed to enter as members of teams. Since the individual portion of the competition is open only to high school seniors, team entries enable younger students (who partner with a senior) to enter the competition. Be aware that team entries are judged according to some additional criteria including the collaboration skills and effective teamwork exhibited by project members.

SOROPTIMIST YOUTH CITIZENSHIP AWARDS

Target Recipient

Entrants must be high school seniors under the age of 21. Youth Citizenship Awards are given "in recognition of the outstanding contributions made by young people to home, school, community, country, and the world."

Money Matters

One $2,000 cash award is given to the overall international winner. Also, 54 cash awards of $1,250 are given to regional winners—two winners in each of the 27 Soroptimist International of the Americas regions. Smaller cash awards are also granted at the local level.

Entry Requirements

Entrants complete a three-page application form. The application features three short-response essay questions (125 words each) discussing family responsibilities, community responsibilities, and views on global citizenship. The application also includes lists of school and community activities, and a description of future career plans. Students must also submit letters of recommendation from three adults outside of the school environment who are familiar with three different aspects of the applicant's activities. Judging is based upon four criteria: service, dependability, leadership, and clear sense of purpose. Grades are not considered.

Application Deadline

Mid December

Contact Information

Attn: Youth Citizenship Program
Soroptimist International
   of the Americas
2 Penn Center, Suite 1000
Philadelphia, PA 19102

Phone: (215) 557-9300
Fax: (215) 568-5200
E-mail: yca@soroptimist.org
Web site: www.soroptimist.org

Sleuth Says:

Diana Pineda, program coordinator for the Soroptimist Youth Citizenship Awards, advises students to focus their applications on community service and to eliminate extraneous information. "We often get applicants who are confusing extracurricular activities with community service," says Pineda. "Being captain of the football team isn't a school service activity." Pineda also stresses the importance of commitment. "The most important thing we look for is a sense that the student is deeply committed to the concept of community service," she emphasizes. "Some students send us three-page lists of community service involvement, but the judges begin to question their commitment to each activity."

TARGET ALL-AROUND SCHOLARSHIP

Target Recipient

Applicants may be high school seniors, high school graduates, or current full-time college students (age 24 and under) who are planning to attend a two- or four-year college, university, or vocational-technical school in the coming academic year. A minimum GPA of 2.0 is required.

Money Matters

Scholarships of $10,000 are awarded to the top five national applicants. Each of the approximately 915 Target stores awards two $1000 scholarships to students who reside in the community where the store is located.

Entry Requirements

The scholarship program is designed to reward students who help their communities. Entrants submit an application form that includes a list of community service activities (including total number of hours spent volunteering); a list of volunteer-related awards, honors, and leadership positions; a brief appraisal by a volunteer supervisor or leader; and a one-page, double-spaced essay describing a significant volunteer experience. Applications are judged by the Citizens' Scholarship Foundation of America (CSFA).

Application Deadline

Early November

Contact Information

Target All-Around Scholarship
c/o Citizens' Scholarship
   Foundation of America
1505 Riverview Rd.
P.O. Box 480
St. Peter, MN 56082-0480

Phone: (800) 316-6142
   or (800) 537-4180
Web site: www.target.com/
   schools/

Note: Application forms are also available at the Community Relations kiosk located near the front of Target stores.

Sleuth Says:

This contest isn't just about the community service you have performed, or the positive effect it has had on those you're trying to help. The program also appears to emphasize the effect that performing community service has had on *your* life and that of your family. Therefore, try to communicate what you've learned through community service in all parts of your application.

THINKQUEST INTERNET CHALLENGE

Target Recipients

The ThinkQuest Internet Challenge is an international program for students ages 12 through 19. Students form teams consisting of two or three students (and one to three coaches). Team members are encouraged *not* to be of the same age group, nationality, gender or grade level, enrolled at the same school, or even from the same country.

Money Matters

ThinkQuest awards prizes totaling over $1 million, including college scholarships ranging from $3,000 to $25,000 for each member of a winning team. Approximately 35 teams are chosen as finalist teams, and are invited to the ThinkQuest Awards Weekend.

Entry Requirements

Each team submits a Web site based upon an educational theme. Teams submit their entries in any one of five categories: Arts & Literature, Science & Mathematics, Social Sciences, Sports & Health, and Interdisciplinary. The judging is based upon the following criteria: technological diversity among students' schools; diversity of team members; team collaboration; educational value; entry quality; growth potential; and entry usage. Judging at the final stage of the competition may also include an interview component.

Entry Deadlines

Late February (application form) & Mid August (submission of entry)

Contact Information

Advanced Network & Services
200 Business Park Drive
Armonk, NY 10504

Web site: www.thinkquest.org
Phone: (612) 359-0990
E-mail: helen@connors.com

Sleuth Says:

ThinkQuest places a premium on the ability of the Internet to facilitate cooperation among groups of people from diverse locations, backgrounds, experiences, and nationalities. In fact, the judges substantially reward team diversity. So a big part of doing well in this competition is putting in the effort to form a diverse team. Check out ThinkQuest's electronic meeting place to find other team members.

One applicant commented that the choice of teammates is also important because you will typically face vastly conflicting schedules, very different ideas on how a project should be structured, and varying levels of Web design proficiency.

Finally, choose the topic of your Web site wisely. Not all categories of the competition are equally competitive, so scan through past entries, and pick an area of interest where it looks like you have the strongest chance to win.

TOSHIBA/NSTA EXPLORAVISION AWARDS

Target Recipient

Entrants must be full-time students in grades K-12, who are U.S. or Canadian citizens or legal residents, living within the U.S., U.S. Territories, or Canada. Students are grouped into four categories: Primary Level (Grades K-3), Upper Elementary Level (Grades 4-6), Middle Level (Grades 7-9), High School Level (Grades 10-12).

Money Matters

The award is a $10,000 U.S. Savings Bond for each member of the 4 first-place teams; a $5,000 savings bond for each member of the 8 second-place teams; and a $100 bond for members of the 36 regional winning teams.

Entry Requirements

Students work in groups of three or four, along with a teacher advisor and an optional community advisor. Each team selects a technology or aspect of a technology that is relevant to their lives. Students use their imaginations to develop a vision of a future technology. Each team must complete a 10-page project description and submit 10 storyboard scenes from a video they might make about their project. The 48 regional winning teams (one per grade level category in each of twelve regions) each receive $500 to be used to produce and submit a videotaped presentation of their project. The judging is conducted by the National Science Teachers Association, and criteria includes creativity, scientific accuracy, communication, and feasibility of vision.

Application Deadline

Early February

Contact Information

Toshiba/NSTA
ExploraVision Awards
1840 Wilson Boulevard
Arlington, VA 22201-3000

Phone: 1-800 EXPLOR-9
   or (703) 243-7100
Fax: (703) 243-7177
Web site: www.toshiba.com/
   tai/exploravision/

Sleuth Says:

What do winning topics look like? Listed below are the topics of the first-place winners of a recent contest year in each grade level category:

Grades K-3: Attaching a microchip to important items helps you locate it instantly.

Grades 4-6: An ingenious system filters air and converts hog waste into fuel for power generation.

Grades 7-9: Doctors custom-fit knee replacements that grow inside the kneecap.

Grades 10-12: Advances in shape memory alloy technology improve airplane travel.

TOYOTA COMMUNITY SCHOLARSHIP

Target Recipient

Entrants must be high school seniors who are nominated by their schools. Each high school may nominate one student for the scholarship (schools with over 600 seniors may nominate two students).

Money Matters

12 national winners receive $20,000 college scholarships. 88 regional winners receive $10,000 scholarships.

Entry Requirements

Entrants submit a written application form in which they exhibit their academic achievement, leadership skills, and dedication to community service. Winners are selected by a panel of college and university admissions officials from across the U.S. The program is administered by the Educational Testing Service. Interested students should first contact their high school guidance counselors. If your school has not received any applications, only counselors are permitted to request them from the ETS using the above contact information.

Application Deadline
Early December

Contact Information

Attn: Scholarships &
    Recognition Programs
Educational Testing Service
Rosedale Road
Princeton, NJ 08541

Phone: (609) 921-9000
Fax: (609) 734-5410
E-mail: etsinfo@ets.org

Sleuth Says:

Winners in the Toyota Community Scholarship Program have been notable for their community service efforts. One winner spent the past three summers in Latin America, helping build schools and churches. Another student started a soup kitchen that serves meals to hundreds of people on a weekly basis. A third winner raised puppies from birth, trained them as guide dogs, and donated them to organizations that help the blind.

TYLENOL SCHOLARSHIP

Target Recipient

This scholarship is open to high school seniors, as well as college freshmen, sophomores, and juniors. All applicants must reside in the United States (but not necessarily be U.S. citizens).

Money Matters

The Tylenol Scholarship Fund awards ten $10,000 scholarships and five hundred $1,000 scholarships. The scholarships can be used at an accredited two- or four-year college, university, or vocational-technical school.

Entry Requirements

Students must complete a short application which includes a brief essay (100-200 words) on goals and aspirations, a list of school activities, and a list of community and volunteer activities. Applicants must also submit a recent grade transcript. All applications are first screened on the basis of leadership responsibilities in community and school activities and on grade point average. Final judging criteria is weighted as follows: Academic record (50 percent); community and school activities, including leadership responsibilities, length of commitment, and awards and honors (40 percent); a clear statement of education and career goals (10 percent). Recipients are selected by the Citizens' Scholarship Foundation of America.

Application Deadline

Early January

Contact Information

McNeil Laboratories
Attn: Scholarship Office
7050 Camp Hill Road
Fort Washington, PA 19034

Phone: (800) 676-8437
  or (215) 233-8505

Administering organization:
Citizens' Scholarship
  Foundation of America
1505 Riverview Road
P.O. Box 297
St. Peter, MN 56082

Note: Applications are available in October in stores where Tylenol is sold. During November and December, call the above 800-number to request an application.

Sleuth Says:

The first thing that you can do to prepare for this contest is to see Chapter 7 for a detailed description and analysis of how my winning application was constructed—using all of the strategies in this book. Note that there is very little room on the application form for all of the requested information. So don't limit yourself to the area provided; Attach several additional sheets that match the application format.

UNITED STATES SENATE YOUTH PROGRAM

Target Recipient

Entrants must be high school juniors or seniors who are elected student government officers. Students must also be permanent residents of the United States, or else attending Department of Defense (DoD) schools overseas.

Money Matters

The program, sponsored by the William Randolph Hearst Foundation, awards 104 $2,000 scholarships to state winners (two in each state plus the District of Columbia and DoD schools). The administrating body in each state also frequently awards scholarship awards to state finalists. State winners receive an all-expenses paid week in Washington D.C. in which they will meet U.S. senators, Cabinet members, Supreme Court justices, and other high officials.

Entry Requirements

Students are selected on the state level, and each state has its own application process. A chief school officer in each state is chosen to administer the program, and frequently the selection process involves personnel from the Department of Education in each state. The state application process generally includes a written application (focusing on extracurricular activities), an essay, letters of recommendation, and an interview.

Application Deadlines

Late September to Early October
(each state has a different deadline)

Contact Information

Program Director
United States Senate Youth
The William Randolph Hearst
   Foundation
90 New Montgomery Street,
   Suite 1212
San Francisco, CA 94105-4504

Phone: (415) 543-4057
   or (800) 841-7048
Fax: (415) 243-0760

Sleuth Says:

The purpose of the 1962 Senate Resolution that founded this program was to expose teens serving in high school student governments to the federal government—hopefully sparking an interest in government service as a career. The applicants who get selected, therefore, demonstrate that they have the skills and qualities to be future leaders in government.

In this contest, the scholarship money is treated secondary to the week in Washington. As a result, it's wise to focus on communicating how you will benefit from the unique opportunity to see our government up-close. Also, be prepared to answer questions about current events and societal issues during selection interviews.

VFW YOUTH ESSAY CONTEST

Target Recipient

The contest is open to students in the 7th or 8th grade who are enrolled in an accredited school (public, private, parochial, or home) in the U.S., U.S. territories, or in an overseas school as a dependent of U.S. military or civilian personnel.

Money Matters

The first-place national winner receives a $10,000 U.S. savings bond. 2nd place through 6th place each receive savings bonds ranging in value from $6,000 to $2,500. 7th place through 11th place each receive a $1,000 savings bond. Department, district, and post winners receive $500, $200, and $100, respectively. The overall national winner also receives a free trip to the VFW National Convention.

Entry Requirements

Students submit a 300-400 word essay on the annual theme (such as "How Should We Honor America's Veterans?"). Essays are judged using the following criteria and point values: addresses theme (20 points), clarity of ideas (30 points), and theme development (50 points). The contest is conducted on the post, district, department, and national levels. One winner from each level advances to the next level of the competition. The contest is sponsored by the Veterans of Foreign Wars (VFW) and its Ladies Auxiliary.

Application Deadline

Mid December

Contact Information

VFW Youth Essay Contest
VFW National Headquarters
406 West 34th Street
Kansas City, MO 64111

Phone: (816) 968-1117
Web site: www.vfw.org/vod/
youth.shtml

Note: Interested students should first contact the Youth Activities Chairman at a local VFW post.

Sleuth Says:

When you are writing a short essay, you don't have room to develop more than a couple of major points and flesh them out with interesting details and descriptions. Two approaches for doing this have been popular in this contest: The first approach is to show examples of patriotic virtues in terms of people and events—especially with wartime or military examples. The second approach is to turn the question on its head, by defining the subject (freedom, for instance) in terms of what it is *not* (i.e., showing what the world would be like if we didn't have freedom). For a sample winning essay, see page B-9 in Appendix B.

VOICE OF DEMOCRACY

Target Recipient

Entrants must be high school sopho-mores, juniors, or seniors in the U.S. or U.S. territories. Children of U.S. military or U.S. civilian personnel in overseas schools are also eligible (foreign exchange students are excluded).

Money Matters

The Veterans of Foreign Wars (VFW) awards its top three national winners scholarships of $20,000, $15,000, and $10,000. 4th through 9th place win scholarships ranging from $6,000 to $2,000. 10th through 16th place receive $1,500. 17th through 39th place receive $1,000 scholarships. A variety of cash prizes are also awarded at the local, district, and state levels.

Entry Requirements

Students write and record on audio cassette tape a three to five minute essay covering the year's assigned patriotic theme (such as "My Vision for America"). Voice should be normal and conversational, not oratorical (no singing, either). No background music or other enhancements are allowed. The essay should not refer to the entrant's race, national origin, disabilities, or geographic region. Point values in judging are assigned as follows: originality (40 points), content (40 points), delivery (20 points). Contestants are *not* required to personally read their essay during any portion of the judging. All entries must be submitted to your local Veterans of Foreign Wars Post, or through your high school.

Application Deadline
Mid November

Contact Information

Voice of Democracy Program
VFW National Headquarters
406 West 34th Street
Kansas City, MO 64111

Phone: (816) 968-1117
Web site: www.vfw.org/vod/

Note: Interested students can contact their local VFW Post.

Sleuth Says:

Just as in the American Legion Oratorical Contest, it has been popular for winners to open with a descriptive passage taken from a dramatic event during a period of American history. Voice of Democracy topics are always concerned with a particular American principle, value, or virtue. From analyzing past winners, it appears that the key in this competition is to show how the particular topic affects <u>you</u> on a personal level.

It should also be noted that many winners in this contest are not particularly great public speakers. So if you weren't born reciting the Gettysburg Address, don't be discouraged. Besides, all speeches are performed on tape, so you'll be able to keep recording yourself until you get a performance you like.

WASHINGTON CROSSING SCHOLARSHIP

Target Recipient

Entrants must be high school seniors who are U.S. citizens and are planning careers in government service. A broad definition of government service is used: Past winners include students who have gone on to become an army doctor, a high school teacher, a public prosecutor, and a member of the White House staff. Recipients are free to major in any field.

Money Matters

The Washington Crossing Foundation hands out a variety of scholarships ranging from $1,000 to $10,000. The number of awards and amounts vary each year.

Entry Requirements

Students submit a one-page essay (not to exceed 300 words) stating why the entrant is planning a career in government service—including any inspiration to be derived from the leadership of George Washington in his famous crossing of the Delaware River. The essay should address the applicant's viewpoint, attitude, and purpose in the particular career choice. Applicants must also submit a letter of recommendation from the entrant's principal or counselor, as well as a high school transcript and standardized test scores. Selection is based on six criteria: an understanding of career requirements, purpose in career choice, career preparation, leadership qualities, sincerity, and historical perspective.

Application Deadline

Mid January

Contact Information

Vice Chairman
Washington Crossing Foundation
1280 General DeFermoy Road
P.O. Box 17
Washington Crossing, PA 18977

Phone: (215) 493-6577
Fax: (215) 949-8843

Note: Students requesting contest applications should enclose a self-addressed, stamped envelope.

Sleuth Says:

This competition *isn't* just limited to those expecting to run for public office someday. Because service to the nation is broadly defined, students with interests in a wide variety of fields can enter and win these awards.

Because of the stipulation that the essay include any inspiration derived from Washington's crossing of the Delaware River, it is a good idea to thoroughly research this historic event so you can work in key ideas.

In addition, this contest allows great flexibility in the submission of additional support materials—such items as recommendation letters, résumés, and lists of activities and awards. So be sure to include these "extras" in your application.

YOUNG AMERICAN CREATIVE PATRIOTIC ART AWARDS

Target Recipient

The contest is open to students in grades 9-12 in the U.S. Foreign exchange students, however, are not eligible.

Money Matters

The Ladies Auxiliary to the Veterans of Foreign Wars awards scholarship prizes to the top five (5) entrants: first prize ($3,000), second prize ($2,000), third prize ($1,500), fourth prize ($1,000), and fifth prize ($500).

Entry Requirements

Students submit a work of patriotic art on paper or canvas. Water color, pastel, charcoal, tempera, crayon, acrylic, pen-and-ink, or oil may be used. The art should be no smaller than 8 inches by 10 inches, but no larger than 18 inches by 24 inches. If the American flag appears in the artwork, it must conform to the Flag Code in terms of color, number of stars and stripes, and other considerations. A copy of the code can be found at a local Auxiliary chapter or local library. Judging, on all levels, is conducted by teachers, professionals, and others knowledgeable in art. Comments of local and state judges will be attached to each work and forwarded along with the art. Each entry will be judged on the originality of concept and patriotism expressed; the content and clarity of ideas; the design, use of color and technique; and the total impact or execution and contrast. Prior first- and second-place national winners may not enter again.

Contact Information

Ladies Auxiliary VFW
   Headquarters
406 West 34th Street
Kansas City, MO 64111

Phone: (816) 561-8655
Web site:
www.ladiesauxvfw.com/
   ypatart.html

Sleuth Says:

What can you do to increase your chances of winning scholarship money in an art contest? Although skillful artistic execution is essential—winning entries typically exhibit meticulous attention to detail—the concept behind the artwork appears to be equally important. An original way of looking at and depicting patriotism seems to win out over more clichéd concepts. I provide samples of winning entries on page B-6 in Appendix B.

Application Deadline

April & May (varies on local level)

YOUNG NATURALIST AWARDS

Target Recipient

Entrants must be students in grades 7-12 who are enrolled in a public or non-public school in the U.S., Canada, U.S. territories, or U.S.-sponsored schools abroad.

Money Matters

Twelve students—two in each grade level—receive U.S. treasury bonds. The amounts vary for each grade: 12th grade, $2,500; 11th grade, $2,000; 10th grade, $1,500; 9th grade, $1,000; 8th grade, $750; 7th grade, $500.

Entry Requirements

Students select one of three possible projects based upon an annual theme (past themes include "biodiversity," "earth science," and "planetary science"). Each project includes an essay writing component and an illustrations component. Entrants write essays of varying length depending on their grade level: grades 7-8, 500-2,000 words; grades 9-10, 750-2,500 words; grades 11-12, 1,000-3,000 words. Entrants then add drawings, photographs, graphs, charts, or other illustrations of their own creation to complement their essay. (Internet images and copies are discouraged.) Students are judged only against others in their grade. Judges include museum scientists, science writers, and science educators. Judges look for evidence of observation, research, analysis, and interpretation. Projects are then evaluated on the basis of accuracy, clarity, and the presence of a personal voice.

Application Deadline

Early January

Contact Information

American Museum of
    Natural History
Young Naturalist Awards
c/o Alliance for Young
    Artists & Writers, Inc.
555 Broadway, 4th Floor
New York, NY 10012-3999

Phone: (212) 343-6492
E-mail: sfewster@scholastic.com
Web site: www.amnh.org/
    youngnaturalistawards/

Sleuth Says:

This is obviously a terrific scholarship contest if you enjoy the great outdoors. It's even better if you can arrange for a science teacher to accept your contest submissions as a replacement for a class project, paper, or exam.

Winning projects exhibit "a deep interest and passion for observing the changing environment. . ." When you read the work of contest winners you can't help but be impressed with their powers of observation and attention to small details. To do well in this contest, you should also take care to communicate your observations in an interesting way—this means employing appropriate illustrations or photos. If you lack experience, find a mentor.

WANT MORE SLEUTH?

An insider's directory of big contests, hot tips & winning entries

By Benjamin R. Kaplan

Author of *How to Go To College Almost For Free*

We hope that the preceding directory of scholarships, specially excerpted from *The Scholarship Sleuth*, has been helpful to you.

But the Appendix A listings are only the beginning. . .

To get the comprehensive *Scholarship Sleuth* directory, order your copy on the Web at:

www.waggledancer.com

The complete *Scholarship Sleuth* directory features:

- Comprehensive listings of big-money scholarship contests that award funds for use at any college

- In-depth, full-page descriptions of entry rules, requirements, and judging criteria—plus insider tips for winning the awards

- Insightful interviews with scholarship administrators, judges, and past award winners

- An essential reference library of winning essays, artwork, stories, poetry, inventions, research reports, orations, and other contest submissions

APPENDIX B

Library of Sample Materials

The following pages contain extensive sample material drawn from winning essays, orations, stories, inventions, drawings, projects, research papers, and much more. I've chosen to include material from a wide range of scholarship contests so that you can see the many different types of opportunities available for transforming your time and talents into money for college.

Due to space limitations, I wasn't able to fit in these pages all of the sample materials that I had hoped to include. So for additional examples of contest submissions that brought home the big bucks, be sure to check out my Reader's Resource Room (at **winscholarships.com**). Because some of the winning material contained in this library is better experienced in a multimedia format (orations, for instance), you may want to log on to the Reader's Resource Room at the same time as your peruse these pages.

With each example, I've included some comments on the merits of the submission or on other areas of interest related to the particular scholarship. For more insights on each contest, see the directory of scholarships in Appendix A.

Contest: Voice of Democracy

Type: Oratorical

Award Won: First Place ($20,000)

My Service to America

In the early morning hours in March, 1945, a young man floated cold and frightened to near delirium in the tropical waters near Okinawa in the South Pacific. This eighteen year old boy had retired to his bunk the evening before only to be awakened by a sickening thud, then <u>silence</u>, then absolute pandemonium aboard the troop transport ship. The ship had been hit by Japanese aircraft. He remembers racing up on deck dressed only in his "skivvies." Dazed and confused, with no time for a life jacket, he followed many dozens of his fellow shipmates into the black abyss of the Pacific Ocean. Within minutes his ship had vanished beneath the rolling sea.

The pure force of the event had sucked him under so far he was sure he would never surface. He had no idea which way was up or down. As his lungs were bursting with a piercing pain, he suddenly surfaced to so much thrashing, screaming, and <u>such</u> human misery he prayed that this was a dream and he would wake up at any instant. There would be no escaping this nightmare.

He floated for nearly four hours until dawn. He was miraculously uninjured physically, but emotionally the scars would last a lifetime. He spent those hours bobbing aimlessly, listening to the panicked cries of the other young sailors, and then to the ever-deafening silence as fewer and fewer survivors hung on. As dawn broke, a rescue ship arrived and plucked the remaining men from the water. My **Poppy** was one of them.

I only had the honor of knowing my quiet, unassuming grandfather for thirteen years, but in that short time Poppy demonstrated to me <u>everything</u> I ever needed to know about the importance of service, sacrifice, giving, and unconditional love of family and country (He taught me how to fix a few things

too!). These were just things he did as easily and naturally as breathing or sipping his morning coffee.

Poppy only talked about his war ordeal once to me but it showed me in one giant example everything about why the United States of America is strong and wonderful. I realized at his death a few years ago that it was now <u>my</u> responsibility to carry on the ability to make life better for all Americans just as he did—one person at a time doing small but significant acts for other people. I learned from him <u>never</u> to take the political process lightly. To actively participate and voice my opinion. I learned that when the community needs a helping hand, like when the floods hit us in 1996, that you pick up and <u>go</u> to a shelter and help prepare meals for evacuees. I learned how <u>good</u> it feels to help run a community food closet. I learned that the graffiti wars can be won when a group of my friends and I quickly painted over scribbled buildings at local business and roadside walls for a full year until the offenders grew tired of us and went away.

My service to America can never come close to the drama of my Poppy's experience in the South Pacific, but it gives me reason to keep plugging away at the small things. The small things, that's what my Poppy taught me. I know these things will make things just a little bit better for America. As for me, it just makes me feel good.

My service to America means dedication of my life to <u>decency</u> and <u>compassion</u>. I want to instill in my children the importance of protecting every freedom we have been granted as Americans. I will protect and teach these freedoms <u>fiercely</u>.

Robert Brynne once said, "The <u>purpose</u> of life is a life of purpose." I will serve my family and my country with a search for excellence in every aspect of my life just as my **Poppy** did. Sometimes when I feel like I am bobbing aimlessly through the ocean of life, struggling to keep my head above water, I can feel the invisible hands of my grandfather lifting me up and giving me that strength and courage to be a proud part of what makes America strong and wonderful.

COMMENTS

Jennifer Gray became the first three-time ThinkQuest award winner, competing in the contest three consecutive years with different design partners each time. Jennifer captured first place ($15,000) in the Sports category (for Runner's Oasis) as a sophomore; third place ($9,000) in the Sport & Fitness category (for Cyber Cycle) as a junior; and second place ($12,000) in the Interdisciplinary category (for The Living Africa) as a senior. Her ThinkQuest scholarship winnings totaled $36,000!

Contest: ThinkQuest

Type: Web site design

ThinkQuest is a Web design competition for students around the world. Over $1 million in scholarships and cash is awarded annually to the winning teams, their coaches, and schools.

The ThinkQuest Web page shown here, **http://library.advanced.org/library/index.html** is your gateway for checking out what it takes to become a ThinkQuest winner. What's great about this page is that for each of the five entry categories, you can browse both winning and non-winning Web sites—learning about what to do and what *not* to do. Keep in mind that as the technology for Web design continually improves, the winning entries typically get better and better. So, all else being equal, what it took to win three years ago probably won't bring home the money today.

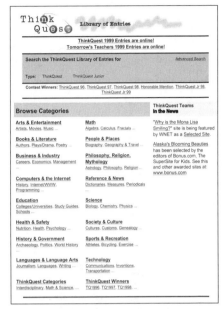

http://library.advanced.org/library/index.html

COMMENTS

The sample shown at right is a small excerpt from a piece titled "Dagoba" by Sarah Ann Jaworski—one of 20 writing awardees who attended ARTS Week in Miami and received anywhere from $500 to $3,000 in prize money.

Space limitations forced us to end this short story where we did. In this relatively small amount of space, however, we can appreciate the author's ability to draw the reader into the mind of the main character.

Contest: ARTS Scholarship

Type: Creative writing

I'm fat. Not beautiful-girl-with-slightly-rounded-hips-who-could-stand-to-lose-five-pounds fat, but large-and-apple-shaped-with-thighs-that-touch fat. I figured I should bring that up before you start picturing a slender hot-to-trot street walker as the heroine. By the way, this is not a fat-girl-loses-weight story.

Somewhere, I think, there is a rule that fat girls cannot under any circumstances be in a story unless it involves them triumphing over their weight problem. Nope. Sorry. I have a little more to say than that.

Don't go and start cooing, "Oh, you're not fat," like all the thin girls do to make you feel okay about yourself when really they are thinking they would kill themselves if they ever got to be my size. I know I am fat because people tell me. These great people whose very souls are torn to shreds as they are tormented by the possibility that I have never seen myself in a mirror, never glanced down at my round belly, never passed a dull oil puddle and paused to study my visage; these people who feel I must be informed just in case I do not know, who feel it is their responsibility and thin-born duty to tell me I am fat.

I am standing in front of one of those clothing store walls, the kind made up of shiny, squarish vertical bars, and I am looking at my distorted shape, peering at my reflection through a row of tight shirts. The sales women look at me as if I do not belong here, wondering why I have not dragged my elephantine behind into the camping supply store to try on a tent. They cast odd glances in my direction, annoyed by my presence, disturbed by the amount of time I have spent standing here in front of a size six blouse. I feel awkward, but I do not leave.

I am waiting for my mother.

My mother loved these stores. She would dance me in and out of malls in search of the perfect pink dress, the perfect leather belt, the perfect pair of cigarette pants. I would stand alone, crammed between the closely-placed racks of clothing, and wait for my mother to come out of the dressing room. My mother was beautiful.

Contest: Scholastic Art & Writing Awards

Type: General Writing Portfolio (Poetry & Prose)

Award Won: First Place, $5,000 (one of four)

COMMENTS

Shown here are excerpts from the creative writing portfolio of Jonathan Braman, age 17, a high school senior from New York.

"All pure writing in my mind becomes poetry, and poetry is music to me," says Braman. "It is joyous understanding and exhilarating awareness. My poetry is an extension of myself, as transparent as the stubble on my face. I love not hiding myself through poetry."

As a writer, Braman employs a very relaxed, flowing style. "Some of my poems and writings are raw. I write them without conscious regard for clarity, effectiveness, economy, direction," says Braman. "Only intuition guides me. At the very least I can communicate with myself effectively and openly."

And close to me you are

I grew up in a house with
more books than I could ever
have read. I did not try
to read all of them. Acquainting
rather casually myself with
certain volumes to visit
like old friends on the shelf
when in need I was of light. In the rooms
dancing came naturally or not at all.
It was a curious kind of lacking,
a selective literary disability
and social inconsistency.
I grew up in a house with a dictionary which
demanded an inordinate quantity of respect
yet somehow neglected, vigorous
vinyl explorations, the needle
needs two or three minutes of anticipation
to spin fast enough. There was never
a piano, but enough guitars,
with soft strings, sliding out of tune
to keep your ears tipped
to the music, untrustingly
exposing your voice
to the polished wood, balancing
jewel on jewel,
couplet on couplet
atop the rise, the release of
familial cycles
of washing dishes with the music on
barely audible above the sound of the water.
There are corners of my house
which disappeared
as I got older.
Yet there are so many levels of exploration
the basic understanding of space
far less accessible,
than anthologies of nameless poets,
the vanity of textbooks
far easier to denounce
than the silence of walls.
You are terrifying, my home
you are undiscovered, pristine
and I wonder can I know
and live in you at once?
Or is there a bridge only to be formed
in separation? I think
that sometime later I walk
beside a river. Familiar windows
appear to me on the opposite bank.
There are doors I see
in distant hillsides, and close to me
you are my home.

a few pages from the log of a boy meeting the mountains

The summer I was sixteen I found the human wilderness quite a bit wilder
than I had expected, noticed in people my own age bignesses, realnesses, I
had reserved previously for rocks and the like. Underestimation. Intimations
of inadequacy. Howling shirtless on the ledges of Hunter Mountain,
chanting mindlessly pursued by my friends in the cushion of sky and
sandstone and spruce. Following tears with my eyes in the saddle between
Sugarloaf and Twin. Not doubting the voices I heard. Crying in the backseat
of my minivan as we zoomed north toward the Adirondacks. Compassless
traverses late into the evening with people I didn't care for outside of the
woods. Finding my head in a cave inside Indian Head and freer under the
headlamp, than in the living room. Finally seeing the mountain and losing
my clothes in a frenzy alone atop Mt. Stevens after a month in the prison of
cigarette smoke and meanness. Affirming the human wilderness on a
midnight raft approaching Skylerville. The Hudson. Diving into the river off
the brace of an old stone bridge in Waterford. Later feeling the sun melt into my
skin and singing with birds and blueberries on the Cape. The ocean is
my friend. I need to skinnydip.

Then I find a human wilderness to sing with my own. But I forget that the
fields of catclaw I crawled bloodily through in the redrocks in Arizona
looked like smooth ground from a quarter mile. Pounding my forehead and
ripping my ears as close other patterns change. And my January saddle
partner, my raft partner turns from me, or I turn from him, and there is a

great experience like riffing, and the way the canyon walls curve and fall off
and litter the slide with sharp-edged boulders like great misshaped
arrowheads is like a grating to my heart and pieces are falling like meteors
into the distance between.

O mother let me sink into you soon!
as the river water and as the bay water.
Let me fry into your deserts
through the shallow black wild eyes like a lizard
and crest out the edge along your ridges.
Let me scream in your valleys
and wail in your fields.
Let my fertile tears flow into your leaf beds
like the blood of a young sheep in a bed of mud and flowers. Do not delay
my return.

COMMENTS

Sarah Drummond, a 12th-grader from Colorado, was a (pun intended) "natural" to take top honors. in a contest that involves researching and observing the geology of local environments.

Sarah has lived next door to shale outcrops and excavations for much of her life. Drawing, writing, and exploring the natural world is what Sarah loves doing, and she even keeps a nature journal to document her observations in words and sketches.

Contest: Young Naturalist Award

Type: Research Report

Award Won: First Place, $2,500 (One of two in 12th-grade Division; other awards exist for grades 7-11)

A brief excerpt from:

From Uplift to Glaciation: Geological History of the Pikes Peak Region

SHADOWS OVER THE PEBBLY TERRAIN, AND A CARPET OF PINE NEEDLES CRACKLES BENEATH MY FEET, AS I SCALE A STEEP HILL ON THE FLORISSANT FOSSIL BEDS NATIONAL MONUMENT IN CENTRAL COLORADO.

Four-mile Creek shimmers down in the valley below, slicing its path through the fossil-rich shales of prehistoric Lake Florissant and the ancient volcanic deposits surrounding them. The surrounding forest of ponderosa pine shrouds the lower portion of a massive granite form. This is Pikes Peak, one of the many mountain summits that comprise Colorado's Front Range in the southern Rocky Mountains.

I sit down on the crest of the hill, absorbing the mountain shapes, muted by the crisp winter light, that ring the horizon around my home: Pikes Peak in the east, Crystal Peak to

the north, the long fringe of the Sangre de Cristos in the distant south, and, bisecting the state as part of the Continental Divide, the Sawatch Range in the west.

Living in the shadow of these mountains, I've gradually become acquainted with their habitats and seasons, but the granite soil eroding from Pikes Peak and rounded boulder outcroppings that pattern the landscape remind me that the land's present character is only the most recent facet of an epic saga.

Looking now at the rugged, ice-sculpted northern shoulder of Pikes Peak, I sense the vast scale on which events took place during the mountain's existence. For Pikes Peak, my human life represents but a single instant in the eternally changing pageant of geologic time.

The Rising Batholith

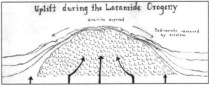

Uplift during the Laramide Orogeny

FIRST PLACE

SECOND PLACE

COMMENTS

I'm not an expert on art, but comparing the first- and second-place winners with fourth and fifth place reveals notable differences. Whereas the top two works appear to be built around an original idea and theme, the fourth- and fifth-place compositions are collages of traditional American symbols. Perhaps the idea and concept behind the artwork is just as important as the artistic execution.

Contest: Young American Creative Patriotic Art

Type: Visual Arts

Out of 44 entries in the national contest, submissions of 4 of the top 5 cash award winners are shown on this page.

The first place ($3,000) winner, Rachel Aydt, described her submission as such: "In southern Indiana, almost everyone flies a flag from their house on the Fourth of July. When you see them lined down a city street, you can almost hear 'land of the free and home of the brave.'"

The second place ($2,000) winner, Beka Stanley, depicted a still life of her father's military boots. Fourth place ($1,000) winner, Robert Bond, combines major symbols of the United States. Fifth place ($500) winner Melissa Burruss, portrays various symbols of American courage and pride.

FOURTH PLACE

FIFTH PLACE

COMMENTS

Shown at right is the first half (plus the final paragraph) of a winning essay submitted by Reuben Olinsky.

Reuben's essay stands out from the pack because of his interesting premise that the resources already around us will help cure some of today's worst diseases.

The Dupont Challenge is a good science-related scholarship contest to enter when you haven't done an independent research project. Unlike scholarship programs such as the Intel Science Talent Search, this contest doesn't require a long-term investment of time and energy.

Contest: Dupont Challenge

Type: Science Essay

Award Won: First Place ($1500) in Senior Division (Grades 10-12)

An excerpt from:

Right Under Our Noses

The media claims that rain forests contain myriad numbers of undiscovered organisms that will help cure today's worst diseases. Focus is placed on the South American tropics and these organisms previously unknown to man. With all this hype, most people forget about resources that have surrounded humans for centuries.

For years, the Pacific yew, *Taxus brevifolia*, had simply been a tree lumberjacks burned when chopping down more valuable trees (Nicolaou et al., 1996). In the 1960s, studies on the yew determined that mixtures derived from its bark destroyed many tumor and leukemia cells (Gelmon, 1994). The bark's effective ingredient, dubbed "taxol," was isolated by 1967. "Taxol" is now a registered trademark of Bristol-Myers Squibb, and is generically referred to as "paclitaxel" (Nicolaou et al., 1996).

Taxol's pharmaceutical applications were not realized until 1978, when Susan Horwitz and Peter Schliff of Albert Einstein College of Medicine discovered that it was unique with respect to how it killed cancer cells. During their research, they determined the exact method by which this agent works within the body (Nicolaou et al., 1996).

The taxoids are a family of antineoplastic agents, similar to taxol, that slow cell growth (Gelmon, 1994). Microtubules are crucial cell elements because they form an apparatus necessary for mitosis, the spindle (Nicolaou et al., 1996). Taxoids attach themselves to tubulin the major component of microtubules, and stop microtubule depolymerization, thereby encouraging build-ups of immobile microtubules ("Medical Letter...," 1996). This build-up obstructs the cell during the G2 (growth-2) and M (mitosis) phases of the cell cycle. A normal spindle cannot form and the cell can-

not divide (Gelmon, 1994). When the affected cell attempts to undergo mitosis, it dies (Nicolaou et al., 1996).

Because taxol seemed to kill cancer cells in a new way and it was found that cancer becomes resistant to certain treatments, researchers became eager to use taxol in oncology. Many hospitals started human testing by 1984. Researchers at Johns Hopkins found that more than 30% of those tested patients whose tumors had grown resistant to conventional chemotherapy decreased in size. These and other similar findings caused taxol to quickly become a globally known cancer-fighting drug (Nicolaou et al., 1996).

Although taxol seems very effective against cancer, it has some dangerous side effects (Nicolaou et al., 1996). Because cancer is marked by uncontrollable, rapid cell division, taxoids mainly affect tumors and cancer cells. However, other cells that undergo division at a fast rate, like hair and white blood cells, may be targeted as well. Patients treated with taxoids may lose hair, have weakened sensory nerves, or lessened immunities to disease (Nicolaou et al., 1996). Also, several patients in taxol testing during the 1980s had allergic-like reactions. Doctors and scientists remain unsure of why this happened, but dosage changes were made to decrease the chance of such reactions (Nicolaou et al., 1996).

A second major drawback of taxol was that its supply was very limited due to a steadily decreasing number of Pacific yew trees and the fact that a tree died after taxol was extracted from it. Furthermore, it took many century-old trees to prepare just one treatment.

.

.

Taxoid research continues today. With a further understanding of taxol, hopefully new cheaper, safer, and more effective taxoids may be synthesized (Nicolaou et al., 1996). Even now, taxol has come quite a distance from those ancient Pacific yews. This drug is sending a message to the scientific world. During searches for illness panaceas or improved treatments, scientists must look right under their nose in addition to the South American tropics. The final cure for one of today's worst diseases could very well be found in a unique organism that festers only in New York subways.

COMMENTS

In the Century III Leaders competition, the following essay question was posed to me: "What is a problem facing America in its third century and what is your solution?"

Choosing which societal problem to write about was my key strategic decision. I selected education as a topic because it tied in well with a community service project I had initiated. This allowed me to back up my theoretical solutions by citing a practical program I had implemented on the local level.

For a description of how I edited and refined this essay, see Chapter 8, page 193.

Contest: Century III Leaders

Type: Leadership

Award Won: First Place ($11,000)

Leveraging the Future: Solving the Challenge of Educating America's Youth

As America continues to assert world leadership during her third century, the current crisis in our educational system looms as one of our greatest national challenges. According to the Department of Education's (DOE) latest National Assessment of Educational Progress (NAEP) report, the small gains in math and science achievement over the last decade hasn't been accompanied by an improvement in reading and writing skills. As a whole, academic ability is still far below national goals. Commenting on the overall outlook, Secretary of Education Richard Riley said: "Holding our own in the information age is simply not good enough. It just doesn't cut it any more."

At the core of this crisis lies changes in attitudes towards education. There has been a significant loss in student motivation and concentration, a decay of belief in the importance and benefits of education, as well as a lowering of parental expectations for their children's potential achievement. Scholastic focus has been shifting away from core academic disciplines while a new "assembly-line mentality"—with an emphasis on just getting students safely through the public system with minimal skills—has crept into our schools. Youth violence, substance abuse, teen pregnancy, the spread of AIDS, and the pervasiveness of broken families have compounded the situation: While schools have been losing programs to funding cutbacks, society has been steadily dumping its ills and social problems onto their backs. Teachers are now expected to take on additional roles as counselors, policemen, mediators, social workers, and informants.

The pursuit of homework as an *effective* adjunct to class time is also under attack. In fact, many schools, unable to get students to complete homework, have practically given up on the concept altogether. According to the NAEP report, one-third of 17-year-olds said they were not required to do daily homework in all subjects. And even when homework is assigned, many students are frustrated by it because there is no way for them to get individual feedback and encouragement. As a result, they never cultivate the habit of completion, nor develop the critical learning skills which will be in high demand in the increasingly sophisticated job market of the future.

Lowering standards so as to get more high school students through the system and into college each year is *not* the panacea for this debilitation in learning. Today, business rightly complain that they must reeducate even *college* graduates in basic academic skills. Some policy makers would have us believe that simply bolstering programs with more money will solve our problems. Unfortunately, money isn't the panacea either: Positive change demands wisdom and discipline, and a lack of money often becomes a convenient scapegoat for failure. In fact, as an active student government member, I have learned how workable solutions are achievable without always allocating new funds—by harnessing underutilized resources, such as the students themselves.

Educators must make the commitment to deliver a quality product. Schools must refocus their energies to ensure that basic core subjects are adequately covered *before* expanding content. By minimizing distractions, we can increase the critical time allotted to developing the building blocks of learning—reading, writing, and math.

Next, we must motivate and inspire students to go far beyond minimum expectations. And in the process, we must *raise* the expectations of students as well as their parents. Furthermore, we need to emphasize and teach *how* to learn, not merely *what* to learn. We should encourage students to pursue learning outside of what is covered in class.

Last, we must find new ways to customize education to help students better prepare for the 21st century. The communications and computer revolutions have forever changed our lives. We need to train students and teachers to maximize resources by sharing information over electronic networks. We should create lower-tech programs that will act as supplementary "training wheels" for the interactive, multimedia resources of tomorrow.

In this portion of the essay I took the broad question of educational reform and narrowed the focus to one particular aspect of that reform. This made the topic more manageable, and helped me segue into a discussion of the Homework Helpline tutoring program I had created.

The difference between present practicalities and future possibilities is only a matter of the technological level of the networking links.

Because in-school hours are limited, accomplishing what I have proposed requires supplementing class time with other support programs. According to former Secretary of Education William Bennett, homework is an integral part of education: "Time on task... how much time you spend on a subject tells you an awful lot about what you will learn." The proper integration of homework has the potential to get families more involved in education, help develop a strong work ethic, cultivate perseverance, and promote confidence and a sense of achievement. We should, therefore, target and engineer this process as a primary way to impact student success in school.

The *Homework Helpline* program I created at my school is one way we can do this. The student-run telephone service provides help and feedback on homework during the evening hours, as well as useful study tips and learning skills. Calls are logged, analyzed, and trouble spots are referred back to teachers. Core curriculum is thus reinforced, other more specialized subjects receive the additional attention they deserve, and both students and teachers log some training-wheel time in preparation for cruising down tomorrow's information superhighway.

During her third century, America must continue to build upon the strong foundation of our educational heritage. In the future, as both journalist and policymaker, I intend to significantly impact the way in which we teach our children. A quality education for all our youth must be achieved if we hope to maintain our leadership position in the world. By courageously taking on this challenge, we can repair the existing damage to our educational superstructure, and continue to build a successful and prosperous America. This is the best way we can leverage the future.

Heather Hull, a ninth grader, crafted this first-place essay on the topic, "What does patriotism mean to you?"

In the body of the essay, Heather discusses the men and women who made great sacrifices for our country through military service. In a scholarship contest sponsored by the Veterans of Foreign Wars, this was an important point to highlight.

Contest: VFW Youth Essay

Type: Essay

Award Won: First Place ($5,000)

Patriotism, to me, is the spirit and soul of a country. It is what keeps a country together not only through war and hardships, but also through victory and triumph. What else could keep a soldier from losing heart and hope in battle? A disheartened country from losing the burning desire to rebuild itself? A nation of divided citizens from losing each other?

It is patriotism that keeps our love of freedom alive. It is not money or wealth; it is not social acceptance. It is the pure good will of every true American that keeps our nation's dreams alive. Everyday we show our patriotism in large and small ways: by proudly saluting the flag, by saying the Pledge of Allegiance, by celebrating the Fourth of July with its bursts of fireworks. Americans show their patriotism when soldiers give their lives serving our country and when citizens cast a vote in support of a candidate whose ideals represent their own.

Behind our many freedoms, including the freedoms of speech and religion, stand all the men and women who, through dedication to their dreams and perseverance through their struggles, have made so many opportunities ours. Although we may only recognize their sacrifices and suffering on certain holidays, such as Memorial Day and Veterans Day, their legacy is all around us everyday. In every military cemetery, the gravestones there represent hundreds of other patriots who have served our country and who continue to do so.

To me, patriotism is a kind of heroism. When I saw my face reflected in the shiny granite of the Vietnam Veterans Memorial ("The Wall") in Washington, D.C., I was reminded of the valor of those whose names are etched there and of the courage of their loved ones.

We Americans have always shown our patriotism by honoring our values and envisioning freedoms for all. To me, patriotism is the optimistic spirit and the deep-rooted soul of our country, the United States of America.

COMMENTS

In this essay, first-place winner Tim Shenk used conflicts in South Africa and Bosnia-Herzegovina to illustrate his views on the handling of war crimes and human rights violations.

The strength of this essay lies in its organization and research. Tim has structured the body of his essay around Professor Lederach's four cornerstones of reconciliation—peace, truth, justice, and mercy. His use of quotes and citations from other sources are well-chosen and demonstrate his research skills.

Due to space constraints, I'm not able to print the final three paragraphs of Tim's essay. For the full text, see the Reader's Resource Room at the winscholarships.com Web site.

Contest: National Peace Essay

Type: Essay Contest

Award Won: First Place ($10,000)

An excerpt from:

How Should Nations Be Reconciled?

The challenge of achieving national reconciliation is an issue of great importance, particularly in the nations of Bosnia-Herzegovina and South Africa. Both of these countries have in recent years experienced brutal violations of human rights; the evils of apartheid and "ethnic cleansing" have divided the populations on racial or ethnic lines. How should these nations reconcile their grievances and create a peaceful future? John Paul Lederach, Professor of Conflict Studies and Sociology at Eastern Mennonite University and an expert on international peacemaking, presents a model of reconciliation: The four cornerstones of truth, mercy, peace and justice, although often in conflict with each other, are together the vital components for creating reconciliation. South Africa's focus on these four fundamentals of reconciliation shows that this approach to peacemaking better assuages the horrors of the past than have the efforts of the international community and the Balkan governments toward the future of Bosnia-Herzegovina.

Peace, meaning a cessation of violence, is necessary before reconciliation can begin. In a broader sense, peace is security, safety, and a trust in one's neighbors; but there is little of these in Bosnia. Violence has uprooted whole populations and allegations of horrible war crimes abound on all sides, leaving neighbors of differing ethnic groups fearful and bitter. Balkan leaders such as Slobodan Milosevic and Franjo Tudjman have come to power by fanning the flames of ethnic hatreds and introducing racist policies. Yet while some Balkan leaders have been indicted for war crimes, the UN Implementation Force has not made efforts to capture the high-profile criminals—an example of an unofficial policy not to get too involved.

Many residents of Bosnia fear that this peace will fail on account of the international community's wavering interest in peacekeeping. Roy Gutman, one of the first international journalists to report on war crimes in Bosnia, describes his criticism: "European and American leaders wasted time and distracted public attention as they search for a negotiated solution where none was available. To dampen public concerns, they denied the visible facts." Another failing of the international community is that the Dayton Peace Accords reinforce the "spoils of war" mentality, awarding to the victor the areas that had been captured through the Nazi-like policy of ethnic cleansing.

Peace in South Africa is of a different type. A notable difference is that the old regime of apartheid—oppression and minority rule—has given way to a fully democratic government which places a high value on human rights. South Africa still has many deep wounds from the past, but the Truth and Reconciliation Commission has given the safe opportunity for victims to speak openly of their pain.

Truth is another difference between Bosnia-Herzegovina and South Africa. Roy Gutman describes hideously false accusations against Croats and Muslims created by the Bosnian Serb government. One tract being circulated by the Bosnian Serb authorities accuses Muslims and Croats, stating "necklaces have been strung of human eyes and ears, skulls have been halved, brains have been split, bowels have been torn out. . ." etc. The television station in Pale, Bosnia-Herzegovina "tells its viewers that NATO used low intensity nuclear weapons against Serbs, and [the station] denies the evidence of eyewitnesses and mass graves around Srebrenica." Croatian national television roused its viewers to further hatred, hammering on crimes against Croats and co-operating in the cover-ups of atrocities against Serbs. With press and governmental denials, many Bosnians will never know what happened to their loved ones.

The South African government, on the other hand, prizes truth highly. The Truth and Reconciliation Commission, founded to reveal the truth of South Africa's horrible past, offers amnesty to perpetrators of political crimes who disclose the whole truth. The hearings are widely made public—a stark contrast to the governmental denial and deception in

South Africa's past. As of November 19, 1996, ninety-three people have complied with these terms and have been granted amnesty. Many families have found out the fate of their loved ones through the commission, and there have been incredible stories of forgiveness and reconciliation. Apart from the Commission, apartheid-era rulers such as former President F. W. de Klerk have publicly apologized for apartheid, and many important figures have chosen to talk about the past.

Justice and mercy are the most difficult aspects of reconciliation. Justice in Bosnia is too much a hostage to international and local politics to be effective. The only mercy in Bosnia goes to numerous indicted war criminals who are too influential to be arrested.

Actions by the UN Implementation Force have often been against the small-time war criminal (if such a thing exists) and have avoided, for the sake of local stability, arresting powerful leaders such as Radovan Karadzic and Ratko Mladic. This aspect of international politics is revealed in a statement by NATO generals that "arresting [indicted war criminals] is not worth the blood of one IFOR soldier." Richard Goldstone, first Chief Prosecutor of the International War Crimes tribunal and an earnest critic of the current policies toward justice in Bosnia, said, "If international justice is to be used as a cheap commodity only to be discarded when Realpolitik so requires, then it would be preferable to abandon justice and leave victims to seek revenge in their own way."

COMMENTS

In this contest, entrants were asked to answer the question, "What would you do if you could give freedom away?"

In the essay shown here, the author has written a compelling and powerful piece by making it personal, and by drawing upon his own unique experiences. He mentions quite a few negative things from his past (and the fact that he's in jail), but skillfully keeps the focus on what these experiences have taught him about the meaning of true freedom.

Contrast this essay with another winning submission in the Optimist contest (shown on page B-12). Both essays were successful, even though each writer took a very different approach.

Contest: Optimist International

Type: Essay

Award Won: 1 of 3 international winners ($2,000 to $5,000)

I came to this country when I was eight or nine years old. I'm Hispanic and now I am 17 years old. I was living in a small city full of gangs, violence, drugs, and prostitution before I got arrested.

After seeing all this for a long time, I got used to it; I even got involved with it and liked it. I did not see that I was not free at all; I was in slavery to my surroundings. I didn't have the freedom that a gangster is supposed to have. I was a follower of people who did not have any future and were in the same low place as I was. I didn't realize that or I just didn't care. Everything was fun for me and that was all I lived for. I thought freedom was just like that, but I was dead wrong. Nothing I was involved in freed me.

Being foolish and not wanting to accept the reality of my captivity cost me much of my life and I'm still paying. In March, 1998, I committed a crime for reasons that I could easily forget, put them aside, and keep on going with my life. But I didn't. I plunged ahead in my crazy life. I got caught, and I lost what I once considered freedom.

I never thought people could take my freedom away in just a few minutes. I'm not talking about the freedom to get drunk or high; what I lost was much more valuable than that. Now I am incarcerated and can never forget how much I have lost that I never paid attention to in the past. Real, authentic freedom was taken from me and I didn't even know I had it.

I see now that genuine freedom has to do with making your own decisions—good decisions. It's practicing your own religion and letting God have His way in your life. It is going where you choose and doing it when you feel it is right. Most importantly, freedom that I lost was all about not being controlled by anything or anybody. I knew that drugs once controlled me, but I didn't realize how all the gang members and wrong attitudes also had a grip on my soul.

Now I'm locked up and I can only plan for a free future; but if I could give my potential freedom to a group of people, I would try to find those who could appreciate what a gift it is, people who were truly alive in their hearts and would use their freedom to help heal a sick society.

I believe that all the people in the world were born with the potential to love freedom. Unfortunately, few of them ever find it. Shame on individuals like me who had it and threw it away so carelessly. Please don't throw your freedom away; it's a piece of your life.

Just like the essay on the previous page, this composition was written on the topic of what you would do if you could give freedom away.

The style and approach used in this essay is much more intellectual and theoretical than the other winning Optimist essay shown on page B-11.

These two examples illustrate how even among winning essays, questions can be interpreted very differently. Some of the best essays I've seen, however, combine an intellectual treatment of the question with illuminating descriptions of personal experiences.

Contest: Optimist International

Type: Essay

Award Won: 1 of 3 international winners ($2,000 to $5,000)

If I could give freedom away, I would have to be a god for it is impossible to freely distribute liberty as one would a gift. Freedom lies in every individual, whether it only dwells in the solemn soul or is exercised daily in an open-minded society. One cannot give freedom away for the simple reason that every human being cannot merely receive such an intangibly magnificent gift, rather each must find this liberty inside himself or herself.

Each man and woman possesses freedom to a certain degree. While some enjoy more liberties than others such as the cherished rights to free speech or religion, every person does experience some level of freedom. John Milton once wrote, "Thou canst touch the freedom of my mind." Freedom of thought is often looked upon as insignificant, yet it is as precious a natural right as any.

Oftentimes, man finds that he must free himself from an oppressive government, but even this freedom could not possibly be a present hastily bestowed. It must be fought for, believed in, and supported to be prized. As Thomas Paine masterfully concluded in *The Crisis, Number One*, "What we obtain too cheaply, we esteem too lightly: it is dearness only that gives everything its value." Yes, the blessings of life such as liberty are much more treasured and appreciated when they are ob-

tained through one's personal hard work, commitment, and dedication.

Any physical suppression is often viewed as the depletion of all liberty, yet is it not an axiomatic right of man to be free? During the time of tyranny by Great Britain, the American colonies were incessantly taxed and deprived of legal freedom. However, in actuality, these colonies could have rebelled at any time and followed their own will as they finally realized and strongly declared in the seditious Boston Tea Party. They had freedom all along, maybe not legally, but they did own the liberty of choice, which was a "gift" they had to find the strength to exercise.

Perhaps the gift of freedom cannot be found by solely lifting political oppression. Are not the chains of society and its priorities just as heavy and enslaving? Is not the pursuit of money, success, fame, and glory equally oppressing? Just as in political suppression, freedom cannot be dealt to deliver one from the clutches of these worldly, oppressive desires. One must personally liberate oneself from these societal values, and how much more exhilarating it is to discover individual independence rather than receiving it, were it possible, on a silver platter.

Liberty must be realized and applied so that it may be cherished and truly appreciated. Each individual possesses this freedom to some extent, and for some, it is only a matter of discovering this inner quality. Liberty and independence are axiomatic rights that free one from political as well as societal oppression, and they are much more treasured when they are personally discovered instead of being simply given.

The essay shown to the right was part of a winning application I submitted to a local scholarship program for students from Oregon. I was asked the question, "What is the importance of a college education?"

Contest: Blazers Scholarship

Type: Overall Achievement

Award Won: First Place ($2,000)

As a sapling pushes its limbs skyward, its roots burrow deeper into the dark, moist sanctuary of soil. It is here, where the foundation lies—at the source of stability and strength—where probing tentacles soak up the very sustenance of life. And, just as the young tree draws its strength from this underlying

foundation, a college education empowers its graduates with the strong roots of lifelong learning: the impetus for intellectual growth, work-skill enhancement, and personality development.

Through this solid educational base, youth is instilled with the discipline and perseverance to stand tall in a world permeated with the winds of challenge and the storms of adversity. Providing both stability and nourishment, a college education excites the mind and spirit—drawing out the inner faculties, as personality, convictions, perspectives, and attitudes blossom. To educate, after all, is to develop from *within*.

College provides an environment where resources for personal growth are readily available, thus extending one's mental horizons by helping elevate taste, refine imagination, clarify ambition, and raise ideals. And in doing so, it helps each student discover and navigate the *best* career course. The potential is here to discover hidden talents and to overcome fears and weaknesses—preparing one to seize the opportunities which can make life rich and meaningful.

But a college education is only the *beginning*. The habits developed in college prepare us to be lifelong learners, responsible citizens, and more fulfilled individuals. This promotes abilities which allow graduates to grasp new information, apply knowledge, and learn new skills as situations change. College doesn't just supply facts; it stimulates inquiry and provides experience in locating sources of knowledge. Academic assignments cultivate the fertile soil of curiosity and teach students *how* to learn.

Furthermore, a college education will become even more important as our society continues to adapt to the new information age. Most new jobs in the 21st century will be for "knowledge workers," requiring qualifications that the high school-educated worker does not possess, and is poorly equipped to acquire. Instead, these future jobs will be dependent upon one's ability to learn quickly, as well as to garner and apply theoretical and analytical knowledge. A college education is the best way to develop these abilities.

For America to initiate a new era of prosperity, we must educate our citizens and instill these prerequisite skills. By making a college education more accessible to our young citizens and more relevant to future needs, we will continue our role as the political, economic, scientific, and creative leader of the world.

And with the roots of a strong college education supporting and nourishing *my* chosen career, I need not fear the future. As I venture forth through the gates of opportunity, I will have the strong foundation, preparation, and confidence to achieve my goals. I will be ready to succeed in a world of infinite possibilities, and thus enjoy the abundant fruits from the tree of life.

COMMENTS

This competition is manageable for all types of students—even those having little or no prior experience with science, electronics, and technology.

All of these inventions exhibit creative thinking and require persistence and follow-through when developing prototypes. But winning projects need not be technically complicated—just functionally intriguing. For more information on this contest, please see page A-11 in Appendix A.

Contest: Duracell/NSTA Invention Challenge

Type: Invention competition

Awards Won: First place ($20,000) and second place ($10,000) winners in two age divisions (grades 6-9 and grades 10-12).

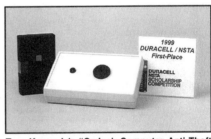

Tom Kennedy's "CoJack Computer Anti-Theft System" was a First Place $20,000 winner.

This picture depicts several first- and second-place inventions from the Duracell competition— including a color reader for the visually impaired, a firefighting safety boot, an outdoor thermometer, and a soda can opener.

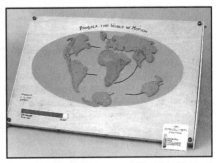

Iliana Jaatmaa's "Pangaea, A World in Motion" was the $20,000 winner for grades 6-9.

COMMENTS

In scanning first-place winner Natalia Toro's abridged report, it's apparent that the Intel Science Talent Search is not for the faint of heart. In fact, many of the winners have spent years working on their research projects.

Don't be intimidated, however, if you don't have a clue about what Natalia is describing; projects of this type often sound much more complicated than they really are. In addition, while first-place projects in this competition are always quite impressive, projects that take home lesser scholarship awards are often not nearly as technically sophisticated.

If you're serious about doing well in this prestigious contest, find a mentor. Most winners in the competition receive guidance and access to research opportunities and resources by working with a research scientist or university professor.

At the bottom of this page, I've also included profiles of the second- and third-place winners in the Intel contest.

Contest: Intel Science Talent Search

Type: Science Project

Award Won: First Place ($50,000)

Independent Analysis of $\nu_\mu \leftrightarrow \nu_\tau$ Oscillations in the Super Kamiokande Atmospheric Neutrino Data

Natalia Toro
Fairview High School, Boulder, Colorado
1999 First Place Winner

(This is an abridged version of Natalia's report. The original report included Summary, Abstract, Introduction, Mathematical Derivation of the Oscillation Formula, The Super-Kamiokande Experiment, Data Analysis, Results, Discussion, Conclusion and Acknowledgments.)

Summary: This study analyzes data from the Super-Kamiokande neutrino detector and finds evidence for flavor oscillations, in which neutrinos, the least understood of all known fundamental physical particles, change from one type into another over time. Such oscillations would prove that neutrinos have non-zero mass, a result with profound implications for the standard model of particle physics.

Introduction: Neutrinos are uncharged fundamental particles that were first hypothesized by Wolfgang Pauli in 1930 and shown to exist experimentally in 1956. According to the Standard Model of particle physics, there are three different types, or flavors, of neutrinos: namely electron (ν_e), muon (ν_μ), and tau (ν_τ) neutrinos. In 1968, Bruno Pontecorvo proposed the theory of neutrino oscillations, in which neutrinos change back and forth between different flavors. This is a uniquely quantum phenomenon, and neutrinos must have mass for oscillations to occur.

In this paper, we study the data from the Super-Kamiokande neutrino detector to look for evidence that electron and muon neutrinos generated in the earth's atmosphere are oscillating. These results were studied by the Super-Kamiokande collaboration, and the researchers reported significant evidence for oscillation. The intent of this study is to verify these results independently. This involves deriving the theoretical neutrino oscillation probabilities and comparing them to the experimental results by means of a χ^2 regression. The results differ somewhat from those obtained by Super-Kamiokande, but strongly imply that something is happening to the neutrinos and that oscillations are one feasible explanation.

Data Analysis Procedure: Two sets of data from Super-Kamiokande are used, describing the distribution of the neutrino counts as a function of the angle at which the neutrinos enter the detector and of momentum. The theoretical angular distribution of neutrino counts is calculated for a wide range of the two parameters that control neutrino oscillations (mixing angle and mass squared difference) and is then averaged over the distribution of momentum, thus smoothing the shape of the distribution. The resulting distributions are compared to the experimental angular distribution of neutrino flux by means of a χ^2 statistic, which also includes the effects of the major uncertainties in the atmospheric neutrino flux. This comparison allows us to determine the values of the oscillation parameters that are most consistent with the experimental data and the associated confidence regions.

Discussion: The data demonstrate convincingly that a no oscillation solution is highly unlikely to produce the experimental results observed by Super-Kamiokande for muon neutrinos. The probability of obtaining data as distant from the predicted values as those observed is just under one in ten million. The data for electron neutrinos, on the other hand, are not indicative of significant oscillations. The no-oscillation hypothesis fits the ν_e data with 20% probability, and this is in fact the best fit to the data. This is not necessarily an indication that electron neutrinos do not mix at all with the other flavors. While this is possible, electron neutrinos may also be oscillating with period too great to be detected over the distances traveled by atmospheric neutrinos. The observed solar neutrino data favors the latter of these possibilities.

One might suggest that the discrepancy between predicted and observed neutrino flux can be explained by errors in the model of the cosmic-ray interactions that produce atmospheric neutrinos. The uncertainty in the atmospheric-neutrino flux, however, is well accounted for in the analysis, and quantum-mechanical considerations are necessary to explain the skewed neutrino distribution. $\mu \leftrightarrow \tau$ or $\mu \leftrightarrow$ sterile oscillations, examined here, are one possible explanation. Another possible explanation is neutrino decay, where mass and flavor eigenstates are allowed to mix—as in the simple oscillation case--but one of the mass eigenstates is unstable.

The values obtained by this study for the oscillation parameters are $\sin^2(2\Theta)=0.59$, $\Delta m^2=4.7\times10^{-4}$ eV^2, whereas those obtained by Super-Kamiokande are $\sin^2(2\Theta)=1.0$, $\Delta m^2=2.2\times10^{-3}$ eV^2. Why such a large difference? Several differences between the analysis of this study and that of the Super-Kamiokande collaboration, as well as limitations on the data available for this study, can explain this discrepancy.

Conclusion: This study derives theoretical expressions for two-state neutrino oscillation and provides evidence, through analysis of the Super-Kamiokande neutrino oscillation data, for a neutrino-mixing scenario. It also demonstrates that two-state $\mu \leftrightarrow \tau$ oscillations are an acceptable solution to the atmospheric neutrino problem. This study also analyzes possible sources of the observed discrepancy between Super-Kamiokande's results and those presented here, and concludes that the two analyses are not inconsistent. ◆

Profile: David C. Moore, Second Place

David, age 18, used detailed quantum modeling techniques to determine the electrical properties of a newly proposed design for molecular electronic switches—devices that promise digital logic circuits a million times smaller than today's tiniest conventional solid-state circuits. David is an Eagle Scout and member of his school's cross-country team. His hobbies include computer programming.

Profile: Keith J. Winstein, Third Place

Keith, age 17, focused on steganography—techniques for embedding information in host data without making any perceptible change to the original material. He pushed beyond the standard techniques that have been developed for concealing data in video, audio and print, to create a framework suitable for digital media. Keith is a member of the American Computer Science League and the Sound F/X, a jazz choir.

APPENDIX C
State Scholarship Agencies

The following listings are of state agencies that administer government-funded scholarship programs in each of the 50 states. The agencies generally administer both federal-funded scholarships (such as the Robert C. Byrd Scholarship) and state-funded programs. In selected states, such agencies may also be contracted out to administer privately-funded scholarship programs. In states with more than one listing, administrative functions may be divided between both agencies.

ALABAMA
Alabama Commission on Higher Education
P.O. Box 302000
Montgomery, AL 36130
(334) 242-2274

State Department of Education
Gordon Persons Office Building
50 North Ripley Street
Montgomery, AL 36130
(334) 242-8082

ALASKA
Commission on Postsecondary Education
3030 Vintage Blvd.
Juneau, AK 99801
(907) 465-6741

State Department of Education
Goldbelt Place
801 West 10th Street, Ste. 200
Juneau, AK 99801
(907) 465-8715

ARIZONA
Commission for Postsecondary Education
2020 North Central Ave., Ste. 275
Phoenix, AZ 85004
(602) 229-2531

State Department of Education
1535 West Jefferson
Phoenix, AZ 85007
(602) 542-3053

ARKANSAS
Arkansas Department of High Education
114 East Capitol
Little Rock, AR 72201
(501) 371-2000

Arkansas Department of Education
4 State Capitol Mall, Room 304A
Little Rock, AR 72201
(501) 682-4474

CALIFORNIA
California Student Aid Commission
Suite 500, P.O. Box 510845
Sacramento, CA 94245
(916) 445-0880

California Student Aid Commission
1515 S Street, North Bldg.
Suite 500, P.O. Box 510845
Sacramento, CA 94245
(916) 323-2146

COLORADO
Colorado Commission on Higher Education
Colorado Heritage Center
1300 Broadway, 2nd Floor
Denver, CO 80203
(303) 866-2723

State Department of Education
210 East Colfax Avenue
Denver, CO 80203
(303) 866-6678

CONNECTICUT
Connecticut Department of Higher Education
61 Woodland Street
Hartford, CT 06105
(860) 566-3910

DELAWARE
Delaware Higher Education Commission
Carvel State Office Bldg.
820 North French Street, 4th Floor
Wilmington, DE 19801
(302) 577-3240

State Department of Public Instruction
Townsend Bldg.#279 /Federal & Lockerman
P.O. Box 1402
Dover, DE 19903
(302) 739-5622

DISTRICT OF COLUMBIA
Department of Human Services
Office of Postsecondary Education, R&E
2100 MLK,Jr. Avenue, SE / Ste. 401
Washington, D.C. 20020
(202) 727-3688

District of Columbia Public Schools
Division of Student Services
450 Lee Street, NE
Washington, D.C. 20019
(202) 724-4934

FLORIDA
Florida Department of Education
Office of Student Financial Assistance
State Programs - 255 Collins
Tallahasse, FL 32399
(904) 488-1034

GEORGIA
Georgias Student Finance Authority
State Loans & Grants Division
2082 East Exchange Place, Ste. 245
Tucker, GA 30084
(770) 414-3000

State Department of Education
2054 Twin Towers East
205 Butler Street
Atlanta, GA 30334
(404) 657-0183

HAWAII
Hawaii Postsecondary Education Comm.
2444 Dole Street, Room 209
Honolulu, HI 96822
(808) 956-8207

Hawaii Department of Education
2530 10th Avenue, Room A12
Honolulu, HI 96816
(808) 733-9103

IDAHO
Idaho State Board of Education
P.O. Box 83720
Boise, IF 83720
(208) 334-2270

State Department of Education
650 West State Street
Boise, ID 83720
(208) 334-2113

ILLINOIS
Illinois Student Assisance Commission
1755 Lake Cook Road
Deerfield, IL 60015
(847) 948-8500

State Board of Education
100 North First Street
Springfield, IL 62777
(708) 948-8500

INDIANA
State Student Assistance Commission
150 West Market Street, Ste. 500
Indianapolis, IN 46204
(317) 232-2350

Indiana Department of Education
State House, Room 229
Center for School Improvement
Indianapolis, IN 46204
(317) 232-2350

IOWA
Iowa College Student Aid Commission
200 10th Street, 4th Floor
Des Moines, IA 50309
(800) 383-4222

State Department of Education
Grimes State Office Building
Bureau of Instruction & Curriculum
Des Moines, IA 50319
(515) 242-6716

KANSAS
Kansas Board of Regents
700 S.W. Harrison, STE. 1410
Topeka, KS 66603
(913) 296-3517

State Department of Education
Kansas State Education Building
120 East Tenth Street
Topeka, KS 66612
(913) 296-4876

KENTUCKY
Kentucky Higher Education Assistance
1050 U.S. 127 South, Ste. 102
Frankfort, KY 40601
(800) 928-8926

State Department of Education
500 Mero Street
1919 Capital Plaza Tower
Frankfort, KY 40601
(502) 564-3421

LOUISIANA
Louisiana Office of Student Financial Assist
P.O. Box 91202
Baton Rouge, LA 70821
(800) 259-5626

State Department of Education
P.O. Box 94064
626 North 4th Street, 12th Floor
Baton Rouge, LA 70804
(504) 342-2098

MAINE
Finance Authority of Maine
P.O. Box 949
Augusta, ME 04332
(207) 623-3263

Maine Education Assistance Division
State House Station #119
One Weston Court
Augusta, ME 04330
(207) 287-2183

MARYLAND
Maryland Higher Education Commission
Jeffrey Building, 16 Francis Street
Annapolis, MD 21401
(410) 974-5370

Maryland State Department of Education
200 West Baltimore Street
Baltimore, MD 21201
(410)767-0480

MASSACHUSETTS
Massachusetts Higher Education
   Coordinating Council
330 Stuart Street
Boston, MA 02116
(617) 727-9420

State Department of Education
350 Main Street
Malden, MA 02148
(617) 388-3300

MICHIGAN
Michigan Higher Education Assistance
Office of Scholarships and Grants
P.O. Box 30462
Lansing, MI 48909
(517) 373-3394

State Department of Education
P.O. Box 30008
608 West Allegan Street
Lansing, MI 48909
(517) 373-3394

MINNESOTA

Minnesota Higher Education Services
Capitol Square Building, Ste. 400
550 Cedar Street
St. Paul, MN 55101
(800) 657-3866

State Department of Education
712 Capitol Square Building
550 Cedar Street
ST. Paul, MN 55101
(612) 282-5088

MISSISSIPPI

Mississippi Postsecondary Education
Financial Assistance Board
3825 Ridgewood Road
Jackson, MS 39211
(601) 982-6663

State Department of Education
P.O. Box 771
550 High Street, Room 501
Jackson, MS 39205
(601) 359-6619

MISSOURI

Miissouri Coordinating Board for High Ed.
3515 Amazonas Drive
Jefferson City, MO 65109
(573) 751-2361

State Dept. of Elementary & Secondary Ed.
P.O. Box 480
205 Jefferson Street, Sixth Floor
Jefferson City, MO 65102
(573) 751-2931

MONTANA

Montana University System
2500 Broadway, P.O. Box 203101
Helena, MT 59620
(406) 444-6570

State Office of Public Instruction
State Capitol, Room 106
Helena, MT 59620
(406) 444-4422

NEBRASKA

Coordinating Comm. for Postsecondary Ed.
P.O. Box 95005
Lincoln, NE 68509
(402) 471-2847

Nebraska Department of Education
P.O. Box 94987
301 Centennial Mall South
Lincoln, NE 68509
(402) 471- 2784

NEVADA

Nevada Department of Education
400 West King Street
Capitol Complex
Carson City, NE 89710
(702) 687-3100

State Department of Education
700 East Fifth Street
Carson City, NE 89701
(702) 687-9228

NEW HAMPSHIRE

New Hampshire Postsecondary Ed. Comm.
2 Industrial Park Drive
Concord, NH 03301
(603) 271-2555

State Department of Education
State Office Park South
101 Pleasant Street
Concord, NH 03301
(603) 271-2632

NEW JERSEY

Office of Student Financial Assistance
4 Quakerbridge Plaza, CN 540
Trenton, NJ 08625
(800) 792-8670

State Department of Education
CN500, 100 Riverview Plaza
Trenton, NJ 08625
(609) 984-6314

NEW MEXICO

New Mexico Comm. on Higher Education
1068 Cerrillos Road
Santa Fe, NM 87501
(505) 827-7383

State Department of Education
Education Building, 300 Don Gaspar
Santa Fe, NM 87501
(505) 827-6648

NEW YORK

New York State Higher Ed. Services Corp.
One Commerce Plaza
Albany, NY 12255
(518) 474-5642

State Education Department
111 Education Building, Washington Ave.
Albany, NY 12234
(518) 474-5313

NORTH CAROLINA

North Carolina Educational Assist. Authority
P.O.Box 2688
Chapel Hill, NC 27515
(919) 821-4771

State Department of Public Instruction
Education Bldg., 116 West Edenton Street
Raleigh, NC 27603
(919) 715-1161

NORTH DAKOTA

North Dakota Student Financial Assist. Pgm
600 East Blvd. Avenue
Bismarck, ND 58505
(701) 328-4114

State Department of Public Instruction
State Capitol Building, 11th Floor
600 East Boulevard Avenue
Bismarck, ND 58505
(701) 328-3546

OHIO

Ohio Board of Regents
309 South Fourth Street
P.O. Box 182452
Columbus, OH 43218
(888) 833-1133

State Department of Education
65 South Front Street, Room 1005
Columbus, OH 43266
(614) 466-2761

OKLAHOMA

Oklahoma State Regents for Higher Ed.
Oklahoma Tuition Aid Grant Program
P.O. Box 3020
Oklahoma, City, OK 73101
(405) 858-1840

State Department of Education
Oliver Hodge Memorial Education Bldg.
2500 North Lincoln Blvd.
Oklahoma, City, OK 73105
(405) 521-4122

OREGON
Oregon State Scholarship Commission
1500 Valley River Drive, #100
Eugene, OR 97401
(541) 687-7400

PENNSYLVANIA
Pennsylvania Higher Ed. Assist. Agency
1200 North 7th Street
Harrisburg, PA 17102
(800) 692-7435
(717) 783-7975

RHODE ISLAND
Rhode Island Higher Ed. Assist. Authority
560 Jerrerson Boulevard
Warwick, RI 02886
(800) 922-9855

State Department of Education
255 Westminister Street
Providence, RI 02903
(401) 277-3126

SOUTH CAROLINA
South Carolina Higher Ed. Tuition Grants
1310 Lady Street
P.O. Box 12159, Ste. 811
Columbia, SC 29211
(803) 734-1200

State Department of Education
1114 Rutledge Building
1429 Senate Street
Columbia, SC 29201
(803) 734-8999

SOUTH DAKOTA
Department of Education & Cultural Affairs
Office of the Secretary
700 Governors Drive
Pierre, SD 57501
(605) 773-3134

TENNESSEE
Tenessee Student Assistance Corp.
Parkway Towers, Ste. 1950
404 James Robertson Parkway
Nashville, TN 37243
(615) 741-1346

State Department of Education
100 Cordell Hull Building
Nashville, TN 37219
(800) 343-1663

TEXAS
Texas Higher Ed. Coordinating Board
P.O. Bos 12788, Capitol Station
Austin, TX 78711
(800) 242-3062

Texas Educational Agency
William B. Travis Building
1701 N. Congress Avenue
Austin, TX 78701
(512) 427-6331

UTAH
Utah State Board of Regents
355 West North Temple,
 #3 Triad Center, Ste. 550
Salt Lake City, UT 84180
(801) 321-7200

Utah State Office of Education
250 East 500 South
Salt Lake City, UT 84111
(801) 538-7779

VERMONT
Vermont Student Assistance Corporation
Champlain Mill, P.O. Box 2000
Winooski, VT 05404
(800) 642-3177
(802) 655-9602

VIRGINIA
State Council of Higher Education
James Monroe Bldg., 101 North 14th Street
P.O. Box 2120
Richmond, VA 23219
(804) 786-1690
(804) 225-2877

WASHINGTON
Washington State Higher Ed. Coord. Board
917 Lakeridge Way, S.W.
P.O. Box 43430
Olympia, WA 98504
(360) 753-7800

State Department of Public Instruction
Old Capitol Building FG11
Olympia, WA 98504
(360) 753-2858

WEST VIRGINIA
State College & Univ. System/Central Office
P.O. Box 4007
Charleston, WV 25364
(304) 558-4016

State Department of Education
1900 Washington Street
Building B, Room 358
Charleston, WV 25305
(304) 588-2691

WISCONSIN
Higher Educational Aids Board
P.O. Box 7885
Madison, WI 53707
(608) 267-2206

State Department of Public Instruction
125 South Webster Street
P.O. Box 7841
Madison, WI 53707
(608) 266-2364

WYOMING
Wyoming Community College Commission
2020 Carey Avenue, 8th Floor
Cheyenne, WY 82002
(307) 777-7763

State Department of Education
Hathaway Building
 2300 Capitol Ave., 2nd Floor
Cheyenne, WY 82002
(307) 777-6265

INDEX

A

ABC/Capitol Cities
    family scholarship of 48
academic achievement **142-144**
    bad grades, compensation for 171
activity lists 219
    customizing master list 221
    ranking 221
administrators. *See* contests
Adobe Pagemaker 220
Advanced Placement (AP) 128, 250
    college savings 250
All-USA Academic Team 37, 40, 46, **A-2**
AltaVista 79
American Association of School Administrators 52
American Legion 51, 82
    Oratorical Contest **A-3**
America's Junior Miss 35, **A-4**
anecdotes, power of 213
AP. *See* Advanced Placement
application components **216-226**
    activity lists 219
    attachments 217
    awards & honors lists 222
    blank spaces 217
    mailing applications 226
    multiple copies 216
    saving drafts and revisions 218
    "Stat Sheet", 219
    supplementary materials 226
    transcripts 223
    trimming out the fat 218
    typing application 216
application
    fees for 56
    theme. *See* theme
Arizona Jeans 85
Arts Recognition and Talent Search (ARTS) 36, 43
    A-5, B-3
Ask The Coach
    About bad grades 171
    About ethnic themes 134
    About fee-based services 72
    About finding the time 101
    About older applicants 227
    About small-town opportunities 149
    About younger students 157
"Ask the Coach" 24
athletic prowess 55
awards & honors lists 222
awards and honors 39
Axe, The 123
Ayn Rand Scholarship Contest 97, **A-6**

B

Bayer/NSF Award for Community Innovation 46
Better Business Bureau 44
bias, of judging 56
Blazers Scholarship **B-12, 13**
BMI Student Composer Awards 35, **A-7**
Boston Globe, The 175
Boy Scout 47
Boy Scouts/Girl Scouts of America 51, 82
Bureau of Consumer Protection 44

C

calendar, use of 93, 108
CASHE Online Scholarship Search Service 73
CD-ROM Databases 77
Century III Leaders (scholarship) 40, 167, 193,
    B-8, 9
Chamber of Commerce 82, 84
Citizens' Scholarship Foundation of America 52, 169
Coca-Cola 51
Coca-Cola Scholars Program 35, 52, 55, 200,
    248, **A-8**
College Board Scholarship Search 71
College Board, The 82, 250
college credit. *See* Advanced Placement (AP)
college students, strategies for 227
CollegeNET MACH25 71
community service. *See* service
company sponsors
    employer of parents 84
content strategies **160-163**
    demonstrate virtues 163
    expand strong points 160
    shore up weak areas 162
    combined with packaging 169, 170
contest detective
    ideal applicant 164
Contest Detective, The **164-166**

contests
    administrators 52
    comparison of local and national 41
    fees 43
    judges for 53
    sponsoring organizations 51
    Types 1, 2, 3 138
Craftsman/NSTA Young Inventor Awards 46

D
database searches. *See also* searching Internet
        databases
    limitations of 76
Daughters of the American Revolution 83
Daughters of the Confederacy 83
Department of Education 175
depth evaluators **142-147**
    awards & honors 147
    awards and honors 144, 146
    class balance 143
    class difficulty 143
    class ranking 142
    grade point average 142
    impact 142, 147
    leadership 142, 146
    organization size 147
    positions held 147
    test scores 143
    time commitment 142, 146, 147
Discover Card 16, 51, 120, 122, 123
Discover Card Tribute Awards 19, 35, 38, 42, 167,
        170, 189, **A-9**
Dupont Challenge, The **A-10**, **B-7**
Duracell/NSTA Invention Challenge **A-11**, **B-13**

E
eligibility, criteria of **46-50**
    age 46
    gender 50
    geographic region 47
    grade in school 46
    grades and test scores 47
    organizational membership 47
    race and ethnicity 50
Elks Club 51, 83
e-mail, for free
    hotmail.com 74
Encyclopedia of Associations 85
ESPN SportsFigures Scholarship 166, **A-12**

essay topics 197
essay topics, tips for
    a person you admire 198
    future career aspirations 197
    growth experiences 199
    solving a pressing issue 198
    your greatest achievement 197
essays **182-200**
    consult other works 192
    honing by rewriting 193
    keep things personal 183
    make it unique and memorable 185
    metaphor 191
    metaphor, extended 186
    move locations 193
    record yourself 192
    recycling 170, 187. *See also* reusability
    show, don't tell 182
    talk it over 192
    the "free write" 192
    tips for revising 196
    use effective organization 183
    word count 185
    zoom in 193
ethnic heritage. *See* theme
Eugene, Oregon 16, 174
Excite (Web search) 79
ExPAN software 73
extracurricular activities 55, 144. *See also* activity lists
    compiling lists of 37

F
FastWEB 70
fee-based services 72
financial aid 32
Foundation Center, The 86
Foundation Directory, The 86
Fountainhead, The 97
Future Business Leaders of America 47
Future Farmers of America 47

G
Gale Research 85
game plan, the
    intangible benefits 252
    seven components of **92-100**
gender. *See* eligibility
Georgia-Pacific Foundation Community
        Scholarship 190

Golden Rule 68
"GPA" Plan 104
   action 110
   goal setting 105
   prioritizing 108
grade point average
   principles of raising 239
grade trend 170
grants, types of
      merit-based 32
      need-based 32
Guerrilla Tactics
   #1, multiple searches 75
   #2, tapping other schools 78
   #3, electronic school visits 81
   #4, recycle and rethink 95
   #5, using school assignments 97
   #6, independent study 98
   #7, questioning past winners 99
   #8, convey virtues 156
   #9, fill in resume gaps 162
   #10, match ideal applicant 168
   #11, read out loud 196
   #12, get more recommendations 205
   #13, letters on disk 210
   #14, expanded descriptions 217
   #15, addendum to transcript 224
   #16, leaving samples behind 233
Guideposts' Young Writers Contest **A-13**

H

Harvard 17, 20, 23, 175, 251
Hatfield, Mark U.S. Senator
   internship with 174
   photo with 175
"hidden" criteria 54
hidden judging criteria **138-142**
   depth evaluators 139
   service to others 141
   width evaluators 139
"hidden rules" 18
HOBY World Leadership Congress 41
Homework Helpline, The 169, 183, 196
Hugh O'Brian Youth (HOBY) Foundation.
     See HOBY World Leadership Congress

I

ideal applicant, the 56, 168
Intel 51

Intel Science Talent Search 35, 52, **A-14**, **B-14**
Intermissions
   #1. What Parents Can Do To Help **59-63**
      Letter From My Parents 62, 63
   #2. The Unforgiving Minute **103-112**
   #3. Creating Opportunities **173-177**
   #4. Being Smart About Your Studies **239-242**
International Baccalaureate (IB) exams.
     See Advanced Placement (AP)
international students
   scholarships for 49
Internet search engines 79
interviews 38
interviews, mastering of **230-238**
   anecdotes 231
   anticipate questions 232
   ask the interviewer 233
   college admissions 233
   conducted by phone 231
   dress for success 234
   key points 231
   "pepper" yourself 232
   person-to-person tips
      annoying habits 237
      finding common ground 235
      handshake and eye contact 235
      listening 235
      making points 236
      monologues 235
      enthusiasm 237
   prepare answers 232
   preparing for 230
   preparing samples of work for 233
   reviewing written application for 233

J

Jaycees 51
judges. *See* contests

K

Kaplan Education Centers 82
Key Club 47, 51, 83
Kinkos copy centers 216
Kiwanis International 83
KLCC, NPR affiliate 161
Knights of Columbus 83

L

leadership **146-148**

letters of recommendation 38, 121, 122, 204
    famous people, from 214
    thank-you notes 212
letters of recommendation, strategy for **204-212**
    communicate effectively 207
    cover letter 209
    cultivate relationships 206
    develop a menu 204
    minimize the work 210
    qualities of a great letter 212
Lions Club 83
local resources
    using your school's 76
    visiting other schools 78
Lucent Global Science Scholars **A-15**
Lycos (Web search) 79

M

mailing 226, 227
margin comments 25
Massachusetts Institute of Technology 41
McNeil Products (Tylenol) 51
Meals on Wheels 125
metaphor, extended 186
Miami, Florida 36
Microsoft Word 220
middle-school students 22, 157
"middle-income financial aid crunch" 21
Milky Way/AAU High-School All-American
    Scholarship 166
minorities, strategy for 134
Minority On-Line Information Service(*MOLIS*) 74
music competition 36, 54
Myths, Exploding the Seven **54-57**
    #1, academic achievement 54
    #2, star athletes 55
    #3, extracurricular activities 55
    #4, applying to college 56
    #5, level playing field 56
    #6, track record 57
    #7, multiple applications 57

N

National Alliance for Excellence Scholarships **A-16**
National Association of Press Women 50
National Association of Secondary School
    Principals 52
National Conventions
    Democratic and Republican, reporting from 175

National Fraud Information Center 44
National Geography Bee 46
National History Day Contest **A-17**
National Honor Society 43, 47, 51, 83
National Honor Society Scholarship 52, 167, **A-18**
National "Make It Yourself From Wool" Contest 36
National Merit program 40
National Peace Essay Contest **A-19**, **B-10,11**
National Public Radio affiliate (KLCC) 162
New York Times, The 24, 175

O

Odd Fellows. *See* United Nations Youth
    Pilgrimage Program
Odd Fellows & Rebekah Lodges 83
odds, stacking the 177
Optimist International 51, 83
    Essay and Oratorical Contests 35, **A-20**, **B-11, 12**
Oregon 52, 84, 123, 188
Oregonian, The 175

P

packaging strategies **163-168**
    combined with content 169
page layout
    Adobe PageMaker 97
Painting Your Portrait. *See* theme
PaperMate 85
paperwork. *See* application components
parents, help from **59-63**
    letter from my 62
Pell Grant 32
Portland Trailblazers 188
Principal's Leadership Award 35, 52, **A-21**
Prudential Spirit of Community Awards 52, 53,
    A-22
public speaking 151

Q

questions
    for Contest Detective 164
    short-answer 36, 199

R

race & ethnicity. *See* eligibility
Rand, Ayn. *See also* Ayn Rand Scholarship Contest
    author of *The Fountainhead* 97
Reader's Resource Room 34, 69, 220, 249

recommendations. *See* letters of recommendation
recycling. *See* essays
Register-Guard, The 174
Research Science Institute 41
reusability 170
Robert C. Byrd Honors Scholarship 84, **A-23**
Rotary Club 51, 83

S

Sample Material, Library of 26
"scams" 43, 72
schedule setting 100
scholarship directories
 Scholarship Handbook, The 82
 Scholarship Sleuth, The 82
 Scholarships, The Essential Guide 82
scholarship, payment plans 246
 flexibility 247
 special exceptions 248
 tracking the details 248
Scholarship Resource Network 73
Scholarship Sleuth, The 25, 69, 80, 82
scholarships, merit-based
 Type 1 35
 Type 2 36
 Type 3 40
Scholastic Art and Writing Awards, The 35, **A-24**, **B-4, 5**
Science Service. *See* Intel Science Talent Search
searching Internet databases **69-76**
self-initiated projects 141
"serendipity" 81
service **139-142**
 community-based 141
 school-based 141, 142
Service to Others, an example 139
Siemens Westinghouse Science & Technology Competition 35, **A-25**
snowball effect 173
Sons of the American Revolution 83
Soroptimist International 83
 Soroptimist Youth Citizenship Awards **A-26**
South Eugene High School 123
sports 166
state scholarship agencies **C-1, 2, 3, 4**
state scholarship commissions 84
"stepping stone" programs 41
supplementary materials 226
synergy 169

T

Target All-Around Scholarship 35, **A-27**
"task paralysis" 104
taxable money 43, 247
Ten Golden Virtues 199. *See also* virtues
tennis 60, 122, 123, 213
test results 39
test scores 225
theme **117-134**
 9 Winning Themes **124-133**
  The Activist 129
  The Athlete 133
  The Brainiac 128
  The Creative Talent 126
  The Do-Gooder 125
  The Entrepreneur 130
  The Leader 131
  The Scientist 132
  The Survivor 127
 employing your 119
 enhancing credibility 119
 ethnic heritage 134
 finding your 134
 primary and secondary 118, 169
 staying balanced 122
ThinkQuest Internet Challenge 35, **A-28**, **B-3**
time management 103
Toshiba/NSTA ExploraVision Awards 46, **A-29**
Toyota Community Scholarship **A-30**
transcripts 37, 223
 test scores included on 225
tuition costs, rising trend 23
Tylenol Scholarship 35, 37, 169, **A-31**
Type 1 contests 35
Type 2 contests 36-40
Type 3 contests 40, 41

U

U.S. News & World Report 24, 175
U.S. Senate Youth Program 174, 223, **A-32**
unions, local chapters as sponsors 83
United Daughters of the Confederacy Scholarship 48
United Nations Youth Pilgrimage Program 41
USA Today. *See* All-USA Academic Team

V

Veterans of Foreign Wars 51, 83. *See also* Voice of Democracy
VFW Youth Essay Contest **A-33**, **B-9**

virtues, "10 Golden Virtues" **150-154**
    1. Hard Work 150
    2. Overcoming Obstacles 151
    3. Teamwork 151
    4. Perseverence 151
    5. Individual Initiative 152
    6. Passion & Enthusiasm 152
    7. Responsibility 153
    8. Civic Duty 153
    9. Purpose 154
    10. Character 155
Voice of Democracy 168, **A-34**, **B-2**

W

Washington Crossing Foundation 48, 61
    Washington Crossing Scholarship **A-35**
Washington, D.C. 174
Web sites, primary and secondary 80
width evaluators **141-147**
    academic clubs and teams 143
    academics 145
    ahletics 144
    communications 144
    community service 146
    community-based service 141
    creative arts 144
    culture and language 145
    entrepreneurial 145
    individual research projects 143
    individual study 143
    internships 145
    issue-oriented 145
    issue-oriented leadership 146
    jobs 145
    organizational leadership 146
    peer-directed leadership 147
    religious groups 146
    representative leadership 147
    school-based service 141
    schoolwork 142
    self-initiated projects 141
    standardized tests 142
    student government 144
    vocational 145
Will, George, as a writing mentor 175
William Randolph Hearst Foundation
    U.S. Senate Youth Program 51
winscholarships.com (Web site) 25, 70, 220
word count 185
word processing program
    Microsoft Word, 97

Y

Yahoo! (Web search) 79
YMCA/YWCA 83
Young American Creative Patriotic Art Awards
    A-36, **B-6**
Young Naturalist Awards **A-37**, **B-5**

Symbols

4-H Club 47, 51, 83

You could...

pay more for college

waste countless hours surfing the Web

never get your questions answered

miss the scholarship boat

... but why?

Introducing **winscholarships.com**

The Web's Ultimate Resource for Scholarship Seekers

- Links and reviews of the top scholarship search databases
- A free scholarship newsletter that alerts you to the latest contest news.
- A discussion board for posting questions to other scholarship winners
- A special "Ask the Coach" feature
- Our scholarship contest of the week

As a special service to readers of *How to Go to College Almost For Free*, we feature a **Reader's Resource Room**—providing access to interactive scholarship coaching, ready-to-use forms, updates and changes to profiled contests, author postings, and much more. For your entry password, follow the instructions at the bottom of this book's Copyright page.

Proudly introducing...

The Best of 'Ask the Scholarship Coach'
A three-part audio series

Through his *Ask the Scholarship Coach*™ service on the **WinScholarships.com** Web site, Ben Kaplan has received many thousands of questions on all aspects of the college scholarship game. Now in this breakthrough audio series, Ben has selected the most provocative of these questions, and has answered them in his trademark conversational style. This series is a must-have audio set for all those who recognize that the fastest way to scholarship success is to ask the right questions. The three volumes in this series include:

- **Volume I: The Essential Questions and Answers.** This volume tackles the most common questions asked of The Scholarship Coach. If you don't have a lot of time to waste, then this volume is the turbo boost you need.

- **Volume II: Personalizing Your Scholarship Quest.** This volume addresses scholarship questions specific to students with particular interests, backgrounds, and goals. Learn how to adapt your scholarship approach to fit your unique circumstances.

- **Volume III: Troubleshooting Your Application.** Any decent consumer electronics manual includes a troubleshooting guide that helps you remedy problems that arise. Likewise, this volume helps you find and fix trouble spots in your scholarship submissions.

The Scholarship Coach National Tour™ Official Workshop Video

As part of *The Scholarship Coach National Tour*, Ben Kaplan delivered workshop presentations in more than two dozen cities across the U.S. In this video, we distill some of the most important insights and anecdotes from these lively presentations, provide extra instructive material based upon audience questions, and include special footage from events, scholarship search demonstrations, and interviews along the bus route. If you weren't able to make it to one of these unique scholarship workshops, or want to share the information and inspiration with someone else, then this video is for you.

For more information see **www.waggledancer.com**
(Or write us at: Waggle Dancer Books • P.O. Box 860 • Gleneden Beach, OR 97388)

ABOUT THE AUTHOR

Benjamin Kaplan won more than two dozen merit-based scholarship contests while in high school—accumulating nearly $90,000 in scholarship funds. In 1999, after attending only six academic semesters at Harvard University, he graduated *magna cum laude* with a degree in economics. Virtually the entire cost of his Harvard education had been covered by his scholarship winnings.

Kaplan has written numerous articles on winning scholarships, including columns for *The New York Times* and *U.S. News & World Report*, that have been syndicated in publications nationwide. He has also served as a writing coach and scholarship advisor for the College Summit program.

In 1996, he attended both the Democratic and Republican National Conventions, and wrote a series of political commentaries from the youth perspective for *The Oregonian* and *The Boston Globe* newspapers. Kaplan also co-authored the book and lyrics for the Hasty Pudding Theatricals' 151st annual musical, "I Get No Kick From Campaign."

Prior to college, Kaplan attended public high school in Eugene, Oregon, where he played varsity tennis, served as student body president and editor-in-chief of his school newspaper, and founded the "Homework Helpline" telephone tutoring service. Among other honors, Kaplan was selected the "Top Student Leader in America" by the National Association of Secondary School Principals.

In addition to his book projects, Kaplan conducts scholarship seminars, consults with organizations desiring to set up scholarship programs, and serves as the resident scholarship coach at the *winscholarships.com* Web site.